TOXIC TORTS

IN A NUTSHELL

By

JEAN MACCHIAROLI EGGEN

Professor of Law

Widener University

ST. PAUL, MINN.

WEST PUBLISHING CO.

1995

Nutshell Series, In a Nutshell, the Nutshell Logo and the WP symbol are registered trademarks of West Publishing Co. Registered in the U.S. Patent and Trademark Office.

COPYRIGHT © 1995 By WEST PUBLISHING CO.
610 Opperman Drive
P.O. Box 64526
St. Paul, MN 55164-0526
1-800-328-9352

Library of Congress Cataloging-in-Publication Data

Eggen, Jean, 1949–
    Toxic torts in a nutshell / by Jean Eggen.
       p.   cm. — (Nutshell series)
    Includes index.
    ISBN 0–314–06542–3 (soft cover)
    1. Toxic torts—United States. I. Title. II. Series.
KF1299.H39E37 1995
346.7303'2—dc20
[347.30632   95–36804
                                         CIP

ISBN 0–314–06542–3

TEXT IS PRINTED ON 10% POST
CONSUMER RECYCLED PAPER

Printed with Printwise
Environmentally Advanced Water Washable Ink

*For Jeffrey and Don
and for Edie*

*

PREFACE

When I began teaching toxic torts eight years ago, the field consisted of a sparse collection of mostly unrelated cases. Developing an image of toxic tort law has been much like putting together a puzzle without knowing the picture that will appear after the puzzle is completed. Although that puzzle is still far from being complete, the picture is coming into focus. What has become clear over the years is that toxic torts is neither a mere offshoot of tort law nor a mere extension of environmental law. Its unique problems and challenges, and particularly its blending of private law and public law, have carved a special niche that is coming into prominence as we approach the twenty-first century. By necessity, it is evolving its own jurisprudence. The growth and continuing development of the body of law that is known as toxic torts is as exciting and challenging for the student and the practitioner as for the legal academic community.

In this Nutshell, I present the legal doctrine of toxic torts less as black-letter law than as an evolving process, a kind of metamorphosis of traditional law into a new, independent form addressing a specific set of problems. The interactions between private and public law, substance and procedure, and science and law all contribute to this process. It is a process enlivened by public policy debate. As a result, many issues have not reached a consensus in the judicial or legislative community. I present the give-and-take of the evolution of the law of toxic torts within the context of the important policy issues and demonstrate the failure of traditional law to solve the host of new problems presented by toxic exposure claims.

As this law has evolved, special note should be taken of one jurist whose contribution to legal discourse on toxic torts has been untiring, inspiring, and always stimulating. The Honorable Jack B. Weinstein of the Eastern District of New York, who presided over most of the "Agent Orange" toxic tort litigation through its settlement in 1984 and beyond, has tackled dozens of daunting and complex issues in that litigation and numerous others. His prolific written opinions on these issues have helped to set the standard since the mid-1980s for the development of the law of toxic torts.

Several research assistants have contributed much time and effort to the substance of this Nutshell. It is with gratitude and appreciation that I acknowledge the assistance of Wendy Bleczinski, Christopher McDemus, and Mark Bleczinski. I am also grateful for the assistance of Susan Gordon in the final preparation of the book. Several colleagues have contributed along the way as well: Peter Bell for sharing his approach to teaching the subject; Francis McGovern and Dr. Jack Snyder for sharing their ideas; and John Culhane, Patrick Johnston, and Jim May for reading and commenting on portions of the manuscript in progress. Finally, I am deeply grateful to the students to whom I have taught toxic torts over the past eight years for openly sharing their opinions and ideas.

JEAN MACCHIAROLI EGGEN

Wilmington, Delaware
June, 1995

*

OUTLINE

TABLE OF CASES

References are to Pages

A

TABLE OF CASES

B

C

D

E

F

G

H

I

J

K

P

R

S

TABLE OF CASES

W

Z

TABLE OF STATUTES

UNITED STATES

UNITED STATES CODE ANNOTATED
7 U.S.C.A.—Agriculture

15 U.S.C.A.—Commerce and Trade

18 U.S.C.A.—Crimes and Criminal Procedure

21 U.S.C.A.—Food and Drugs

TABLE OF STATUTES

TABLE OF STATUTES

POPULAR NAME ACTS

———

CIVIL RIGHTS ACT OF 1964

COMPREHENSIVE ENVIRONMENTAL RESPONSE, COMPENSATION AND LIABILITY ACT

TABLE OF STATUTES

UNIFORM COMMERCIAL CODE

STATE STATUTES

ALABAMA CODE

ALASKA STATUTES

ARIZONA REVISED STATUTES

ARKANSAS CODE ANNOTATED

TABLE OF STATUTES

TABLE OF STATUTES

TABLE OF STATUTES

FEDERAL RULES OF CIVIL PROCEDURE

FEDERAL RULES OF EVIDENCE

TOXIC TORTS

IN A NUTSHELL

*

CHAPTER ONE

INTRODUCTION TO THE STUDY OF TOXIC TORTS

A. WHAT IS A TOXIC TORT?

The term "toxic torts" encompasses a wide variety of claims, both private and public. To some extent, characterizing these claims as "torts" is a misnomer. A toxic tort action may be a civil lawsuit, an administrative action for clean-up of hazard waste, a workers' compensation claim, or any other of a multitude of actions. What do these actions have in common? What themes tie them together? And why should these particular kinds of torts be treated as a separate category in the law? It is initially important to understand the answers to these questions and to comprehend the various contexts in which a toxic tort may arise. This chapter explores the characteristics of a toxic tort to provide the basis for a more detailed understanding of the kinds of claims and defenses that this book will discuss.

1. Exposure to a Toxic Substance

Typically, toxic tort actions involve substances as diverse as asbestos, silicone breast implants, prescription drugs, chemical compounds, radiation, or

hazardous waste. The harm claimed may be equally diverse. Claims may seek compensation for personal injuries or property damage. But claimants
may also seek to recover for discrimination in the
workplace or for the costs of cleaning up a contaminated site. In general, however, the claims involve
the release of and exposure to—or threatened release of and exposure to—one or more substances
alleged to be "toxic." The definition of what is
"toxic" may vary, depending upon the context in
which it appears. Generally, the use of the term in
legal circles is broader than its use in medical or
scientific circles. A broad, workable definition is
given in the Toxic Substances Control Act (TSCA),
15 U.S.C.A. § 2606(f) (West 1982), where, in the
context of the manufacture of chemical substances
and mixtures, imminent hazard is described as involving "the manufacture, processing, distribution
in commerce, use, or disposal of [a substance that]
is likely to result in ... injury to health or the
environment." Similarly, in the Hazard Communication Standard promulgated by the Occupational
Safety and Health Administration (OSHA), a
"health hazard" is defined as "a chemical for which
there is statistically significant evidence based on at
least one study conducted in accordance with established scientific principles that acute or chronic
health effects may occur in exposed employees." 29
C.F.R. § 1910.1200(c).

Human or property exposure may occur in a wide
variety of ways. The New York statute of limitations that governs actions relating to toxic expo-

sures enumerates the methods of exposure as follows: "absorption, contact, ingestion, inhalation, implantation or injection." N.Y. Civ. Prac. L. & R. 214–c (McKinney 1990). Exposure may be knowing, as with a prescription drug, or unknowing, as with a contaminated drinking water supply.

The substances that appear in toxic tort actions have certain characteristics that distinguish them from the instrumentalities that appear in a traditional tort action, such as a motor vehicle accident. These also tend to be many of the same substances selected by the federal Government for regulation, either generically or specifically, in programs administered by a variety of agencies, such as the Environmental Protection Agency, the Food and Drug Administration, and OSHA. For example, in the Hazard Communication Standard, OSHA has required certain actions to be taken with regard to chemicals that may be classified as "carcinogens, toxic or highly toxic agents, reproductive toxins, irritants, corrosives, sensitizers, hepatotoxins [(toxic to liver)], nephrotoxins [(toxic to kidneys)], agents which act on the hematopoietic [(blood)] system, and agents which damage the lungs, skin, eyes, or mucous membranes." 29 C.F.R. § 1910.1200. Substances and processes of concern under TSCA include those causing such effects as "carcinogenesis, mutagenesis, teratogenesis, behavioral disorders, and cumulative or synergistic effects." TSCA, 15 U.S.C.A. § 2603(b)(2)(A) (West 1982). Carcinogenesis relates to the capability of the substance to cause cancer. Teratogenesis refers to a birth defect caused by certain stimuli during fetal development that may cause the fetus to be malformed. Mutagenesis is somewhat different. It refers to the inducement of genetic mutations caused by changes in DNA. Genetic mutations may express themselves at various times and in various ways. The injurious effects can appear directly in the person exposed to a particular substance. Or, the gene may be inherited, and the harmful expression of the gene may manifest itself in a subsequent generation. For example, a plaintiff might allege that her cancer was caused by her grandmother's ingestion of a certain prescription drug while the grandmother was pregnant with the plaintiff's father, who has remained healthy. The plaintiff might allege that the in utero exposure caused a genetic mutation in the father that was passed on to the plaintiff, causing her to develop the cancer.

Often the substances that are involved in toxic tort actions are new compounds, and sometimes they can be obscure. In addition, the complaint in a toxic tort action may set forth circumstances in which several or many substances were commingled in some fashion. Thus, it may be necessary to examine the synergistic effects associated with the combination of substances alleged. Two or more separate substances may combine and interact in a way that becomes harmful only upon interaction or in a way that enhances the harmful effects of the substances. Further, some substances may cause deleterious effects only upon prolonged or cumulative exposure. The subtleties of the scientific issues involving the toxicity of substances indicate the need for attorneys practicing in this area of the law to have a basic understanding of scientific or engineering principles as well as to keep current on scientific knowledge relevant to their cases.

2. Latency Period

In general, in a toxic tort action, the full effects of exposure are not immediately apparent. This is either because the injury has not manifested itself or because the harm goes undiscovered for a period of time. Injuries such as cancer, birth defects, and genetic mutations necessarily require a latency period for their development. Asbestos exposure presents a classic example of a long latency period between exposure and the onset of symptoms. Asbestos workers rarely exhibited any evidence of asbestos-related disease at the time of initial exposure or shortly thereafter. It was not uncommon for workers to develop asbestosis, a chronic and degenerative lung condition, or malignant mesothelioma, a form of lung cancer associated with asbestos exposure, many years after initial exposure and often many years after exposure had ceased. Latency periods of ten to thirty years appear frequently in the cases. *See* Borel v. Fibreboard Paper Prods. Corp. (5th Cir.1973). Latency periods may not stop at several decades. The example given earlier of genetic harm demonstrates the possibility that injuries could manifest themselves generations after the initial exposure.

The long latency periods associated with toxic tort claims generate many problems that were unusual in the standard tort action. For example, statutes of limitations and rules of accrual needed to be modified to encompass toxic tort actions, in which the time of the defendant's action and the discovery of the injury are separated by expanses of time. Furthermore, the collection of evidence and even the identification of tortfeasors becomes more difficult with the passage of time due to missing records and lapsed memories. Virtually every aspect of tort law has been challenged by the novel claims and scientific issues that are presented in a toxic tort action.

3. Scientific Uncertainty and Causation Problems

Due to the long time period between exposure to the substance and the onset of the symptoms, it becomes difficult for a plaintiff to establish the necessary causal link between the substance and the injury. The likelihood of multiple intervening causes is greater with the passage of time. Further causal complications arise from the fact that many of the diseases alleged by toxic tort plaintiffs occur in background levels in the general population, and not just among those persons who have been exposed to the substance in question. For example, persons who were exposed to radiation during the United States Government's atomic testing program in the 1940s and 1950s have claimed that they developed leukemia and other cancers as a result of their exposures. The same illnesses occur in the general population as a result of numerous other causes, such as heredity, exposure to other substances, or exposure to radiation in other contexts; sometimes, they occur inexplicably and, apparently, spontaneously. *See* Allen v. United States (D. Utah 1984). As a result, in many instances it is virtually impossible to determine with any measure of certainty whether a plaintiff's illness arose from the defendant's product or conduct, or whether that plaintiff still would have developed the illness in the absence of the alleged exposure.

A related complicating factor in toxic tort litigation is the inability of science to connect many illnesses to their precise causes. The etiology of many illnesses, such as many cancers, autoimmune diseases, and neurological damage, is not completely understood in the medical community. Often, matters related to levels of exposure that could cause injury, and the kinds of injury produced by certain exposures, are open to reasonable debate in the scientific literature and among scientific researchers generally. Accordingly, clinical evidence of the plaintiff's physical condition or of the progression of the disease may not provide the solid evidence of causation that the same information may provide in other kinds of tort claims.

Consequently, it is not unusual for a plaintiff in a toxic tort action to allege a claim for which evidence of the cause-in-fact is lacking. Courts are now faced with the issue of whether or to what extent to allow such claims. The strongest evidence of causation in a toxic tort action is probabilistic evidence. Such evidence by its very nature can only demonstrate whether the particular substance to which the plaintiff was exposed *was capable* of producing the injury alleged. Probabilistic evidence cannot establish that exposure to the substance was the actual cause of the particular plaintiff's injury. It merely deals in probabilities, never in certainty.

Even where plaintiffs have been allowed to maintain actions without traditional cause-in-fact evidence, the end result has not necessarily been favorable to plaintiffs. In numerous cases in which plaintiffs have alleged birth defects as a result of in utero exposure to the prescription drug Bendectin, the actions have been dismissed either because the plaintiff's primary probabilistic evidence was deemed inadmissible under the applicable evidentiary standard or because the court deemed the probabilistic evidence to be insufficient to raise a triable question of fact. *See, e.g.*, DeLuca v. Merrell Dow Pharmaceuticals, Inc. (D.N.J.1992) (summary judgment dismissing action for insufficient expert evidence).

4. Reliance on Expert Scientific Testimony

The problems of causation outlined above render it necessary for the parties to a toxic tort action to focus closely on establishing or refuting a legally cognizable connection between the exposure alleged and the injury suffered by the plaintiff. In a conventional tort action, causal connections could be established to the jury by circumstantial evidence on matters often within the jury's knowledge and experience. The scientific and medical nature of toxic torts, however, requires the development of evidence about which few persons have the requisite level of knowledge or experience.

Often, in a conventional personal injury action, the testimony of a treating physician will be sufficient to establish the relationship between the defendant's product or conduct and the plaintiff's injuries. In toxic tort actions, the testimony of a treating physician is rarely sufficient. For example, in a traditional kind of tort—the motor vehicle accident—a plaintiff suffering from traumatic head injury typically will rely upon the treating physicians to describe the condition and to offer opinions from their professional knowledge and experience on the existence of brain damage and the degree of recovery expected. In a toxic tort, however, the treating physicians may know relatively little about the causation of the illness and, in some cases, may not even know of the exposure. Their task of treating the illness in many instances will be the same regardless of whether it was caused by exposure to a toxic substance or arose otherwise. To prove causation, toxic tort plaintiffs often must rely instead upon statistical information and reports of a variety of laboratory studies.

In determining the role that scientific evidence will play in the resolution of a toxic tort claim, courts are being called upon to consider the relationship between medical or scientific causation and legal causation. The level of certainty required to establish a causal relationship in scientific matters is upwards of ninety-five percent certainty. In contrast, the preponderance of the evidence standard applied in most civil actions in the United States is a mere fifty-one percent standard. Courts have been reluctant to recognize legal causation in the absence of scientific concurrence, however. Consequently, parties and their attorneys must focus their attention on the reliability of the type and quality of the expert testimony that supports their respective positions.

In addition, toxic tort claims have involved an unprecedented variety and number of experts. For example, a claim for personal injuries arising out of seepage of hazardous chemicals into the groundwater system beneath a disposal site and, ultimately, into the plaintiffs' drinking water supply could involve all of the following experts: chemist, industrial toxicologist, chemical engineer, environmental engineer, hydrogeologist, epidemiologist, and a wide variety of medical subspecialists, depending upon the injuries alleged. Considering that both plaintiffs and defendants will need experts to support their positions, the expert component of the litigation could become very time consuming and costly, and those costs could dictate the course of the litigation.

5. The Role of Risk

The causation problem is one example of the role that risk plays in toxic tort litigation. Probabilistic evidence is based upon risk; that is, it provides the court or jury with evidence of the risk of acquiring a certain illness as a result of exposure to a particular substance. Statisticians skilled in the area of epidemiology have created models that estimate the level of risk of illness from exposure to a substance. This is one form of risk analysis and is frequently used by both plaintiffs and defendants in toxic tort litigation. *See generally* Abraham M. Lilienfeld & David E. Lilienfeld, Foundations of Epidemiology 342–47 (2d ed. 1980). Translating statistical risk into legally cognizable standards has been problematic, however, and resistance to employing concepts of risk to form the basis of legal claims is pervasive.

Contemporary life carries with it certain risks that citizens perceive to be dangerous. Whether those fears are reasonable or not, aggrieved persons have sought relief both in the courts and through governmental regulation for claims based upon those risks, and courts have increasingly been willing to consider risk as a basis for the claims. Claims by toxic tort plaintiffs for emotional distress absent signs of physical injury (sometimes referred to as "cancerphobia"), for increased risk of disease, and for medical surveillance without a current medical condition all rely to some degree on risk as their foundation. In each of these types of claims, the plaintiff is seeking some form of relief purely on the basis of the risk of contracting some disease in the future.

Risk also forms the basis for environmental regulation. Regulatory officials consider the health and environmental effects of substances when determining whether to develop standards for or limitations on the manufacture, use, and disposal of those substances. Regulatory response to risk is often substance-specific and relatively narrow in focus. For example, OSHA standards exist for only a small percentage of the many substances that could be regulated in the occupational setting. This has led some to be critical of the current approach to use of risk in the regulatory process. *See* Hon. Stephen Breyer, Breaking the Vicious Circle 10–51 (1993) (arguing that Congressional and regulatory responses to risk tend to reflect public perceptions rather than risk analysts' priorities).

The disciplines of risk assessment and risk management have blossomed in recent decades and have become important tools with respect to the management and reduction of toxic and environmental risks, both by means of regulation and through the judicial system. In general, risk assessment involves the identification of potentially hazardous substances and a determination of the effects on humans of certain levels of exposure to the substances. Through the use of interdisciplinary methodologies and statistical extrapolation, the analysts attempt to predict the effect on populations of exposure to the identified substances. They also seek to characterize the substances with regard to the hazards they pose, such as whether a particular substance is carcinogenic.

Risk management, on the other hand, is a broader process and, in many ways, is more subjective than risk assessment. The risk manager's task is to determine the optimum means for addressing the risks identified by the risk assessment process. Ideally, the risk manager would be aware of the limitations of the data used. The risk management process is conducted in light of society's goals and policies, including the manner in which the risk information will be used by the legal system. *See generally* Carnegie Comm'n on Science, Technology and Government, Risk and the Environment: Improving Regulatory Decision Making (1993) (discussing and evaluating the roles of risk assessment and risk management in the environmental regulatory process).

The appropriate use of the risk assessment methodologies and proper interpretation of the data collected through the process are matters that continue to be open to dispute. Public perceptions, policy goals, and partisan political affiliations all play a role in the assessment and management of risk, whether through the regulatory process or in the court system.

6. Massive Scope

The exposures that form the basis of toxic tort lawsuits often affect many people. On occasion, the numbers have reached into the thousands. Some exposures occur at approximately the same time and under the same circumstances, as with the incident in Bhopal, India, which involved the release of the lethal gas methyl isocyanate from a plant that was a subsidiary of Union Carbide. *See generally* In re Union Carbide Gas Plant Disaster at Bhopal, India in Dec. 1984 (2d Cir.1987) (dismissing action on ground of forum non conveniens subject to condition that defendant submit to courts of India and not assert limitations defense). In contrast, some mass exposures have occurred to many people over a long period of time, up to several decades, and under a variety of circumstances.

A special problem emerging in many mass toxic tort actions involves the extent to which future claimants—those who have been exposed, but who have not manifested any symptoms of disease at the time of the litigation—should be or can be included in the settlement or judgment. The inclusion of future claimants in current litigation stretches the scope of the litigation indefinitely, as it would be a rare case indeed where the number of ultimate claimants could be predicted with accuracy.

The sheer magnitude of much toxic tort litigation has created significant judicial management problems. Judges may be faced with questions involving the use of the class action device or other available aggregative procedures to manage the litigation more efficiently. Pretrial practice, including discovery, necessarily takes on a heightened role in mass toxic tort litigation. Moreover, the wealth of scientific evidence that the parties seek to introduce calls for special expertise and specialized judicial management. All these factors combine to make the road to resolution a protracted process.

B. CONVERGENCE OF PUBLIC LAW AND PRIVATE LAW

The developing law of toxic torts exhibits a blending of principles arising from the common law and standards and approaches rooted in the regulatory aspects of public law. In 1980, when the Comprehensive Environmental Response Compensation and Liability Act (CERCLA), 42 U.S.C.A. §§ 9601–9675 (West 1983 & Supp. 1994) (also known as the "Superfund" statute), was enacted, Congress declined the opportunity to include remedies for personal injuries within the statute. Instead, the statute offered a remedial scheme allowing administrative and judicial actions by the Government—and, in some limited circumstances, by private parties—for matters relating to the clean-up of hazardous substances released into the environment. With a great deal of overlap, the law of toxic torts has evolved in the gap between traditional tort doctrine and public law. The result has had a synergistic effect, spinning off new legal territory that requires a jurisprudence of its own.

Attorneys whose practice encompasses what is now known as toxic torts may in fact be spending significant amounts of time involved in OSHA matters, handling claims in workers' compensation court, or defending citizen suits for administrative penalties authorized under the federal environmental laws. The methodologies and standards employed in the public sector with respect to toxic substances often differ from the standards that have evolved under the common law. A case filed by airline attendants for injuries alleged to have been suffered as a result of their exposures to environmental tobacco smoke while working allows reflection on some of these issues. As workers, the claimants would have workers' compensation claims against their employers. They would also have product liability claims against the cigarette manufacturers. Public law issues emerge as well, with the Government regulating smoking on airplanes, and OSHA and EPA seeking to regulate passive smoke in the workplace.

An understanding of the interaction between private law and public law, particularly in a complex piece of litigation, is crucial for attorneys practicing in this area.

CHAPTER TWO

THEORIES OF LIABILITY

The law of toxic torts has several provenances. One major source has been the relatively new law of product liability. Another major source has been the more traditional law of torts related to the land, such as nuisance and trespass. A third source has been the regulatory arena of environmental and occupational regulation. This Chapter will focus primarily on the uniquely *tort* aspect of these claims, but note will be taken of the areas in which interaction with public law is inevitable.

A. CLAIMS AGAINST SELLERS OF PRODUCTS

1. Product Liability Law and Toxic Torts

Early actions evinced a reluctance on the part of courts to extend the law of product liability to claims of injury due to exposure to toxic substances. In Bassham v. Owens–Corning Fiber Glass Corporation (D.N.M.1971), the court refused to treat a claim by an asbestos worker under the law of product liability, holding that occupational disease claims were not injury claims of the sort contemplated by the law of product liability. The long latency period between exposure to the asbestos and manifestation of the disease was a major factor in distinguishing the claim from the standard product liability claim in which an immediate injury occurs as a result of contact with a defective product. The judicial attitude in *Bassham* was fairly common until the mid–1970s.

Borel v. Fibreboard Paper Products Corporation (5th Cir.1973), is the seminal case that applied the law of strict product liability to workplace-related asbestos injury. The plaintiff, an industrial insulation worker, brought action against several manufacturers of asbestos-containing insulation materials for failure to warn of the hazards associated with handling asbestos. The plaintiff alleged that he had contracted asbestosis and mesothelioma (a form of lung cancer) from his exposure to asbestos in the workplace over a thirty-three year period.

Applying Texas law, the court held the manufacturers strictly liable for failure to adequately warn the plaintiff of the hazards of the asbestos-containing products with which he worked. In so doing, the court examined the medical literature regarding the effects of asbestos on workers and concluded that evidence of causation existed. The court's decision to hold the manufacturers strictly liable was significant as the leading departure from the line of cases from which *Bassham* was derived. It was also noteworthy in that although the jury had apportioned some measure of fault to the plaintiff in the action, the plaintiff was still able to recover. Under the applicable law of contributory negligence, the plaintiff was unable to recover on his negligence claim; but under the law of strict product liability, in which contributory negligence was not a defense, the plaintiff's fault was no impediment to recovery.

Once the *Borel* court presented its well-reasoned opinion in applying strict product liability to asbestos-related occupational disease, a flood of asbestos litigation entered the court systems. Furthermore, strict product liability law was applied to a variety of other products alleged to cause latent illness in plaintiffs. Toxic tort product liability claims are presented under a variety of theories, ranging from the more traditional negligence theories to strict liability theories.

2. Restatement (Second) § 402A Strict Liability Theories

Strict product liability law embodies the policy position that the costs of injuries can best be borne by the manufacturers and sellers of the products because the costs of accidents associated with those products can be spread among the purchasers of the products. As a matter of equity, the law reflects public expectations that sellers stand behind the products that they develop or sell. Section 402A of the Restatement provides as follows:

> (1) One who sells any product in a defective condition unreasonably dangerous to the user or consumer or to his property is subject to liability for physical harm thereby caused to the ultimate user or consumer, or to his property, if

    (a) the seller is engaged in the business of selling such a product, and

    (b) it is expected to and does reach the user or consumer without substantial change in the condition in which it is sold.

(2) The rule stated in Subsection (1) applies although

    (a) the seller has exercised all possible care in the preparation and sale of his product, and

    (b) the user or consumer has not bought the product from or entered into any contractual relation with the seller.

Thus, no privity between the injured party and the manufacturer or seller is required for liability to attach. And, no attention to the manufacturer or seller's fault is necessary, at least theoretically. *See generally* Greenman v. Yuba Power Products, Inc. (Cal.1963) (initially stating rule allowing tort actions against sellers of defective products without need to prove culpable conduct).

The only requirements of Section 402A are that the defendant be "in the business of selling" the product, that the product be "in a defective condition unreasonably dangerous," and that the plaintiff be an "ultimate user or consumer." Implicit in Section 402A is the additional requirement that the plaintiff prove that the product caused the injuries alleged. Claims for toxic products so far have tended to center on asbestos, cigarettes, and prescription drugs and medical devices. A product may be defective in several different ways, and it is not uncommon to find more than one type of defect alleged in a plaintiff's complaint.

a. Design Defect

Much of the controversy generated by Section 402A has been directed at the interpretation of the meaning of "defective condition," with respect to both design defects and manufacturing defects. With respect to design defects, two distinct approaches have emerged for defining the concept. The first is commonly known as the consumer expectation test. This test derives from Comment i of 402A, which defines "unreasonably dangerous" as "dangerous to an extent beyond that which would be contemplated by the ordinary consumer who purchases it, with the ordinary knowledge common to the community as to its characteristics." Although this test appears to be relatively easy to apply, it is much more difficult to apply in cases involving alleged toxic products, where the reasonable consumer's expectations may be unclear. Moreover, anomalous results could be achieved in situations in which the danger was known or obvious (no liability), even though the product could have been designed to be safer.

More recently, in design defect cases, courts have begun to favor a risk-utility, or risk-benefit, balancing test, according to which the product will be deemed defective where the danger outweighs the product's utility. This test incorporates an examination of whether alternative designs were available that would have eliminated the risks of the product in question. It also necessarily includes consideration of the costs of developing a safer product. Courts are in disagreement as to the relative weight to be given to these various factors when applying a risk-utility analysis. In addition, consumer groups have complained that the risk-utility test allows manufacturers to be immunized from liability for design defects for very hazardous products simply because of the products' high degree of utility. Despite the fertile ground for disagreement over application of the risk-utility test, the Reporters for the revision of the Restatement of Torts have proposed to eliminate the consumer expectation test from the Restatement (Third) of Torts: Products Liability, now in draft stages, and endorse the risk-utility test.

b. Manufacturing Defect

A manufacturing, or production, defect relates to a product that was produced out of conformity with the product's design and the manufacturer's intent. The classic example of a manufacturing defect is one of the cases in which a decomposed mouse was found in a bottle of soda. *See, e.g.*, Shoshone Coca–Cola Bottling Co. v. Dolinski (Nev.1966). Although toxic tort actions may certainly arise from manufacturing defects, such claims are less frequent in the toxic tort context than design defects or failure to warn. Nevertheless, a manufacturing defect claim may, for example, arise where a foreign chemical contaminates a batch of a particular product. This was exemplified by the situation in the 1970s in Michigan, when farm feed containing PBBs (a fire-retardant chemical not intended to be in the feed) was fed to farm animals, causing loss of livestock and initiating a variety of claims. *See* Oscoda Chapter of PBB Action Committee, Inc. v. Department of Natural Resources (Mich.1978) (addressing issues involving the burial of PBB-contaminated livestock).

c. *Failure to Warn*

Failure to warn of the hazards of an allegedly toxic product is generally treated as a separate strict liability theory. It also constitutes a product defect, however. The leading case in the area of toxic torts is Borel v. Fibreboard Paper Products Corp. (5th Cir.1973), previously discussed. A major difficulty in applying the developing law of warning defects to toxic torts is the unknowability of hazards at the time of the manufacture and sale of the product. Thus, an issue has arisen as to whether the seller may defend against the action on the ground that it did not know, nor could it have known, the consequences of the product's use at the time of the plaintiff's exposure. This "state-of-the-art" defense is discussed in more detail *infra*. The more the court allows the finder of fact to consider the knowledge and, in effect, culpable conduct of the defendant in determining liability, the closer the theory of failure to warn inches towards negligence.

In general, the seller of the product is under a duty to disclose only foreseeable risks associated with the product. In *Borel*, for example, the court examined closely the development of scientific knowledge regarding the hazards of working with asbestos insulation products before concluding that the risks were foreseeable as early as the 1930s. Even very small foreseeable risks may trigger liability. In Davis v. Wyeth Laboratories, Inc. (9th Cir. 1968), the court held that a manufacturer of polio vaccine had a duty to warn consumers of the risk that one person in one million would contract polio through taking the vaccine. The court stated:

> There will, of course, be cases where the personal risk, although existent and known, is so trifling in comparison with the advantage to be gained as to be de minimis. Appellee so characterizes this case. It would approach the problem from a purely statistical point of view: less than one out of a million is just not unreasonable. This approach we reject. When, in a particular case, the risk qualitatively (e.g., of death or major disability) as well as quantitatively, on balance with the end sought to be achieved, is such as to call for a true choice judgment, medical or personal, the warning must be given.

Furthermore, the manufacturer will be held to the "knowledge and skill of an expert." *See Borel, supra*. Thus, the manufacturer has an affirmative obligation to keep aware of current scientific developments related to its products, as well as to conduct its own reasonable inquiry into the effectiveness and safety of the products. The *Borel* court stated:

> The manufacturer's status as an expert means that at a minimum he must keep abreast of scientific knowledge, discoveries, and advances and is presumed to know what is imparted thereby. But even more importantly, a manufacturer has a duty to test and inspect his product. The extent of research and experiment must be commensurate with the dangers involved.

Even where a risk/utility analysis leads to the conclusion that the utility of the product outweighs its risks—thereby resulting in the conclusion that the product is not defectively designed—inadequate warnings will not be excused. The court in *Borel* examined the risks and benefits of asbestos insulation products, but emphasized the importance of adequate warning. The court stated: "The utility of an insulation product containing asbestos may outweigh the known or foreseeable risk to the insulation workers and thus justify its marketing. The product could still be unreasonably dangerous, however, if unaccompanied by adequate warnings."

3. Implied Warranties

Article Two of the Uniform Commercial Code, adopted in virtually every state, supplies the basic rules governing claims under implied warranties. Uniform Commercial Code § 2–314 establishes an implied warranty of merchantability in a contract of sale in which the seller is "a merchant with respect to goods of that kind." UCC § 2–314(1). To be merchantable, the product must, at a minimum, be "fit for the ordinary purposes for which such goods are used" (§ 2–314(2)(c)), be "adequately contained, packaged, and labeled as the agreement [of sale] may require" (§ 2–314(2)(e)), and "conform to the promises or affirmations of fact made on the container or label if any" (§ 2–314(2)(f)).

A warranty of fitness for a particular purpose is also implied in the sale of a product. UCC § 2–315 provides that

> [w]here the seller at the time of contracting has reason to know any particular purpose for which the goods are required ant that the buyer is relying on the seller's skill or judgment to select or furnish suitable goods, there is ... an implied warranty that the goods shall be fit for such purpose.

As distinguished from an implied warranty of merchantability, this section does not require the seller of the product to be a "merchant" of the type of goods sold. Furthermore, the section provides that the seller should know that the buyer will be relying on the seller's skill or judgment.

The UCC does not require that the person making the warranty claim be in privity of contract with the seller of the product. The extent to which persons related or unrelated to the buyer may rely upon the implied warranties will depend upon which alternative set forth in UCC § 2–318 the state has enacted. These alternatives range from the more restrictive (family members, household members, and guests of the buyer) to the quite liberal (persons who could bring product liability actions in tort).

Warranty claims have been asserted in many toxic tort actions, typically along with negligence and strict product liability claims. Perhaps because warranty claims derive from the law of contracts, these claims tend to be given less emphasis than the tort claims in judicial decisions in the area of toxic torts. Nevertheless, they continue to be recognized as prominent among the claims in the toxic product plaintiff's arsenal. *See, e.g.*, Cipollone v. Liggett Group, Inc. (S.Ct.1992) (holding that implied warranty claims against cigarette manufacturers for injuries associated with smoking were pre-empted by Federal Cigarette Labeling and Advertising Act).

4. Misrepresentation Claims

a. *Express Warranty*

In addition to implied warranties, product sellers may make express warranties to consumers. The rule of express warranties also derives from the Uniform Commercial Code. UCC § 2–313 provides that a seller makes an express warranty by "affirmation of fact or promise made" (§ 2–313(1)(a)), by "description of the goods" (§ 2–313(1)(b)), or by a "sample or model" (§ 2–313(1)(c)), any of which must have been made a part of the basis of the bargain between the seller and the buyer. Breach of an express warranty essentially creates a strict liability, as the product need not be shown to be defective for the breach of warranty claim to lie. Nor need the plaintiff demonstrate reliance on the warranty, unless the seller affirmatively proves lack of reliance. UCC § 2–313, comments.

b. *Strict Liability for Misrepresentation*

A strict tort liability claim for misrepresentation is set forth in the Restatement (Second) of Torts and is recognized in many jurisdictions. Section 402B of the Restatement provides:

One engaged in the business of selling chattels who, by advertising, labels, or otherwise, makes to the public a misrepresentation of a material fact concerning the character or quality of a chattel sold by him is subject to liability for physical harm to a consumer of the chattel caused by justifiable reliance upon the misrepresentation, even though

(a) it is not made fraudulently or negligently, and

(b) the consumer has not bought the chattel from or entered into any contractual relation with the seller.

Here, as with Section 402A, the seller must be "in the business of selling chattels." The section also focuses on the public nature of the misrepresentation, such as—but not limited to—advertisements and other forms of sales promotions.

Moreover, in contrast to express warranty theories under the UCC, Section 402B expressly requires "justifiable reliance" by the consumer on the representations made by the seller. What constitutes justifiable reliance? In Gunsalus v. Celotex Corp. (E.D.Pa.1987), the court dismissed the plaintiff's misrepresentation claims arising out of cigarette advertisements that the plaintiff alleged misrepresented the health and safety aspects of smoking. The plaintiff alleged reliance on certain advertisements that made representations that the specific brand of cigarettes was soothing to the throat. The court held that the ads were "not the kind of representations upon which reasonable people would rely; they suggest only that a smoker might enjoy Pall Mall cigarettes more than other brands." The court further noted that once the plaintiff had tried the particular cigarette brand, his decision to continue smoking it was based upon his own taste choices and/or his alleged addiction, not upon the seller's representations.

5. Negligence

The *Borel* case evidenced the perils of relying upon a negligence theory in a latent disease case in the era when contributory negligence barred recovery by plaintiffs in most jurisdictions. Without question, most toxic product defendants would prefer to rely upon strict liability theories than upon negligence. But whether negligence is asserted as a fallback position or as the only available claim under the circumstances of the case, plaintiffs will need to prove the standard negligence prima facie case. This traditionally requires the plaintiff to prove the elements of duty, breach of duty, proximate causation, and damages. The standard of care defining the duty, and the existence of a breach of the duty, may be difficult to prove where a latency period exists between the time of the exposure and the manifestation of illness. It requires the plaintiff to demonstrate both the defendant's knowledge of the hazards at the time of exposure and the foreseeability of harm to the plaintiff.

Actions based upon contaminated blood products present an example of the problems that latent-illness negligence claims sometimes may present. While the supplying of blood and other body parts is generally considered a service, rather than a product, negligence claims against the suppliers of blood products are quite similar to negligence claims involving other products. The blood product negligence claims have tended to focus upon the time at which the blood suppliers became aware of the bloodborne nature of AIDS and the availability of steps to screen donated blood for HIV at the time in question. With respect to the applicable standard of care, courts differ as to whether a defendant can rely upon industry practices at the time to establish its duty.

In general, a blood supplier is held to a professional standard for a skilled provider of the same services. In Doe v. American Red Cross Blood Services (S.C.1989), the court interpreted this to mean that the blood supplier must "conform to the

generally recognized and accepted practices in his
profession" at the relevant time. But other courts
have held that mere compliance with industry practices cannot by itself establish the defendant's compliance with due care. In United Blood Services v.
Quintana (Colo.1992), the court stated:

> In a professional negligence case ... a plaintiff
> should be permitted to present expert opinion
> testimony that the standard of care adopted by
> the school of practice to which the defendant
> adheres is unreasonably deficient by not incorpo-
> rating readily available practices and procedures
> substantially more protective against the harm
> caused to the plaintiff than the standard of care
> adopted by the defendant's school of practice....
>
>   . . .
>
> In the instant case, [the blood supplier's] compli-
> ance with the Food and Drug Administration's
> recommendations and with the guidelines devel-
> oped by the national blood banking community
> was some evidence of due care, but was not
> conclusive proof that additional precautions were
> not required.

In *Quintana*, the jury, on remand, found the defendant negligent notwithstanding its compliance with
the industry standards. Not all cases have reached
the same result, however. *See, e.g.*, Doe v. Miles
Laboratories, Inc. (4th Cir.1991) (holding that the
defendant blood clotting factor manufacturer had
not breached the applicable standard of care after
examining industry custom, governmental regula-

tions, and medical profession standards at the relevant times). *See also* McKee v. Miles Laboratories, Inc. (E.D.Ky.1987) (dismissing negligence claims for failure to show violation of standard of care).

The AIDS cases have tended to focus on the timing of the defendant's conduct as well as the reasonableness of the conduct. In Kozup v. Georgetown University (D.D.C.1987), the court apparently held that blood suppliers that complied with industry standards prior to 1985—when the ELISA test for screening blood for the presence of HIV antibodies was developed and implemented in the blood industry—could not as a matter of law be negligent for failure to test blood, notwithstanding the existence of another, less reliable, testing procedure. Similarly, whether a defendant breached its duty by failing to screen out high risk blood donors has depended upon the date of the exposure in relation to the knowledge of the defendant regarding the risk of AIDS transmission in human blood. *See, e.g.,* Hoemke v. New York Blood Center (2d Cir. 1990) (no negligence for transfusion occurring in 1981).

6. Regulatory Duty to Disclose

Product manufacturers have certain regulatory duties that may create liabilities beyond the direct liability to an injured user or consumer. One such liability is imposed by the Hazard Communication Standard, 29 C.F.R. § 1910.1200 (1994), authorized pursuant to the Occupational Safety and Health Act ("OSHAct"), the primary statute governing health issues in the workplace. The Hazard Communication Standard requires chemical manufacturers and importers to evaluate, by considering the available scientific information, the chemicals produced or imported by them to determine the hazards associated with the chemicals. Further, the manufacturers and importers must create a material safety data sheet (MSDS) for each hazardous chemical, which shall travel with the chemical when it leaves the hands of the manufacturer or importer and is transferred to a distributor or employer. The manufacturer or importer is also required to label the chemicals with "appropriate hazard warnings," which should include a description of the target organ effects of exposure to the chemicals. Martin v. American Cyanamid Co. (6th Cir.1993). Subsequently, employers are obligated to pass the information on to their employees who come into contact with the chemical, pursuant to certain defined regulatory procedures. *See generally infra* Chapter 4, Sec. C(4).

B. PRODUCT LIABILITY DEFENSES

Toxic tort claims stretch the law of product liability beyond its originally intended limits. Accordingly, it is within the context of toxic tort actions that courts have been asked to apply certain product defenses in new ways. This has been particularly notable with respect to the unknowable character of many hazards at the time the product was sold. While this information is always relevant to negligence claims, and is usually relevant in strict product liability claims, arguments from dissenting jurisdictions raise important policy questions about the role of strict liability in the legal system. The same may be said of certain other defenses as well.

1.   State-of-the-Art Defense

The state-of-the-art defense has been asserted in strict liability claims where the defendant alleges that it did not know, and could not reasonably have known, of the hazards of the product at the time of the plaintiff's exposure. The defense has been widely recognized in failure to warn cases. *See, e.g.*, Anderson v. Owens–Corning Fiberglas Corp. (Cal.1991).

A vocal—and controversial—minority opinion has been expressed by the New Jersey Supreme Court in an early failure to warn case involving asbestos workers. In Beshada v. Johns–Manville Products Corp. (N.J.1982), the court refused to allow the state-of-the-art defense, even though the extent and timing of the defendants' knowledge of the hazards associated with their asbestos-containing products were in dispute. The court noted that the state-of-the-art defense essentially is a negligence defense because it focuses on the culpability of the defendant at the times relevant to the warning. The court examined the policies underlying the law of strict product liability—most particularly, risk spreading and deterrence—and concluded that un-diluted strict liability best served the goals of the tort system. Moreover, the court expressed concern that undertaking the task of determining what was scientifically knowable at a particular point in time would consume judicial resources and ultimately lead to jury confusion.

The *Beshada* court's opinion points out both sides of the policy argument regarding allowance of the state-of-the-art defense:

> One of the most important arguments generally advanced for imposing strict liability is that the manufacturers and distributors of defective products can best allocate the costs of the injuries resulting from those products. The premise is that the price of a product should reflect all of its costs, including the cost of injuries caused by the product. This can best be accomplished by imposing liability on the manufacturer and distributors. Those persons can insure against liability and incorporate the cost of the insurance in the price of the product. . . .

> Defendants argue that this policy is not forwarded by imposition of liability for unknowable hazards. Since such hazards by definition are not predicted, the price of the hazardous product will not be adjusted to reflect the costs of the injuries it will produce. Rather, defendants state, the cost "will be borne by the public at large and reflected in a general, across the board increase in premiums to compensate for unanticipated risks."

With respect to deterrence, the court noted that the level of the state of the art at a particular moment in time is affected by the level of research and development conducted by the industry at that time. The court stated: "By imposing on manufacturers the costs of failure to discover hazards, we create an incentive for them to invest more actively in safety research."

In 1984, shortly after the *Beshada* case, the New Jersey Supreme Court allowed the state-of-the-art defense in a product liability action against drug manufacturers. Feldman v. Lederle Laboratories (N.J.1984). The court in *Feldman* expressly limited *Beshada* to its facts, presumably the unique circumstances of asbestos litigation. Some courts would disagree as to the propriety of the distinction made by the New Jersey Supreme Court in these cases. When asbestos manufacturers raised the question of the constitutionality of this distinction between asbestos cases and other types of cases, they were rebuffed. *See* In re Asbestos Litig. (3d Cir.1987) (holding classifications not unconstitutional).

Most jurisdictions, however, do allow the state-of-the-art defense in failure to warn cases, whether or not the product involved contains asbestos. *See, e.g.*, Anderson v. Owens–Corning Fiberglas Corp. (Cal.1991). Nevertheless, the *Beshada* opinion continues to be an emphatic, if not compelling, argument against the introduction of the state-of-the-art defense in certain kinds of cases.

2. Unavoidably Unsafe Products

Some products may be incapable of being made safe for the use for which they were intended, but their usefulness may outweigh the risk of harm. The unavoidably unsafe product is the subject of comment k of Restatement § 402A, which states that "[s]uch a product, properly prepared, and accompanied by proper directions and warning, is not defective, nor is it unreasonably dangerous." The policy behind this defense is to encourage the development of useful and highly necessary products by allowing the seller to avoid liability associated with the risks of those products. As comment k states, however, the seller remains under an obligation to provide an appropriate warning to the consumer regarding the risks associated with the product. Thus, comment k applies directly to design defects, but not to manufacturing defects or failure to warn claims.

The classic example of an unavoidably unsafe product is an experimental drug that could be quite beneficial for one therapeutic purpose, but that may carry with it other significant risks. The battle on the application of comment k has been waged primarily in the arena of prescription drugs. Some courts have held that comment k is properly applied on a case-by-case basis. *See* Savina v. Sterling Drug, Inc. (Kan.1990); *see also* Hill v. Searle Laboratories (8th Cir.1989) (holding that only products "with exceptional social need" fall within comment k protection). The case-by-case analysis would seem to be consistent with the language of comment k itself, which provides various examples of the kinds of prescription drugs that would appropriately fall within the comment's protection, but which does not suggest that all prescription drugs—or all of any other class of product—should be considered unavoidably unsafe.

Other courts, in contrast, have read comment k as applicable to certain broad classes of claims. In particular, in Brown v. Superior Court (Cal.1988), a DES case, the California Supreme Court held that all prescription drugs are deemed unavoidably unsafe. The court's concerns were that liability for prescription drug defects could drive manufacturers from the market, that strict liability could lead to protracted delays in new drugs reaching the market, and that manufacturers' insurance rates would soar. In Grundberg v. Upjohn Company (Utah 1991), the Utah Supreme Court agreed, emphasizing the social benefit of prescription drugs. The *Grundberg* court noted that the Food and Drug Administration (FDA) often grants approval to market new drugs that contain known risks on the basis of their beneficial qualities. The court found that the regulatory process for licensing new drugs and providing post-market surveillance adequately balanced the drugs' risks with their benefits and was the proper forum for that analysis.

3. Sophisticated User Defense

In some commercial situations, the party to whom the product is delivered is in a position superior to the seller to know the ultimate uses of the product. Courts have allowed a "sophisticated user" defense in appropriate circumstances where the seller provides adequate warning of the hazards

of the product to the purchaser. This defense is
often employed in the context of bulk suppliers of
chemicals to knowledgeable intermediaries. Thus,
in Adams v. Union Carbide Corp. (6th Cir.1984),
the court affirmed the trial court's grant of summary judgment in favor of Union Carbide, the man-
ufacturer/supplier of the chemical toluene diisocya-
nate (TDI), which Union Carbide had sold to the
plaintiff's employer, General Motors. The plaintiff
alleged that Union Carbide should have given direct
warning to the employees of General Motors. The
court relied on Restatement (Second) of Torts
§ 388, comment n, finding that Union Carbide's
safety manual, the MSDS (the information sheet on
the hazards of the product provided by the supplier), and safety discussion sessions with General
Motors officials satisfied Union Carbide's obligation
to provide adequate warnings. Moreover, Union
Carbide reasonably relied upon General Motors to
communicate the safety information to its employees.

In Oman v. Johns–Manville Corp. (4th Cir.1985),
the court applied a balancing test to determine
whether the manufacturer of asbestos-containing
products had a duty to warn the employees of the
purchaser of its products. The factors set forth in
this test were:

   (1) the dangerous condition of the product; (2)
   the purpose for which the product is used; (3) the
   form of any warnings given; (4) the reliability of
   the third party as a conduit of necessary information about the product; (5) the magnitude of the

risk involved; and (6) the burdens imposed upon the supplier by requiring that he directly warn all users.

In *Oman*, the court did not allow the sophisticated user defense because the product was extremely dangerous and little burden would be placed upon the manufacturer to provide the warning. Furthermore, the record showed that the employer was unaware of the dangers until 1964, and, upon becoming aware, failed to communicate the dangers to its employees. Reaching a similar result, the court in Willis v. Raymark Industries, Inc. (4th Cir.1990), stated that "[t]he fact that an employer possesses knowledge of a product's dangers does not extinguish the manufacturer's liability unless the manufacturer can also show that it had reason to believe that the employer was or would be acting to protect the employees."

On the other hand, where the employer can be shown to be in a position to adequately warn its employees, the existence of adequate warnings from the supplier may be irrelevant. At least one court has applied the sophisticated user defense where inadequate warnings were given by the supplier. Newson v. Monsanto Co. (E.D.Mich.1994), involved the sale of polyvinyl butyryl (PVB) to Ford Motor Company for use in manufacturing shatterproof windshields. When workers brought suit against the supplier for respiratory injuries that they claimed were related to exposure to heated PVB, the court allowed the supplier to avoid liability on the basis that Ford was a sophisticated user of the

PVB. The court so held notwithstanding the fact that the supplier had not provided an adequate warning regarding the hazards of heated PVB. The court determined that Ford, which had several departments engaged in scientific research, could have learned of the hazards of heated PVB by conducting its own research and through its own past experience.

4. Learned Intermediary Defense

Whereas the sophisticated user defense is typically raised in the context of an industrial situation in which the plaintiff is an employee of the party determined to be a "sophisticated user," the learned intermediary doctrine is sometimes raised when the defendant claims that other kinds of parties with superior knowledge had the responsibility to warn the user of the product of its hazards. *See, e.g.*, Swayze v. McNeil Laboratories, Inc. (5th Cir.1987) (applying learned intermediary defense where drug manufacturer only warned prescribing physician). The learned, or knowledgeable, intermediary defense has been asserted in medical malpractice cases, but may arise in other professional contexts. When asserted in a toxic tort action, it is analogous to the sophisticated user defense, relying upon the same underlying principles.

For example, Mazur v. Merck & Co. (3d Cir.1992), involved production of the MMRII vaccine by defendant Merck, which then sold the vaccine to the Centers for Disease control (CDC) for distribution under a mass immunization program. Under an express agreement, the CDC agreed to provide adequate warnings to parents of children receiving the vaccine in the program. The warning eventually transmitted by the CDC to the parents of children in the program was based upon information from Merck and independent studies by the CDC. The plaintiffs alleged that their child had developed a fatal neurological condition from the dose of the MMRII vaccine she had received through the program. Characterizing the product as "unavoidably unsafe," the court held that Merck satisfied its obligation to warn of the hazards of the vaccine and upheld Merck's agreement with the CDC, finding the CDC to be a learned intermediary. Thus, the defense absolved Merck of any liability to warn. *But see* Allison v. Merck & Co. (Nev.1994) (in vaccine program in which manufacturer contracted with CDC to provide product information to patients, manufacturer may not delegate duty to warn and may be liable for failure to adequately warn ultimate user).

5. Blood Shield Statutes

Virtually every state has enacted legislation shielding suppliers of blood and blood products from strict product liability claims for contaminated blood. In Royer v. Miles Laboratory, Inc. (Or.Ct. App.1991), the court interpreted the Oregon blood shield statute in a case brought by a hemophiliac who contracted hepatitis and AIDS from a blood clotting product. The appellate court affirmed the trial court's dismissal of the strict liability claims on the basis of the statutory language, which provided:

(1) The procuring, processing, furnishing, distributing, administering or using of any part of a human body for the purpose of injecting, transfusing or transplanting that part into a human body is not a sales transaction covered by an implied warranty under the Uniform Commercial Code or otherwise.

Or. Rev. Stat. § 97.300. Because the concept of strict liability in tort was essentially an offshoot of breach of warranty under the UCC, the court construed the statute to bar strict product liability claims against the manufacturer of the clotting product.

The policies underlying the blood shield statutes are two-fold. First, the state legislatures feared that allowing strict liability against providers of blood and blood products would cause providers to leave the market. Second, the costs of liability, coupled with a diminished market, would raise the cost of blood products to a prohibitive level. Third, the blood industry had charitable beginnings, and the notion of treating it in a similar fashion to profit-making product manufacturers was distasteful. Consequently, providing blood and blood products has been traditionally viewed as a service, rather than as the sale of a product.

Most state blood shield statutes were developed in the pre-AIDS era, and at a time when the selling of blood and blood products was not considered big business. In many respects, these products are now sold in the same fashion as other products, with non-profit blood suppliers realizing profits from the sale and resale of blood. Blood products are distributed into the stream of commerce with markups in price at every stage leading to their ultimate destination. These factors raise the issue of whether blood shield statutes may be inappropriate for the claims and injuries of the 1990s and beyond.

A further reason for the legislative restrictions on the use of strict product liability claims is the difficulty in viewing contaminated blood and other human body parts as products in the traditional sense. This has been problematic both in a moral sense and as a matter of legal doctrine. Thus, contaminated blood is not seen as the kind of defect that Section 402A was intended to reach. Resembling a manufacturing defect more closely than a design defect, contaminated blood defies strict categorization into any of these theories. The fact that strict product liability is not available for claims arising from the sale of blood and blood products does not preclude claims based upon negligence, however. *See generally* Section A.5 *supra*.

C. CLAIMS RELATED TO ACTIVITIES ON THE LAND

When a toxic tort action arises from the defendant's activities on land, and/or affect the plaintiff's interest in property, the relationship between private law and public law becomes clearest. The activities out of which such claims may arise can be quite diverse, from the disposal of hazardous waste to ordinary industrial activity. While the law of torts provides remedies for such injuries, the law has been asked to stretch traditional causes of action to fit the toxic tort context. In addition, federal and state laws regulate many activities on the land, and defendant companies may be subject to additional regulatory liabilities beyond the strict operation of tort law. Most notably, private toxic tort actions may be associated with clean-up liabilities pursuant to the Comprehensive Environmental Response, Compensation, and Liability Act (CERCLA), also known as the Superfund law. The private actions are set forth in this Chapter, whereas a more detailed discussion of CERCLA is presented in Chapter Three.

1. Strict Liability for Abnormally Dangerous Activities

The concept of land-related strict liability derives from the English case of Rylands v. Fletcher (1865), which provided for absolute liability of owners or occupiers of land on which non-natural and hazardous activities were being undertaken. Under this rule, the plaintiff need not show lack of due care on the part of the landowner. Whereas *Rylands* was limited to situations in which the owner or occupier brings onto the land a thing that is "likely to do mischief if it escapes," modern American courts have expanded this doctrine to include any ultra-hazardous activity, including the storage of hazardous chemicals on the property. *See* Cities Service Co. v. State (Fla. Dist. Ct.App.1975) (holding that phosphate waste stored on property that contaminated adjacent drinking water supply constituted a non-natural use of land and invoked doctrine of strict liability).

The most recent incarnation of *Rylands* appears in the Restatement (Second) of Torts §§ 519–520, which replaced the "ultrahazardous" language contained in the first Restatement with the concept of "abnormally dangerous activity" and a multi-factored test. Section 519 provides:

(1) One who carries on an abnormally dangerous activity is subject to liability for harm to the person, land or chattels of another resulting from the activity, although he has exercised the utmost care to prevent the harm.

(2) This strict liability is limited to the kind of harm, the possibility of which makes the activity abnormally dangerous.

Thus, reasonable care on the part of the landowner will not prevent liability if the activity is abnormally dangerous and the harm is associated with those dangerous qualities. The reasoning underlying strict liability for such activities is to require "[t]he defendant's enterprise ... to pay its way by compensating for the harm it causes." Restatement (Second) of Torts § 519, comment d (1965).

To determine what is abnormally dangerous, Section 520 sets forth several factors:

(a) existence of a high degree of risk of some harm to the person, land or chattels of others;

(b) likelihood that the harm that results from it will be great;

(c) inability to eliminate the risk by the exercise of reasonable care;

(d) extent to which the activity is not a matter of common usage;

(e) inappropriateness of the activity to the place where it is carried on; and

(f) extent to which its value to the community is outweighed by its dangerous attributes.

The factors incorporate a kind of risk-utility analysis in that the value of the activity to the community enters into the calculus and is to be balanced against the degree of harm. Comment f to Section 520 makes clear, however, that all listed factors are to be considered, but that no single factor is to be dispositive and not all of them need be applicable for a finding of abnormal danger.

In Sterling v. Velsicol Chemical Corp. (W.D.Tenn. 1986), the district court examined the activities of the defendant in maintaining a chemical waste burial site that allegedly contaminated neighboring water wells. The court determined that the defendant's activities satisfied both the *Rylands* test and the Restatement (Second) test for strict liability. The court applied the Section 520 factors and held that increased risk of disease and diminished quality of life as a result of exposure to the chemicals constituted a great risk of harm. According to the court, the risk of harm ultimately outweighed any value that the defendant's enterprise had to the community. As in *Sterling*, a number of courts that have considered the issue have held that the disposal or storage of hazardous substances constitutes an abnormally dangerous activity under the Restatement test. *See, e.g.*, State Dep't of Envt'l Protection v. Ventron Corp. (N.J.1983) (concluding that mercury and other toxic wastes are abnormally dangerous substances and that their disposal is an abnormally dangerous activity).

In contrast, however, some courts have held that the handling of hazardous substances does not necessarily constitute an abnormally dangerous activity. *See* Avemco Insurance Co. v. Rooto Corp. (6th Cir.1992); Arawana Mills Co. v. United Technologies Corp. (D.Conn.1992); Richmond, Fredericksburg & Potomac Railroad Co. v. Davis Industries, Inc. (E.D.Va.1992). These cases tend to focus on the ability of the landowner to eliminate the hazards associated with the substances that they handled or stored.

2. Trespass

Historically, the tort of trespass applies to invasive actions that interfere with a person's possessory interest in property. In this sense, it is distinguishable from nuisance, which provides a broader claim for interferences with property, as discussed in the next section. Although the defendant need not have actually entered onto the plaintiff's property, the defendant must have caused the entry of a concrete substance onto the property. *See generally* Prosser & Keeton on the Law of Torts 67–84 (5th ed. 1984 & Supp. 1987). Toxic torts have pushed the technical definition of such an invasion because toxic torts can involve microscopic substances in the air, water, or soil that invade the property of the plaintiff. Notwithstanding this new category of invasive substances, the case law indicates that the tort of trespass accommodates the evolution into toxic torts.

The Restatement (Second) of Torts § 158 sets forth the basic provisions of liability for trespass:

One is subject to liability to another for trespass, irrespective of whether he thereby causes harm to any legally protected interest of the other, if he intentionally

(a) enters land in the possession of the other, or causes a thing or a third person to do so, or

(b) remains on the land, or

(c) fails to remove from the land a thing which he is under a duty to remove.

The Restatement makes clear that liability for trespass exists for both direct and indirect invasions of property. Further, the invasion may be on the surface of the land, beneath the land, or in the air above the land. *See id.*, comment i & § 159. With respect to the requirement of intent in the case of more indirect invasions, comment i explains: "[I]t is not necessary that the foreign matter should be thrown directly and immediately upon the other's land. It is enough that an act is done with knowledge that it will to a substantial certainty result in the entry of the foreign matter." In contrast, an accidental injury, without this requisite intent, would not be actionable as a trespass. *See generally* Prosser & Keeton on the Law of Torts 73–75 (5th ed. 1984).

Historically speaking, a trespass action was maintainable even without a showing of harm, resembling a strict liability standard. Thus, nominal damages could be recovered by virtue of the invasion of the property alone. Toxic torts cases have called upon courts to interpret this principle in a different context from that in which the tort of trespass initially arose. Particularly in cases involving invisible particles containing toxic substances, there may be a reluctance to allow a trespass claim where actual damages are not present.

Courts have recognized that a trespass may still occur where the invasion is by invisible substances. In Martin v. Reynolds Metals Co. (Or.1959), gases and particulate matter composed of fluoride compounds from an aluminum smelting operation that had drifted onto the land of the plaintiff were held to constitute a trespass. The court stated that it "prefer[red] to emphasize the object's energy or force rather than its size." The *Martin* court stated, however, that not all invasions are, as a matter of law, actionable in trespass: "[A] possessor's interest is not invaded by an intrusion which is so

trifling that it cannot be recognized by the law. . . .
[T]here is a point where the entry is so lacking in
substance that the law will refuse to recognize it,
applying the maxim de minimis non curat lex."
This case indicates that despite the rigid historical
pedigree of the law of trespass, courts may impose
their own thresholds in certain categories of cases.

In Bradley v. American Smelting and Refining
Co. (Wash.1985), the court went further and imposed a requirement of actual damages in another
case involving invisible particulate matter. Ac-
knowledging that "our concept of 'things' must be
reframed" in light of modern usages of the land, the
court agreed that invisible particles, at least in
some circumstances, could constitute a trespassory
invasion. Adopting a test announced in Borland v.
Sanders Lead Co. (Ala.1979), the *Bradley* court required a showing by the plaintiff of "substantial
damages to the res." Thus, the *Bradley* court felt
constrained to place a requirement of actual damages on this kind of case.

The rather rigid historical requirements of the
tort of trespass make that tort theory less attractive
to plaintiffs who seek remedies for interference with
their rights and interests in their property. These
requirements also include numerous privileges that
may be asserted as defenses to a trespass claim.
See Restatement (Second) of Torts §§ 191–211
(1965). The much greater flexibility of the law of
nuisance makes nuisance claims a preferable course
of litigation for many plaintiffs.

3. Nuisance

Nuisance is generally defined as an interference with the use and enjoyment of one's property. A nuisance may be the result of intentional or negligent conduct, or it may be associated with the performance of an abnormally dangerous activity. Not only does nuisance not require the physical invasion of the property that the law of trespass requires, but also the nature of the interest protected (use and enjoyment of one's property) is broader than the interest at which the law of trespass is directed (possessory interest in property). Two separate doctrines of nuisance have evolved, private nuisance and public nuisance. The fundamental distinction between these two doctrines is based in the nature of the interest that is protected.

a. *Private Nuisance*

A claim in private nuisance arises from the tortfeasor's unreasonable nontrespassory interference with a private individual's use and enjoyment of the individual's property. Restatement (Second) of Torts § 821D–F. Although the harm suffered generally must be significant, the precise parameters of the right have always been vague, and toxic tort actions have offered courts the opportunity to apply private nuisance in a variety of circumstances. As a result, no unitary, precise definition of private nuisance has emerged. Some examples within the toxic tort context give a sense of the rights encompassed, and excluded, by this tort.

In Ayers v. Township of Jackson (N.J.1987), the New Jersey Supreme Court allowed a private nuisance claim for diminution in quality of life arising from the contamination of the plaintiffs' drinking water supply, which caused inconvenience and discomfort for some time after its discovery. Following Restatement (Second) of Torts § 929, the court stated that plaintiffs could recover in nuisance damages for inconvenience, discomfort, and annoyance in addition to damages for injury to their persons and proprietary interests.

Courts have had to address the limitations on allowable private nuisance claims. In Adkins v. Thomas Solvent Company (Mich.1992), the plaintiffs brought an action in nuisance to recover damages for depreciation in the value of their property as a result of groundwater contamination allegedly caused by the defendant company. The record showed, however, that the plaintiffs' property had not actually been contaminated and, further, that no such contamination was likely to occur in the future. The court refused to allow a nuisance claim under these circumstances, stating that "[c]ompensation for a decline in property value caused by unfounded perception of underground contamination is inextricably entwined with complex policy questions regarding environmental protection that are more suitably resolved through the legislative process." Even though the court acknowledged that in a proper nuisance case depreciation in the value of property could constitute an element of damages, it found this plaintiff's claim to be a " 'loss without an injury, in the legal sense.' "

In Koll–Irvine Center v. County of Orange (Cal. Ct.App.1994), the court rejected a private nuisance claim brought by commercial property owners in the vicinity of jet fuel storage tanks at an airport. The plaintiffs alleged that they feared the construction of the tanks in a location close to a commercial center created a danger of an explosion that interfered with their use of their property. The court held that the plaintiffs' private nuisance claim could not be based upon merely the fear of future injury.

b. Public Nuisance

Restatement § 821B characterizes public nuisance as an "unreasonable interference with a right common to the general public." The precise definition of public nuisance is as elusive as that of private nuisance. *See* Prosser and Keeton on the Law of Torts § 86, at 616–17 (5th ed. 1984). Public nuisance claims may be established by statute with respect to certain enumerated activities. *See, e.g.*, Ariz. Rev. Stat. Ann. § 36–601(A) (1993) (listing certain conditions declared nuisances dangerous to the public health). Whether or not a statute exists, judicial determination has usually been necessary to define unreasonableness and determine who may bring a public nuisance action.

The Restatement defines "unreasonableness" as follows:

(a) Whether the conduct involves a significant interference with the public health, the public safety, the public peace, the public comfort or the public convenience, or

(b) whether the conduct is proscribed by a statute, ordinance or administrative regulation, or

(c) whether the conduct is of a continuing nature or has produced a permanent or long-lasting effect, and, as the actor knows or has reason to know, has a significant effect upon the public right.

Thus, it would not be necessary, except in actions falling within subsection (c), for the plaintiff to prove culpable conduct on the part of the actor. Typically, the public right is sought to be protected by a public entity. *See, e.g.*, State of New York v. Schenectady Chemicals, Inc. (N.Y.1983) (State brought public nuisance claim for cleanup expenses incurred with respect to dump site at which defendant company disposed of waste).

Increasingly, private individuals in toxic tort actions have brought claims sounding in public nuisance. These plaintiffs essentially are acting as private attorneys general, seeking to vindicate public harms on behalf of the public entity. Questions arise as to the circumstances under which private citizens should be allowed to prosecute a public nuisance action. Restatement (Second) of Torts § 821C provides that a private citizen seeking to maintain a public nuisance action for damages "must have suffered harm of a kind different from that suffered by other members of the public exercising the right common to the general public that was the subject of interference." This has come to be referred to as the "special injury rule." With respect to actions seeking to enjoin or abate a public nuisance, the rule is broader, however. The plaintiff must satisfy the special injury rule, be an appropriate public official, *or* have standing to either commence a citizen's suit (pursuant to the federal environmental laws) or be a class member in a class action.

What constitutes a "special injury"? In Venuto v. Owens–Corning Fiberglas Corp. (Cal. Ct.App. 1971), the court held that individuals who complained of emissions from a plant that were polluting the air and causing health complaints among neighboring residents could not maintain an action for public nuisance because the same injuries were suffered by all residents. Likewise, in Brown v. Petrolane, Inc. (Cal. Ct.App.1980), the court refused to allow a public nuisance action brought by private citizens on the basis of fear of the proximity of explosive substances handled by the defendant. The court stated that the plaintiffs' fear did not constitute special injury because it was common to their entire community, even though differing in degree.

In contrast to this strict rule, some courts have held that injuries to an individual's health may be considered a special injury. Restatement § 821C, comment d, provides that physical harm "is normally different in kind from that suffered by other members of the public and [a public nuisance] action may be maintained." In Anderson v. W.R. Grace & Co. (D.Mass.1986), the plaintiffs complained that the defendant had contaminated the groundwater that fed into their drinking water supply, thereby causing a variety of illnesses in the community. The court found the existence of a public nuisance because "[t]he right to be free of contamination to the municipal water supply is clearly a 'right common to the general public.'" The individual health problems of which the residents complained constituted the requisite special injury. *See also* Wood v. Picillo (R.I.1982) (allowing public and private nuisance claims for physical harm to persons residing near chemical depository).

Notwithstanding the continued viability of the special injury rule, its difficulty of application has led some commentators to argue that it is no longer justified. *See* David P. Hodas, *Private Actions for Public Nuisance: Common Law Citizen Suits for Relief from Environmental Harm*, 16 Ecology L.Q. 833, 844 (1989).

Anderson also addressed the elements of damages, which the court stated included compensation for diminution in property value, physical injuries, and emotional distress related to the physical injuries. While allowable recovery is broad, recovery on the basis of economic loss alone, without physical injury, generally has not been allowed. *See* State of Louisiana, ex rel. William J. Guste, Jr. v. M/V Testbank (5th Cir.1985).

4. Claims Against Real Estate Brokers

Some purchasers of residential property have claimed harm as a result of purchasing property that, unbeknownst to the purchaser, was contaminated with hazardous substances or was in proximity to a hazardous condition. Often in such instances the responsible party may be indeterminable, insolvent, or no longer existent. Some plaintiffs have sought a remedy against the real estate broker who may or may not have known of the existence of the hazard.

As a general rule, the real estate broker is deemed to be the agent of the seller. Traditional rules governing the transfer of property always have emphasized the doctrine of caveat emptor. Under this traditional rule, a purchaser of property had little recourse against the seller or the broker for claims arising out of defects on the property. Only where the broker engaged in some affirmative misrepresentation to the purchaser that constituted fraud—either passive or active—would the purchaser have a cause of action against the broker. This traditional rule proved workable when the kind of defect contemplated was termite infestation.

During the 1970s, courts began to erode the traditional rule and to imply a fiduciary relationship between the broker and the purchaser. Courts began to hold brokers liable for making representations without determining the actual condition of the property if the buyer inquired about the specific condition. Moreover, if the broker had information or a suspicion that should have prompted the broker to investigate the condition of the property, the broker could be liable for not so doing. *See* First Church of the Open Bible v. Cline J. Dunton Realty, Inc. (Wash. Ct.App.1978). This development in the law was grounded in the superior position of the broker to know or obtain knowledge about the property. *See* Berryman v. Riegert (Minn.1970).

Some courts have taken the fiduciary relationship a step further. In Bevins v. Ballard (Alaska 1982), the seller had represented to the broker that the water well on the property was adequate, and the broker transmitted the information to the purchaser. Because under state law the seller would have been liable to the purchaser directly for misrepresentations, however innocent, the court imposed a similar liability on the broker for innocently transmitting the seller's misrepresentation. Due to the superior position of the broker, the court recognized an obligation on the part of the broker to investigate before passing along the seller's representations.

A few states have imposed on the broker a full duty to investigate. In these states, even where the broker has made no representations to the seller and is unaware of any latent defects, the broker may be liable for failing to investigate. *See* Easton v. Strassburger (Cal. Ct.App.1984) (holding that real estate broker had affirmative duty to conduct "a reasonably competent and diligent inspection" of property and disclose all material facts to prospective purchasers); Robison v. Campbell (N.M.Ct.App.

1984) (noting that failure to investigate property was considered by trial court in determining that broker misrepresented property condition; appealed on other grounds). Concepts of comparative negligence could mitigate this liability, however, where the purchaser inspected the property and could have learned of the defect.

Such cases raise significant questions regarding the extent of the broker's duty in the era of toxic torts. Must the broker go beyond the listed property and investigate neighboring property to determine the existence of hazardous substances? In Strawn v. Canuso (N.J.1995), the New Jersey Supreme Court held that developers and selling brokers of new homes have an affirmative obligation to disclose to prospective purchasers the existence of off-site hazards that materially affect the value of the property. In *Strawn*, the plaintiffs were purchasers of new homes that were in the vicinity of a closed landfill that had been under investigation by the State because of the hazardous substances contained there.

Noting that the law has been slow to move away from the concept of caveat emptor, the court emphasized two policy issues that guided its decision— (1) the inequitable bargaining positions of the purchasers of residential property vis-a-vis the developers and their brokers and (2) the difference between the parties in relative access to information regarding the site. On this basis, the court limited its holding to professional sellers of real property, such as the developers and builders. Liability was further extended to the brokers, agents, and salespersons representing the professional sellers in the transaction. The court stated:

> We hold that a builder-developer of residential real estate or a broker representing it is not only liable to a purchaser for affirmative and intentional misrepresentation, but is also liable for nondisclosure of off-site physical conditions known to it and unknown and not readily observable to the buyer if the existence of those conditions is of sufficient materiality to affect the habitability, use, or enjoyment of the property and, therefore, render the property substantially less desirable or valuable to the objectively reasonable buyer. Whether a matter not disclosed by such a builder or broker is of such materiality, and unknown and unobservable to the buyer, will depend on the facts of each case.

Thus, the effect of the landfill on the value of the plaintiffs' property was a jury question to be determined at trial.

In circumstances less obvious than a closed landfill, would a broker necessarily possess the requisite expertise to make environmental judgments, and, if not, must an environmental engineer be called upon to conduct an investigation? If so, who pays for it? One solution for real estate brokers may be to shift the responsibility for such investigations to the purchasers via the standard real estate purchase contract.

D. OTHER CLAIMS

1. Battery

Battery may be an available claim in situations in which the conduct of the defendant has gone beyond negligence. A claim of battery was allowed in Werlein v. United States (D.Minn.1990), a complex case that arose from the discharge of toxic chemicals by tenants at an army ammunition plant and another site. The plaintiffs were nearby residents who claimed injury from the release of the chemicals into the environment. The court defined the standard as requiring the plaintiff to prove that the defendant disposed of the toxic substances intending to cause an offensive or harmful contact *or* with the knowledge that such contact was substantially certain to occur. The court found that the plaintiffs had stated a claim for battery under the latter standard by alleging that the defendant "disposed of highly toxic substances into sandy ground directly above a regional aquifer."

The need to rely upon a claim of battery is diminished in toxic tort actions, where plaintiffs usually have available negligence claims and often have available strict liability claims. The level of intent necessary to prove a battery claim may be a deterrent to plaintiffs raising that claim. Plaintiffs seeking punitive damages, however, may include such a claim to complement and support the punitive damages claim, as punitive damages claims typically require proof of conduct that is more egregious than mere negligence. The higher standard of proof set for punitive damages will be satisfied by proof of an intentional tort. Punitive damages are discussed in detail in Chapter Eight, *infra.*

2. Negligence Per Se

Toxic tort claims, with some notable exceptions, typically are not created by statute, but rather arise under the common law. Nevertheless, obligations imposed by statute or regulation may be relevant to the duty of the defendant toward the plaintiff. A plaintiff may attempt to show that the defendant violated a standard of conduct established by statute or regulation and that in so doing must be held to be negligent per se. *See generally* Martin v. Herzog (N.Y.1920). Where negligence per se is recognized, the statute giving rise to the claim must have been enacted to protect the class of persons of which the plaintiff is a member against the kind of harm that the plaintiff has suffered. Courts are less receptive to allowing negligence per se when the standard is embodied in an administrative regulation or ordinance, rather than a statute. *See generally* W. Page Keeton et al., Prosser and Keeton on Torts § 36, at 229–31 (5th ed. 1984).

This kind of presumption of negligence tends to be disfavored in toxic torts litigation; but some plaintiffs have successfully pursued such a theory. In Bagley v. Controlled Environment Corp. (N.H. 1986), the court allowed a negligence per se claim based upon a state statute requiring operators of hazardous waste facilities to obtain a permit. The statute also required the operator to comply with statutory standards, to abide by any rule promulgated by the relevant agency, and to meet the terms and conditions of its particular permit. The court stated that in addition to the explicit standards stated in the statute or regulations, the conditions imposed in the defendant's permit created substantive standards that could serve as the basis for a negligence per se claim.

Some of the difficulties with allowing a negligence per se claim in environmental or toxic torts have been noted in the literature. First, negligence per se is a creature of an earlier time when community standards were embodied in statutory and regulatory standards. Environmental and products standards tend to be based upon sophisticated scientific data of varying degrees of uncertainty. Even what appears to be the most objective standard in a statute or regulation—for example, a numerical standard, such as typically is contained in a permit under the environmental laws—may in fact have been based on scant scientific evidence. Or, the scientific basis may have been open to several reasonable interpretations, only one of which is reflected in the statutory standard. Or, the scientific evidence may be more complete or different at the time the action is brought from the evidence that formed the basis of the standard. Similar difficulties may arise with respect to identifying the harms that the statute or regulation was meant to remedy in relation to the harm that the plaintiff alleges. *See* Sheila Bush, *Can You Get There From Here? Noncompliance with Environmental Regulation as*

Negligence Per Se in Tort Cases, 25 Idaho L. Rev. 469 (1988–1989). These arguments make a persuasive case for not allowing negligence per se in toxic tort actions. They suggest that factfinders must examine the statute or regulation closely in light of the allegations in the complaint and determine on a case-by-case basis whether negligence exists.

3. Civil RICO

The federal Racketeer Influenced and Corrupt Organizations Act (RICO), 18 U.S.C.A. §§ 1961–1968 (West 1984 & Supp. 1995), may provide a cause of action for injured plaintiffs under some circumstances. The case law in this area is undeveloped, and RICO's utility for toxic tort plaintiffs is not at all clear, however. RICO was intended to be primarily directed at organized crime, but the statute has been construed liberally. The reason that RICO may be particularly attractive to toxic torts plaintiffs is the availability of treble damages. It may be difficult, however, for many toxic tort lawsuits to fall within the rather narrow provisions of RICO.

To plead a proper civil RICO claim, the plaintiff must be a "person injured in his business or property by reason of a violation of ... Section 1962" of RICO. 18 U.S.C.A. § 1964(c). The term "person" encompasses individuals, corporations, and partnerships. Section 1962 enumerates several different acts that constitute a violation of RICO, each of which requires a predicate act constituting a "pattern of racketeering activity." Provided that the predicate act was present, the defendant may have violated RICO in a variety of ways, including activities that constitute mail or wire fraud. Furthermore, the plaintiff's injury must be to "business or property." Thus, personal injuries and related emotional and economic losses do not present an appropriate injury to establish a civil RICO claim. *See* Grogan v. Platt (11th Cir.1988).

An example of a case in which the plaintiff properly stated a RICO claim was Standard Equipment, Inc. v. Boeing Co. (W.D.Wash.1985). The case arose out of the storage of hazardous waste, which led to soil contamination affecting the plaintiff's property. The plaintiff claimed decreased property value and lost loans and business as a result of the defendant's improper storage of the waste. The "pattern of racketeering activity" alleged constituted an illegal plan by the defendants to improperly dump waste and conceal the illegal activity. Among other activities, the plaintiff alleged that the racketeering activity was carried out through fraudulent mail and wire transmissions. *But see* Rohrbach v. AT & T (M.D.Pa.1994) (holding that plaintiff had not stated a claim under civil RICO for activities related to discharge of hazardous substances into environment).

In an entirely different context, a California court dismissed a RICO action brought by smokers against the tobacco industry for personal expenses related to treatment for smoking addiction. In Allman v. Philip Morris Inc. (S.D.Cal.1994), the court held that the plaintiffs' alleged economic losses did not constitute injury to property within the meaning of RICO. The court viewed these losses as incidental to personal injuries, which may not form the basis of a RICO claim. *See also* Genty v. Resolution Trust Corp. (3d Cir.1991) (holding that injuries alleged to be caused by exposure to hazardous substances from toxic waste site were not compensable under RICO).

So far, the case law indicates that courts are reluctant to extend RICO to the environmental and toxic products area absent other, more traditional, indicia of racketeering activities. But, as the *Standard Equipment* case demonstrates, some courts may be open to RICO claims involving violations of the federal environmental laws. *See also* Timothy G. Griffin, *Civil RICO and Toxic Tort Litigation*, 15 J. Prods. & Toxics Liab. 229 (1993) (suggesting that failure to fully comply with the various reporting requirements embedded in the federal environmental statutes, or fraudulent reporting, may be means for invoking civil RICO).

E.   EXTENT OF LIABILITY: INTERGENERATIONAL TORTS

Sometimes a toxic tort action is brought for a tort that was committed on a parent of the injured plaintiff prior to the plaintiff having been conceived. In recent years, the question of the liability of defendants for preconception torts has arisen in the context of the "DES grandchildren" litigation. The

classic DES case is one brought by a child of the
woman who ingested the DES while pregnant with
that child. This is essentially a prenatal tort—
alleging that the tortious act of the defendant directly injured the plaintiff by an exposure in utero
prior to birth. The grandchildren, however, cannot
allege that they were exposed directly to the DES,
thus causing courts to question their right to recovery. Courts are divided on public policy grounds as
to the treatment of the grandchildren's preconception claims.

A few courts addressing this type of claim have
allowed it. In Jorgensen v. Meade Johnson Laboratories (10th Cir.1973), the court allowed a cause of
action by the father of twins born with genetic
defects. The twins' mother had ingested birth control pills prior to the twins' conception, and the
complaint alleged that the birth control pills had
caused an alteration in the mother's chromosome
structure that led to the genetic defect in her children. The court did not address, however, the
future implications of allowing recovery on this
kind of claim. Moreover, although *Jorgensen* alleged a preconception tort, it was a "second-genera-
tion" claim, not a "third-generation" claim as in
the DES grandchild situation. This may have made
it more palatable to the court to allow the claim to
stand.

A similar situation was presented in Renslow v.
Mennonite Hospital (Ill.1977), but with a more protracted time frame. This court also recognized the
claim for a preconception tort. The facts of *Ren-*

slow involved a woman who allegedly received incompatible Rh-positive blood transfusions almost a decade before her child was born. The plaintiff claimed that the transfusions caused the injuries with which the child was born. The court found the existence of "a contingent prospective duty to a child not yet conceived but foreseeably harmed by a breach of duty to the child's mother." Thus, the court used an analysis of duty to justify allowing this preconception tort claim in the medical malpractice context.

These two cases, even though they involve preconception torts like the DES grandchildren cases, are actually more akin to the standard DES child case in the generational proximity to the tortious conduct. In fact, the court in *Renslow*, in dicta, drew the line at claims that may be brought by subsequent generations for genetic damage. Because the *Renslow* plaintiff was not claiming a genetic injury, liability was allowed, and the issues raised by intergenerational claims were not directly addressed.

The DES cases have presented the clearest example of the problems of allowing intergenerational liability. In Enright v. Eli Lilly & Co. (N.Y.1991), the grandmother had ingested the prescription drug DES while pregnant with her daughter. In the complaint, the daughter and her daughter ("the granddaughter") alleged that the daughter's exposure to DES in utero had resulted in a condition that prevented her from carrying a baby to term. Such physical problems were known to be associated with in utero exposure to DES. Years later, the granddaughter was born prematurely as a result of this condition. The granddaughter suffered from injuries related to her premature birth. The court disallowed the granddaughter's claim "to confine liability within manageable limits." The court recognized the far-reaching implications if such a claim were allowed: "[T]he cause of action plaintiffs ask us to recognize here could not be confined without the drawing of artificial and arbitrary boundaries. For all we know, the rippling effects of DES exposure may extend for generations."

Similarly, in Grover v. Eli Lilly & Co. (Ohio 1992), the court rejected a DES grandchild's claims on a set of facts similar to those in *Enright*. The court in *Grover*, however, used language of foreseeability and duty to justify its decision. The court stated: "An actor does not have a duty to a particular plaintiff unless the risk to that plaintiff is within the actor's 'range of apprehension'." Citing the Restatement, the court found that the recognizable risk that the DES manufacturers created was to the class of persons actually exposed to the drug and that the manufacturers could not reasonably have anticipated injury beyond that generation of persons. *See* Restatement (Second) of Torts, § 281m, comment c (1965). The court stated:

> It is one thing to say that knowledge of a propensity to harm the reproductive organs is sufficient to impose liability for a variety of different injuries to the reproductive organs. It is yet another thing to say that this generalized knowledge is

sufficient to impose liability for injuries to a third
party that occur twenty-eight years later.

. . .

... [[T]he grandchild's] injuries are not the result of his own exposure to the drug, but are
allegedly caused by his mother's injuries from her
in utero exposure to the drug.   Because of the
remoteness in time and causation, we hold that
[the grandchild] does not have an independent
cause of action.... A pharmaceutical company's
liability for the distribution or manufacture of a
defective prescription drug does not extend to
persons who were never exposed to the drug,
either directly or *in utero*.

Thus, the court kept the litigation within manageable limits.   *See also* Sorrels v. Eli Lilly & Co.
(D.D.C.1990) (applying Maryland law) (rejecting
claim of DES grandchild).   *But see* McMahon v. Eli
Lilly & Co. (7th Cir.1985) (applying Illinois law)
(holding that DES manufacturer's knowledge of
hazards of drug was sufficient to subject it to liability for injuries to grandchildren of women who ingested the drug).

Undoubtedly, the courts in *Enright* and *Grover*
and like cases foresaw the more troublesome class
of intergenerational torts referenced in *Renslow*.
At least one incident of alleged genetic injury, causing the DES "signature" cancer in a granddaughter
of a woman who ingested the drug, has been report-
ed.   *See* Marisa L. Mascaro, *Preconception Tort Liability: Recognizing a Strict Liability Cause of Action*

for DES Grandchildren, 17 Am. J.L. & Med. 435, 449–50 (1991). Genetic injury claims are especially problematic because a genetic mutation may not be expressed for several generations, thus extending the potential period for claims indefinitely. Nevertheless, it is likely that courts will place strict limits on such claims in the same manner that the physical injury claims of *Enright* and *Grover* were prohibited.

F. TORT REFORM MEASURES

No discussion of toxic tort causes of action would be complete without some mention of the reform movement. Tort reform initiatives have taken different shapes. Reform has moved on several fronts, most notably the Restatement and various legislative initiatives both at the state and federal levels.

1. Restatement Revisions

For several years, the work on the updating of the Restatement of Torts on products liability has ensued in the midst of much debate. Professors James A. Henderson and Aaron D. Twerski, the Reporters for the Restatement revisions, have prepared tentative drafts of the Restatement (Third) of Torts: Products Liability. As of early 1995, the proposal continued to undergo comment and revision. The proposal evidences the increasing importance of product liability litigation and takes a position on some major issues that have appeared in the litigation. Although the individual elements of the proposal are too numerous to describe in this book, some mention of the fundamentals is warranted.

The current proposal has expanded the definitions of the three types of product defects and has treated them separately. A major feature of the proposal has been the incorporation of a risk-utility test to determine the existence of a design defect. The consumer expectation test, although abandoned as an independent test, has appeared as one factor in the risk-utility analysis in the proposal. This provision has sparked considerable debate, predictably between members of the plaintiffs' bar and members of the defense bar. In addition, disagreement has been expressed over the proposed requirement that the plaintiff offer a "reasonable alternative design." *Cf.* Banks v. ICI Americas Inc. (Ga. 1994) (applying risk/utility test with availability of alternative design as one factor in rat poison case and referencing proposed Restatement (Third) of Torts: Products Liability). As a result, the Reporters have been working on a compromise approach. The process of shaping the new Restatement is ongoing, with projections for completion to occur by 1997.

2. Joint and Several Liability Reform

Since the 1980s, state legislatures have embarked upon a mission to dramatically alter the operation of the doctrine of joint and several liability. Typically, the states have undertaken to abrogate, or to modify, joint and several liability in favor of sever-

al-only liability. There is a wide variation among
these statutes, but the states are in general agreement that joint and several liability no longer serves
the system effectively in all kinds of cases. Most
states that have addressed the issue have abrogated
joint and several liability and mandated several-only
liability, but have imposed varying numbers of exceptions that would permit joint and several liability in some cases. Several of the exceptions are
noteworthy because of their bearing on toxic tort
litigation.

A common exception to several-only liability is
hazardous waste litigation. *See, e.g.*, Ariz. Rev.
Stat. Ann. § 12–2506(D)(2) (1994) (actions relating
to hazardous waste or solid waste disposal sites);
N.Y. Civ. Prac. L. & R. 1602(9) (McKinney Supp.
1994) (actions arising from releases into environment of hazardous substances or hazardous wastes).
Another exception is certain kinds of product liability actions. *See, e.g.*, Idaho Code § 6–803(7) (1990)
(medical devices or pharmaceutical products); N.J.
Stat. Ann. § 2A:15–5.3(f)(1) (West Supp. 1994)
(negligent manufacture or use of hazardous or toxic
substances). Some states have devised schemes
based upon the defendant's percentage share of
fault as determined by the jury at trial. When the
defendant's liability exceeds a certain threshold percentage, joint and several liability applies. *See, e.g.*,
Haw. Rev. Stat. § 663–10.9(3) (1988) (greater than
25%); Iowa Code Ann. § 668.4 (West 1987) (50% or
more).

The joint and several liability reforms are a logical extension of the comparative negligence movement that overtook the state legislatures a decade earlier. The significant number of exceptions, however, indicates that total abrogation of joint and several liability may be inappropriate and unworkable in certain categories of cases, many of which affect toxic tort claimants.

3. Federal Substantive Law

Efforts at federal product liability legislative reform have been considered for a number of years. These proposals would pre-empt the operation of state tort law in the areas covered by the legislation. The issue of a federal product liability law has been divisive, however, with representatives of industry and proponents of consumer protection facing off on a number of issues. Moreover, Congressional sentiments regarding tort reform have vacillated according to the political winds. Observers of Congress undoubtedly will continue to debate the benefits and disadvantages of such provisions for some time to come.

The 104th Congress has been seen as the one most likely to adopt federal tort reform measures. A comparison of two major product liability reform bills before the 104th Congress offers a view of the range of proposals and also some insight into the obstacles to their passage. The "Fairness in Product Liability Bill" has been before Congress in various versions for several years. Under criticism from consumer representatives, the bill has proposed reform measures with a somewhat soft touch. For example, the bill no longer contains a cap on punitive damages, while it retains a provision for requiring proof of a punitive damages claim by "clear and convincing" evidence. Further, supporters of the bill have refused to include a provision allowing defendants to rely on compliance with government standards or regulations as an absolute defense to an action. The bill does contain a provision for abrogating joint and several liability and limiting a defendant's liability to its percentage of fault.

In comparison, another major proposal considered in the 104th Congress takes a less conciliatory and more industry-oriented approach. Called the "Common Sense Legal Reforms Act" (H.R. 10), the bill—which continues to undergo changes as it proceeds through the legislative process—would make it more difficult to hold the sellers of products liable for defective products. A major feature of the proposed legislation would be to hold drug and medical device manufacturers harmless for injuries caused by their products if the products were approved by the Food and Drug Administration for marketing. It would also impose a cap on punitive damages awards of the greater of $250,000 or three times the amount of economic damages awarded, and would include a "clear and convincing" standard. The bill also contains a notice of claim provision for product liability actions. It further addresses attorney conduct by providing sanctions for frivolous actions or conduct that harasses another party or delays the litigation unduly. It would impose a standard for scientific evidence and make inadmissible the testimony of experts paid on a contingency basis. The bill also contains a provision for the losing party to pay attorney fees to the prevailing party.

These competing bills, and others that inevitably have been introduced, have galvanized both their proponents and their opponents. While it seems likely that the 104th Congress will pass some legislation on this subject, the exact parameters of the legislation are difficult to predict. The treatment of the product liability bills within the political process could prove a bellwether for other reforms relevant to toxic torts. Even though Congressional observers sense that the 104th Congress presents the climate most conducive to action in this area, reform efforts face concerted opposition, mostly from consumer groups. This means that the ultimate product of Congressional efforts at reform may not be realized for some years, or never at all.

CHAPTER THREE

CERCLA LIABILITY

A. INTRODUCTION

The Comprehensive Environmental Response, Compensation and Liability Act (CERCLA), 42 U.S.C.A. §§ 9601–9675, is part of a broad federal scheme of regulation of industry. The role of CERCLA is different from the other environmental statutes in that CERCLA is primarily focused upon cleanup of hazardous substances that have been released into the environment and hazardous substance emergencies, whereas the other federal environmental statutes tend to focus upon the ongoing regulation of various enterprises and activities. When CERCLA was initially enacted in 1980, Congress debated but rejected the option of including a provision for a private right of action for personal injuries. Consequently, CERCLA contains no private right of action for damages for persons who claim to have been injured by the releases encompassed by the statute, although it does contain a savings clause that recognizes the rights of private individuals to pursue their torts claims under state law. CERCLA § 310(h). Instead, the CERCLA provisions focus primarily on the right of the Government to enforce the cleanup regulations against parties deemed to be statutorily responsible. As with the other major federal environmental statutes, CERCLA also contains a citizens suit provision that permits private individuals, under certain circumstances, to step into the shoes of the Government and enforce the statute against alleged violators. CERCLA was significantly revised by the Superfund Amendments and Reauthorization Act of 1986 (SARA), with many of the amendments reflecting case law prior to that date.

B. ENFORCEMENT SCHEME

The applicability of CERCLA is triggered by the release or threatened release of a hazardous substance into the environment from a facility. A "facility" is defined as "any site or area where a hazardous substance has been deposited, stored, disposed of, or placed, or otherwise come to be located." CERCLA § 101(9). The process by which the Government identifies a site appropriate for response action and determines the proper action is the National Contingency Plan (NCP). CERCLA § 105. Appropriate sites are placed on the National Priorities List (NPL) based upon a ranking of hazards. A decision to remedy is based upon cost considerations as well as the nature and magnitude of the hazard. A large portion of CERCLA centers on factfinding: determining hazardous substances, identifying dangerous sites, and requiring the reporting of information regarding releases of hazardous substances into the environment.

CERCLA provides several different mechanisms by which responsibility for the cleanup of hazardous substances in the environment can be imposed upon persons statutorily held responsible for the release or threatened release. These persons are called potentially responsible parties (PRPs). First, the President, through the Attorney General, may commence either an administrative or judicial action against any PRP for abatement of the condition or for other appropriate action. CERCLA § 106. The trigger for such an action is the occurrence of "an imminent and substantial endangerment to the public health or welfare or the environment because of the actual or threatened release of a hazardous substance." CERCLA § 106(a). Failure to comply with such an order could lead to civil penalties of $25,000 a day and treble damages. Second, the Government, or a private party, may conduct the cleanup, through hiring contractors, funded from the Superfund—a fund created pursuant to CERCLA for this purpose through a tax on business—and subsequently seek reimbursement from a PRP. CERCLA §§ 104, 111. The Government or private party may not make a claim against the Fund unless efforts to find the PRPs or require them to conduct the cleanup have been exhausted. If the Government conducts the cleanup, PRPs have no right to pre-enforcement judicial review of the chosen remedial action. CERCLA § 113(h); Lone Pine Steering Committee v. EPA (3d Cir.1985). Third, CERCLA contains provisions for settlement between a PRP and the Government designed to induce settlement and expedite cleanup. CERCLA § 122.

While CERCLA does not provide a private right of action for damages for personal injuries, it does allow a private cause of action for response costs. Section 107(a)(4)(B) makes clear that response costs incurred by "any other person" may be sought from a PRP. No requirement exists that the costs incurred have been generated through a Government cleanup program. Such a right of action may arise where an entity voluntarily cleans up the property to avoid damage to its own property or where statutorily protected innocent landowners choose to clean up their own property.

C. LIABILITY FOR CLEANUPS

For a party to become liable for cleanup, a "release" must have occurred. CERCLA § 101(22) defines "release" as

any spilling, leaking, pumping, pouring, emitting, emptying, discharging, injecting, escaping, leaching, dumping, or disposing into the environment (including the abandonment or discarding of barrels, containers, and other closed receptacles containing any hazardous substance or pollutant or contaminant). . . .

CERCLA does not cover releases within the workplace, from motor vehicle exhaust, or due to a nuclear incident, as those matters are regulated by other federal statutes. CERCLA applies to both active and inactive sites.

When a release has occurred, the cleanup becomes the responsibility of the PRPs enumerated in Section 107. Liability has been deemed to be strict. In general, liability is joint and several, provided that the harm is indivisible. The court in United States v. Chem–Dyne Corp. (S.D. Ohio 1983) so held, stating: "If the harm is divisible and if there is a reasonable basis for apportionment of damages, each defendant is liable only for the portion of the harm he himself caused." Because waste from different sources is often commingled at a site, the burden on the PRP to demonstrate divisibility of harm is considerable. See United States v. Monsanto Co. (4th Cir.1988) (holding that defendants had not established divisibility of harm). CERCLA does provide that a PRP, including one that has settled with the Government, may seek contribution from other PRPs with respect to any liability that may have exceeded the PRP's proportionate share. CERCLA § 113(f).

A PRP is liable for both Government response costs and private response costs, all consistent with the NCP. In addition, a PRP may be liable for natural resource damages and for health assessments pursuant to the Agency for Toxic Substances and Disease Registry, an agency within the Public Health Service established by CERCLA.

1. Owners and Operators

CERCLA § 107(a) sets forth the categories of entities that comprise PRPs. These include current owners and operators of a vessel or facility. CERC-

LA § 107(a)(1). The statutory language refers to "any person owning or operating such facility" or "owning, operating, or chartering by demise, such vessel." No qualifications are placed upon this definition, and because of the strict liability nature of CERCLA, no showing need be made of the culpability of an owner or operator to hold that party liable. In State of New York v. Shore Realty Corp. (2d Cir.1985), the owner of the site was held liable for costs even though it had not participated in the disposal of waste on the site and had not owned the property at the time of disposal. Moreover, the court also held the officer and stockholder of Shore Realty liable as an "operator" of the facility because he managed the corporation and was in charge of the facility under scrutiny.

In addition, at least some past owners and operators are considered PRPs under the statute. CERCLA § 107(a)(2) establishes the liability of

(2) any person who at the time of disposal of any hazardous substance owned or operated any facility at which such hazardous substances were disposed of. . . .

In contrast to current owners and operators, former owners and operators will be liable only if they owned or operated the facility at the time of disposal of any hazardous substance at the facility.

There is some split in authority as to the circumstances under which an individual may be found liable as an "operator" of a facility. In the Fourth Circuit, an individual may be liable as an operator by virtue of the authority granted to that individual, whether or not the individual exercised any actual control over the facility. United States v. Carolina Transformer Co. (4th Cir.1992). Elsewhere, the individual must actually exercise that authority to control the facility to be held liable as an operator under CERCLA. *E.g.*, United States v. Gurley (8th Cir.1994).

2. Generators of Hazardous Substances

Another category of PRP is set forth in CERCLA § 107(a)(3), which establishes liability for

(3) any person who by contract, agreement, or otherwise arranged for disposal or treatment, or arranged with a transporter for transport for disposal or treatment, of hazardous substances owned or possessed by such person, by any other party or entity, at any facility or incineration vessel owned or operated by another party or entity and containing such hazardous substances. . . .

Essentially, liability under the section is triggered by being an "arranger." Industrial generators of hazardous waste are the principal group of entities that fall with the scope of this subsection, although the section certainly is not limited to industrial generators. Contracting and arranging for disposal seem to be the targeted elements for liability, and courts have interpreted this section broadly. Thus, liability may be imposed where a generator did not choose the site, United States v. Wade (E.D.Pa. 1983), and where the generator had no knowledge

that the particular site would be used, United
States v. Aceto Agricultural Chemicals Corp. (8th
Cir.1989). The case law indicates that for a party
to "arrange" for disposal, the party must take some
affirmative steps to the party's own advantage. *See*
United States v. Consolidated Rail Corp. (D.Del.
1990). *See generally* William H. Rodgers, Jr., Environmental Law § 8.7, at 778–81 (2d ed. 1994) (discussing liability of generators and arrangers generally).

For the Government to make a prima facie case
against a generator, the Government need only
show the removal of the generator's waste at some
prior point in time to the site for disposal, the
existence of that kind of waste at the site, a release
or threatened release from the site, and the incur-
rence of costs. United States v. Monsanto Co. (4th
Cir.1988). No tracing of the generator's actual
waste to the release is necessary if these requirements are met.

Some case law has mitigated the harshness of this
rule for generators who are able to demonstrate
that their waste did not contribute to the release or
was a divisible portion of the harm. The burden is
on the generator to demonstrate a reasonable basis
for apportionment or release of liability. *See* United States v. Alcan Aluminum Corp. (2d Cir.1993);
United States v. Alcan Aluminum Corp. (3d Cir.
1992); In re Bell Petroleum Services, Inc. (5th
Cir.1993).

An example of an arranger that was not a generator occurred in Emergency Technical Services Corp.
v. Morton International (N.D.Ill.1993). In that
case, a consultant who actually arranged the disposal, including choice of site, was held liable as an
arranger under § 107(a)(3). *But see* Amcast Industrial Corp. v. Detrex (7th Cir.1993) (no arranger
liability for accidental spill by common carrier
where chemical manufacturer shipped products to
customers using the carrier).

3. Transporters

CERCLA § 107(a)(4) sets forth the liability of a
transporter of hazardous substances by identifying
as a PRP

> any person who accepts or accepted any hazard-
> ous substances for transport to disposal or treat-
> ment facilities, incineration vessels or sites select-
> ed by such person, from which there is a release,
> or a threatened release which causes the incur-
> rence of response costs, of a hazardous substance.

In addition, CERCLA § 101(25) defines the terms
"transport" or "transportation" as follows:

> the movement of a hazardous substance by any
> mode, including pipeline ... , and in the case of a
> hazardous substance which has been accepted for
> transportation by a common or contract carrier,
> the term[s] ... shall include any stoppage in
> transit which is temporary, incidental to the
> transportation movement, and at the ordinary
> operating convenience of a common or contract

carrier, and any such stoppage shall be considered as a continuity of movement and not as the storage of a hazardous substance.

The terms of the statute indicate that the transporter will be liable only if it selected the site, and the majority of jurisdictions interpret the statute broadly. *See* United States v. South Carolina Recycling & Disposal, Inc. (D.S.C.1984). It is irrelevant whether or not the transporter was a common carrier; if the transporter chose the site, liability will attach. United States v. Hardage (W.D.Okla.1990). The transporter may not avoid liability by arguing that the generator or some other PRP collaborated in choosing the waste site or that the transporter did not make the ultimate decision in choice of site. Tippins Inc. v. USX Corp. (3d Cir.1994) (noting, however, that transporter must take some active role in site selection for liability to attach). The precise scope of transporter liability has yet to be delineated.

D. DEFENSES

The primary defenses to a CERCLA action for cleanup costs are located in Section 107(b) of the Act. There is boilerplate language precluding liability for releases caused solely by an act of God or an act of war, CERCLA §§ 107(b)(1)-(2), with the emphasis on the "solely" requirement. Section 107(b) also provides for a third-party defense under limited circumstances. In 1986, SARA included what has become known as the "innocent landowner defense," which appears in the definitional section of CERCLA, Section 101(35), rather than in Section 107. Other procedural and substantive defenses to cost recovery actions may exist, including the possible availability of equitable defenses. *See* William H. Rodgers, Jr., Environmental Law § 8.8, at 793–94 (2d ed. 1994) (discussing division of authority on the availability of equitable defenses in CERCLA actions). To understand the potential CERCLA liability of clients who may also be defending separate toxic tort actions, the third-party defense and the innocent landowner defense are the most important.

1. Third-Party Defense

A defense to CERCLA liability may be available to a PRP in situations in which the release of the hazardous substances was due solely to

> (3) an act or omission of a third party other than an employee or agent of the defendant, or than one whose act or omission occurs in connection with a contractual relationship, existing directly or indirectly, with the defendant....

CERCLA § 107(b)(3). By its terms, the defense is not available to a broad spectrum of persons related to the defendant in a variety of contractual relationships. *See, e.g.*, Shapiro v. Alexanderson (S.D.N.Y. 1990) (no defense where PRP asserting it is landowner and third party is operator of landfill). Not only does "contractual relationship" apply to contracts for disposal, transportation, or other handling of the waste, but it also refers to real property transactions. *See* CERCLA § 101(35)(A) (defining "contractual relationship" to include real property transactions and providing for innocent landowner defense with regard to real property transactions under limited set of circumstances).

Section 107(b)(3) goes on to set forth two additional requirements that must be met for a court to allow the third-party defense:

> [T]he defendant [must establish] by a preponderance of the evidence that (a) he exercised due care with respect to the hazardous substance concerned, taking into consideration the characteristics of such hazardous substance, in light of all relevant facts and circumstances, and (b) he took precautions against foreseeable acts or omissions of any such third party and the consequences that could foreseeably result from such acts or omissions. . . .

The combination of requirements in CERCLA § 107(b)(3) make the defense very difficult to use in most cases, causing Professor Rodgers to refer to it as "nine parts loser." *See* William H. Rodgers, Jr., *supra*, § 8.8, at 797–98 (noting that courts may decide to restrict the defense to third-party "outsiders," commonly referred to as "midnight dumpers").

2. Innocent Landowner Defense

The innocent landowner defense, a creature of the SARA amendments, is found in the exception to the definition of "contractual relationship" in

CERCLA § 101(35). After stating that "contractual relationship" includes real property transactions, the section proceeds to delineate a defense for circumstances in which

> the real property on which the facility concerned is located was acquired by the defendant after the disposal or placement of the hazardous substance on, in, or at the facility, and one or more of the [following] circumstances ... is also established by the defendant by a preponderance of the evidence:
>
> (1) At the time the defendant acquired the facility the defendant did not know and had no reason to know that any hazardous substance which is the subject of the release or threatened release was disposed of on, in, or at the facility.

The other stated circumstances apply to governmental entities and to persons acquiring the property by inheritance or bequest. In addition, the same due care and affirmative precautions requirements set forth in Section 107(b)(3)(a)–(b) for the third-party defense also apply to the innocent landowner defense. The innocent landowner defense is only available if the PRP asserting it did not cause or contribute to the release or threatened release in any way. CERCLA § 101(35)(D).

Case law construing the innocent landowner defense has considered the extent of the inquiry that the defendant must have conducted at the time of acquiring the property. This issue is initially addressed in the statute:

(B) To establish that the defendant had no
reason to know [of the hazard], ... the defendant
must have undertaken, at the time of acquisition,
all appropriate inquiry into the previous owner-
ship and uses of the property consistent with
good commercial or customary practice in an effort to minimize liability. For purposes of the
preceding sentence the court shall take into account any specialized knowledge or experience on
the part of the defendant, the relationship of the
purchase price to the value of the property if
uncontaminated, commonly known or reasonably
ascertainable information about the property, the
obviousness of the presence or likely presence of
contamination at the property, and the ability to
detect such contamination by appropriate inspection.

CERCLA § 101(35)(B). In United States v. Serafi-
ni (M.D.Pa.1988), the court refused to hold as a
matter of law that lack of an on-site visual inspection precluded the defendant from relying on the
innocent landowner defense. This emphasizes that
a defendant's inquiry will be examined on a case-by
case basis in light of the customs and circumstances
presented.

In United States v. Pacific Hide and Fur Depot,
Inc. (D. Idaho 1989), the court established a sliding
scale for evaluating landowners' inquiries, requiring
the most stringent review in commercial property
transactions and the least stringent in cases of
inheritance or bequest. But some courts have been
quite strict in reviewing the defendants' inquiry

about the condition of the site. *See, e.g.*, In re Hemingway Transport, Inc. (1st Cir.1993).

Furthermore, if a PRP who qualified as an innocent landowner at the time of acquisition of the property later obtains actual knowledge of the hazard, then transfers the property without disclosing the hazard, that PRP will be liable. CERCLA § 101(35)(C). Liability will attach notwithstanding the PRP's previous status as an innocent landowner.

As with the third-party defense, the innocent landowner defense presents numerous hoops through which the PRP must jump to be relieved of liability. As courts continue to interpret this provision, its parameters may become clearer.

E. SETTLEMENT

CERCLA § 122 contains settlement provisions that are designed to encourage cost recovery by giving PRPs an incentive to come forward and take responsibility for the release or threatened release. The Government is authorized to give the PRP with which the agreement has been made a covenant not to sue with respect to future liability, but only after all remedial action has been completed. CERCLA § 122(f). An exception exists for releases arising out of conditions unknown at the time of the agreement. CERCLA § 122(f)(6). To further induce settlement, and to protect a PRP who settles its present and future liabilities with respect to a site, Section 113(f) shields the settling PRP from liability for contribution to other PRPs while maintaining the settling PRP's right to seek contribution from others.

A settlement with fewer than all PRPs in no way discharges the remaining PRPs from their statutory liability, unless the settlement agreement so provides. The settlement "reduces the potential liability of the others by the amount of the settlement." CERCLA § 113(f)(2). Although this pro tanto set-off rule appears to allow the nonsettling PRPs to benefit from a high settlement by the settling PRP (a settlement in excess of the settling PRP's percentage contribution to the release), the preservation of contribution claims for the settling PRP renders this advantage illusory. On the other hand, if the settling PRP settles low (below its percentage contribution to the release), the nonsettling PRPs may be required to pay an amount in excess of their percentage shares with no recourse against the settling PRP. Presumably, this scheme would have the effect of inducing PRPs to settle with the Government.

A special settlement provision addresses PRPs who are considered "de minimis" contributors to the release. Section 122(g) provides for an expedited settlement with PRPs whose portion of the response costs is deemed to be minimal, as determined by one of two tests. The first test requires the PRP's contribution to the site to be minimal in *both* amount and toxicity, in comparison to the other hazardous substances at the site. The second test applies only to PRPs who are owners of the real property on which the facility is located, and requires that the owner did not "conduct or permit" any hazardous waste activities at the site and did not contribute to the release or threat of release. Further, the owner must not have "purchased the real property with actual or constructive knowledge that the property was used for the generation, transportation, storage, treatment, or disposal of any hazardous substance." CERCLA § 122(g)(1). In addition, the de minimis settlement must represent a minor portion of the overall response costs associated with the release. As with standard settlements under CERCLA, de minimis settlements relieve the settling PRP from liability for contribution to other PRPs arising out of the release that is the subject of the settlement. *See* CERCLA § 122(g)(5); Dravo Corp. v. Zuber (8th Cir.1994). In 1993, EPA issued a guidance document that authorized a new class of settlements with "de micromis" PRPs. The document recommends a series of calculations based upon the party's percentage contribution of waste to the site, as well as other factors, in determining a settlement amount for this class of PRPs, who presumably have contributed less than even de minimis PRPs to the hazard at the site. *See Guidance on CERCLA Settlements With De Micromis Waste Contributors* (OSWER Directive #9834.17, July 30, 1993).

F. SAVINGS CLAUSE

CERCLA contains a provision expressly saving a person's right to pursue tort claims under state law for matters related to any release of a hazardous substance into the environment.   Section 310(h) provides:

> This chapter does not affect or otherwise impair the rights of any person under Federal, State, or common law....

This section makes clear that CERCLA was not intended to preclude individuals' private rights of action for personal injuries and property damage. Thus, the remedial scheme in CERCLA operates separately from the tort remedies available under state law.

G. CITIZENS SUITS

CERCLA, following the precedent of other federal environmental statutes, contains a citizens suit provision that allows "any person" to bring an action directly against a "person ... who is alleged to be in violation of any standard, regulation, condition, requirement, or order" pursuant to CERCLA. CERCLA § 310(a)(1).   Alternatively, the action may be brought against a government officer (including the EPA Administrator) for failure to perform any non-discretionary act or duty pursuant to the Act.   CERCLA § 310(a)(2).   The term "person" refers to a corporation or a governmental entity, as well as a natural person.   Citizens are not entitled to private monetary damages under this provision. Rather, the remedies available are injunctive relief to enforce the standard or regulation and, with respect to a Section 310(a)(1) citizens suit, civil penalties.

The citizens suit provision permits persons to act as private attorneys general to remedy violations that have not otherwise been dealt with under the regulatory provisions of the Act. As such, in many ways it is the federal statutory complement to the public nuisance action. It is a dramatic illustration of the confluence of public and private remedies in the area of toxic torts.

Much of the case law interpreting the scope of citizens suits has developed within the context of other federal environmental statutes. Many similar issues arise with respect to CERCLA citizens suits. Case law has held that the citizens must be able to show injury-in-fact under standard requirements for standing to be able to bring suit under this section. *See* Lujan v. Defenders of Wildlife (S.Ct. 1992) (general intent to return to locale of endangered species for observation insufficient to acquire standing to sue under Endangered Species Act); Lujan v. National Wildlife Federation (S.Ct.1990) (vague allegations of use of large expanse of land insufficient to acquire standing to sue under Endangered Species Act). The Supreme Court also has addressed the meaning of "in violation" so as to trigger citizens suit liability under the Clean Water Act, 33 U.S.C.A. §§ 1251–1387 (West 1986 & Supp. 1994) (as amended). The Court has held that violations must be ongoing or recurring, and not isolated past incidents, for a citizens suit to be proper. Gwaltney of Smithfield v. Chesapeake Bay Foundation (S.Ct.1987).

The statute sets forth certain threshold limitations on commencement of the action. First, notice of the alleged violation must be sent to the EPA, the state, and the alleged violator at least sixty days before the action is commenced. CERCLA § 310(d)(1). Second, a citizen suit may not be commenced if the government "has commenced and is diligently prosecuting an action" under the Act. CERCLA § 310(d)(2). The definition of "action" within this subsection is open to dispute. The purpose of this second limitation is to allow focus on agency enforcement without the distraction and potential conflict of the citizens suit.

The citizens suit provision and other enforcement provisions of CERCLA point out that a toxic tort defendant may be faced with an assault of actions on several fronts. Common-law torts may be only a portion of the defendant's worries. Attorneys should be prepared to advise and defend their clients in all these areas involving public, as well as private, law.

CHAPTER FOUR

LIABILITY OF EMPLOYERS

Issues of toxic exposures in the workplace present the paradigmatic public and private law model. The product liability theories discussed in Chapter Two may certainly arise within the context of the workplace. But, as this chapter will explore, product liability becomes an option for the injured worker outside of the employer-employee relationship. This chapter addresses liabilities that inhere directly in the employment relationship. Many of the rules that apply in the workplace are not rules that derive from the law of torts, however. The workplace is primarily a public law forum, and statutory regulation and administrative law tribunals play prominent roles in the investigation of the impact of hazardous substances and the resolution of claims related to toxic exposures.

A. WORKERS' COMPENSATION

1. Historical Perspective

Interest in occupational illness in America was piqued in the 1930s with the attention drawn to workplace victims of silicosis. A bias existed, however, against recognizing occupational disease as a legitimate injury meriting compensation. Early

concerns for a flood of claims related to occupation-
al disease that could create economic havoc in in-
dustry caused lawmakers to be reluctant to provide
mechanisms of recovery for occupational disease
victims. *See generally* Arthur Larson, *Occupational
Diseases Under Workmen's Compensation Laws*, 9
U. Rich. L. Rev. 87 (1974); Richard Robblee, *The
Dark Side of Workers' Compensation: Burdens and
Benefits in Occupational Disease Coverage*, 2 Indus.
Rel. L.J. 596 (1978).

The workers' compensation schemes that were
evolving during the early part of the Twentieth
Century, and that were in place in virtually every
state by about 1920, originally did not include a
remedy for occupational disease. Workers' compensation arose as a result of an increase in workplace
accidents directly tied into the industrial revolution.
The quid pro quo arrangement of workers' compensation provided a remedial scheme for employees
injured during the course of employment and protection for employers from liabilities to their employees outside of workers' compensation for employment related injuries. The system was designed to treat worker injuries as a cost of industry
to be spread to consumers of the products manufactured. *See* 1 Arthur Larson, Workmen's Compensation Law § 2.20 (1994). Eventually, occupational
disease claims came to be treated within the workers' compensation system, but with an ambivalence
that has yet to be fully resolved. While workers'
compensation typically provides compensation for

medical expenses and lost wages, as well as a relatively small statutory amount above that, it does not included recovery for pain and suffering.

Although workers' compensation usually bars a separate claim against the claimant's employer arising out of the same incident, tort actions against third parties, such as the manufacturers of equipment used in the production process, have still been allowed. The now common situation of injured asbestos insulation workers presents a perfect example. In such cases, the workers usually may not bring suit against their employers (e.g. contractors) due to the operation of the workers' compensation laws, but may bring tort actions against the third-party manufacturers of the asbestos containing products. *See, e.g.*, Borel v. Fibreboard Paper Prods. Corp. (5th Cir.1973).

Because the workers' compensation system has tended to be less responsive to occupational disease claims than accidental injuries, and because of the attraction of large jury verdict awards for tort claims, workers have attempted to find legal loopholes that would permit them to bring tort actions against their employers, even where their claims fit within the scope of workers' compensation. One must bear in mind, however, that the strict causation requirements of tort law and the difficulty of proving the defendant's culpable conduct, where applicable, make workers' compensation an attractive primary remedy under many circumstances.

2. Occupational Disease Statutes

Because workers' compensation statutes require that the injury have occurred within the course of employment, occupational disease claims have been treated with skepticism due to the difficulty of assuring that the injury was work-related. Two particular problems arise within this context. First, occupational diseases often are identical to illnesses existing in the general population, and may not be unique to the claimant's occupation. Second, the long latency periods associated with the manifestation of many illnesses make it difficult to demonstrate that an illness was in fact work-related and was not the result of intervening causes.

This skepticism led to restrictive treatment of occupational disease in the workers' compensation laws of most states. Limitations on occupational disease claims abound. For example, some statutes allow occupational disease workers' compensation claims only when the worker had been exposed to the toxic substance in the workplace for a certain length of time. *See, e.g.*, Cal. Lab. Code § 5500.5 (West 1989). Or, statutes in some states require employment for a certain length of time before the claim will be covered by workers' compensation. Further, some states require that the illness must manifest itself within a designated period of time following the worker's last exposure to the alleged substance or the worker's last day of employment for the employer. *See, e.g.*, Ill. Ann. Stat. ch. 48, para. 172.36(f) (Smith–Hurd 1986) (within two years of last exposure); S.C. Code Ann. § 42–11–70

(Law. Co-op. 1985) (within one year of last exposure). Limitations such as these obviously cannot
provide equitable rules in all occupational illness
situations, and the distinctions they embody often
seem arbitrary.

In general, occupational disease statutes require
that for an illness to be compensable, it must be
associated with the worker's specific occupation and
not be an "ordinary disease of life." *See, e.g.*, Ill.
Ann. Stat. ch. 48, para. 172.36(d) (Smith–Hurd
1986); Md. Lab. & Empl. Code Ann. § 9–101(g)
(1991). To ensure this, one type of occupational
disease statute provides a list of diseases that are
compensable. *See, e.g.*, Pa. Stat. Ann. tit. 77,
§ 1208 (1952 & Supp. 1991). These scheduled illnesses typically are those that are considered "signature diseases" related to a specific exposure, such
as asbestosis. A claim brought for a listed disease
will be presumed to be sufficiently associated with
the workplace in which the claimant was exposed to
the offending substance as to satisfy the work-
relatedness requirement. Most statutes allow occupational disease claims where the illness is "peculiar to" the worker's occupation, either as a sole
requirement or as a supplement to a schedule of
diseases. *See, e.g.*, Mich. Comp. Laws Ann.
§ 418.401(2)(b) (West 1985 & Supp. 1991–92). For
diseases associated with exposure to toxic substances, determination of whether a claimant's illness falls within this definition may be problematic.
This is particularly true where the disease alleged
has a long latency period and/or appears in back-

ground levels in the general population. "Ordinary diseases of life," to which the general public is exposed outside of the claimant's workplace, will not be compensable, even if the claimant can make a reasonably good showing that he or she developed the disease as a result of a workplace exposure. The line between covered illness and noncovered illness tends to be blurred.

An often overlooked limitation on occupational disease claims is that they be suffered by *employees*. This may seem obvious, but especially in the area of reproductive and genetic injury, persons related to the worker, such as a spouse or children, may claim to have been injured as a result of the worker's employment exposure to toxic substances. For example, a child of a worker may suffer a birth defect that allegedly was caused by the worker's exposure to a substance in the course of his or her employment. These third parties will probably be limited to the tort law—which may or may not provide recovery for the kind of claim brought and which may be subject to more stringent causation requirements than the work-relatedness requirement of workers' compensation law—for a remedy. *See generally* Jean Macchiaroli Eggen, *Toxic Reproductive and Genetic Hazards in the Workplace: Challenging the Myths of the Tort and Workers' Compensation Systems*, 60 Fordham L. Rev. 843 (1992) (discussing the problems third-party family members face in proving a sufficient causal connection between toxic exposure and injury to recover under either tort or workers' compensation law).

This issue remained a troublesome background question in the recent United States Supreme Court case of UAW v. Johnson Controls, Inc. (S.Ct.1991). In *Johnson Controls*, the Court held that an employer's fetal protection policy, which effectively excluded all women of child-bearing age from jobs that might expose them to lead, constituted sex discrimination in violation of federal law. The company had expressed concern that allowing women in lead-exposure jobs would lead to increased liability for injuries to offspring that might be associated with lead exposure. The Court dismissed these concern for an increase in tort liability for employers, however. But issues do remain about how the legal system should address claims by offspring who allege injury as a result of one parent or another's exposure to a toxic substance in the workplace.

3. Exclusivity of Remedy

The concept of workers' compensation as an exclusive remedy bars workers from bringing tort actions against their employers for work-related illness. In return, the worker obtains expedited compensation without the need to show fault on the part of the employer. The worker also is not restricted by the traditional tort doctrines of contributory negligence, assumption of the risk, and the fellow servant rule. One of the seeming paradoxes of occupational disease claims, however, is that the worker need not actually recover under workers' compensation for a tort action to be barred. Consider the example presented by Cole v. Dow Chemical Co. (Mich.Ct.App.1982). In *Cole,* workers complained of sterility as a result of occupational exposure to the chemical DBCP. The claims were held to be covered under the Michigan occupational disease statute, but presented noncompensable injuries. Subsequently, the workers brought personal injury actions against their employer in state court. The court dismissed their actions because the injuries were alleged to arise from exposures in the workplace setting. The court considered it irrelevant that the workers' compensation tribunal had refused to compensate the workers.

In contrast, however, where the occupational illness is deemed to fall outside of the coverage of the relevant occupational disease statute, the claimant should be allowed to commence a tort action against the employer. For example, in McCarthy v. Department of Social & Health Servs. (Wash.1988), the plaintiff had been denied workers' compensation benefits because her chronic lung condition, which she alleged arose from a severe reaction to environmental tobacco smoke in the workplace, was not a covered illness within the state occupational disease statute. The court allowed her civil suit against the employer to proceed on that basis.

The situation presented in the *Cole* case demonstrates the kinds of problems faced by many occupational disease claimants whose injuries are alleged to be related to exposures to toxic substances in the workplace. Because such claims confront numerous statutory hurdles and are often challenged vigorously by employers and insurance carriers, close questions can result in noncompensable injuries. Where, as in *Cole*, claimants have no direct recourse in the courts, legitimately injured workers could be left with no remedy. There is no question that such toxic claims present significant problems for the legal system. Determining precisely how to go about handling these claims to balance all the interests of the parties will continue to be a major challenge in both the public and private legal arenas.

4. Exceptions to Exclusivity

Notwithstanding the result in a case such as *Cole*, most states recognize at least some exceptions to exclusivity, which allow claimants to bring actions directly against their employers. These exceptions exist in addition to the right to bring an action against a third party, such as the manufacturer of equipment or substances used during the course of employment. These exceptions generally are construed quite narrowly, however. Exceptions may appear in the state workers' compensation statute or may arise through judicial interpretation.

a. Intentional Misconduct of Employer

One circumstance that will give rise to special treatment is where the employer acted with the knowledge that injury to the worker was substantially certain to occur. Some jurisdictions treat this situation within the workers' compensation statute, typically establishing an increased benefit for intentional misconduct. In many jurisdictions, however,

the employee may bring an independent civil action
against the employer for injuries arising from such
conduct. "Substantial certainty" of injury is typically a requirement; gross negligence or reckless-
ness usually will not qualify to meet this exception.
See generally 2A Arthur Larson, Workmen's Compensation Law § 68 (1994). With respect to toxic
workplace exposures, the major question becomes
whether workers may bring tort actions against
their employers when the conduct of which they
complain is knowledge of workplace hazards coupled with failure to warn workers or remove the
hazards.

Courts generally have been reluctant to read intentional misconduct into the failure-to-warn circumstances. *See, e.g.*, Wilson v. Asten–Hill Mfg.
(3d Cir.1986); Miller v. Ensco, Inc. (Ark.1985);
Reed Tool Co. v. Copelin (Tex.1985). Most states,
therefore, would prohibit an employee action for
intentional misconduct where the employer failed to
warn of hazards, failed to provide adequate safety
equipment and/or training, or breached workplace
safety regulations, whether or not those acts were
done knowingly. *See also* W.Va. Code § 23–4–2
(1985 & Supp. 1991) (requiring intent to injure and
overruling Mandolidis v. Elkins Industrial, Inc.
(W.Va.1978), which had allowed an exception to
exclusivity for conduct that was willful, wanton,
malicious, and with deliberate disregard for worker's well-being).

Some courts, however, have found these kinds of
circumstances to be sufficiently egregious as to jus-

tify an independent action against the employer for intentional misconduct. In Blankenship v. Cincinnati Milacron Chemicals, Inc. (Ohio 1982), the court read an unwritten exception into the Ohio workers' compensation statute for an employer's failure to act with respect to its employees' exposures to fumes and toxic chemicals. Promoting workplace safety was the overriding policy goal expressed by the court, and the court refused to allow employers to hide behind the limited liability of workers' compensation while committing intentional acts.

Blankenship and similar cases present a question of interpretation of intentional conduct. Some courts view as fraudulent and intentional an employer's acts—whether affirmative or passive—that were likely to lead to injury in the employee. In Cunningham v. Anchor Hocking Corporation (Fla. Dist. Ct.App.1990), the court held that the complaint's allegations that the employer had affirmatively diverted fumes into the workplace and removed manufacturers' warning labels from products used in the workplace could, if proved, constitute claims for "battery, fraud and deceit," thus falling outside the workers' compensation statute. In O'Brien v. Ottawa Silica Company (E.D.Mich. 1987), where the employer allegedly withheld medical information of the worker's occupational illness, the court held that the employer's conduct constituted intentional fraud. The plaintiff in *O'Brien*— the personal representative of the estate of the deceased worker—alleged that the employer knew from information supplied by company doctors that the decedent and other workers were developing asbestos-related disease from exposures in the workplace. The plaintiff further alleged that the employer ignored the doctors' recommendations to take precautions to protect the decedent and failed to inform the decedent of the health problems discovered by the doctors. The court held that these facts, if proven, provided a basis for a direct action against the employer for intentional misconduct because injury was "substantially certain to occur."

These cases indicate that the traditional distinctions between specific intent to injure and endangering the health of workers may become blurred in the toxic torts context. Notwithstanding these developments, however, most states continue to construe the intentional misconduct exception narrowly. Its use by an employee, therefore, as a means of bringing an independent action against the employer may be quite limited, depending upon the relevant jurisdiction.

b. *Aggravation of Injury*

A few states have recognized an exception to the exclusivity of workers' compensation where the employer acted in a manner that aggravated the worker's injury. Under this theory, a tort action could be brought against the employer only for the aggravation of the injury and not for development of the illness in the first place. The chief case applying this theory is Johns–Manville Products Corporation v. Contra Costa Superior Court (Cal.1980). The California workers' compensation statute encompassed intentional conduct, and provided for a one-half increase in benefits if the requisite intent could be proved. In *Contra Costa*, the complaint alleged that the employer had conducted health monitoring of its employees and had knowingly concealed adverse health information from an employee. The court held that under these circumstances, the employer could be liable in tort for the aggravation of the employee's condition. *See also* Millison v. E.I. duPont de Nemours & Co. (N.J.1985) (allowing exception for aggravation of injury, but requiring plaintiff to prove "deliberate corporate strategy" of concealment of health condition).

c. Dual Capacity

This exception has become of extremely limited use in toxic tort actions. It has been applied where an employer undertakes a duty to the employee that is independent of and separate from the employer-employee relationship. The duty is one that the employer owes to the general public, rather than to its employees within the employment relationship. *See* Duprey v. Shane (Cal.1952) (applying dual capacity exception where chiropractor-employer allegedly negligently treated employee for work-related injury). Some questions may arise as to whether an employer that engages in health monitoring of its employees may be open to a tort action for serving in the separate capacity of health care provider. So far, application of the dual capacity exception has not extended that far. In general, employers who provide health screening for their employees are still acting as *employers*. They are not, as the case law seems to require, acting on a duty to the general public.

B. INJUNCTIVE RELIEF FOR UNSAFE WORKING CONDITIONS

When a worker seeks equitable relief for remediation of workplace hazards, rather than monetary compensation, the claim falls outside of workers' compensation and within the jurisdiction of the courts of equity in the state. In Shimp v. New Jersey Bell Telephone Company (N.J.Super.1976), the plaintiff sought to have cigarette smoking enjoined in the area in which she worked because of her severe allergic reaction to passive smoke. The court held that the employee had a right to work in a safe environment, which here included the right to have smoke-free air to breathe while engaged in her work. Taking judicial notice of the toxic nature of cigarette smoke and its association with ill health effects, the court used its equitable powers to fashion a remedy that allowed the employer to provide smoking areas for smoking employees while protecting the right of the plaintiff to be free from smoke.

C. REGULATION UNDER THE OCCUPATIONAL SAFETY AND HEALTH ACT

When Congress enacted the Occupational Safety and Health Act (OSHAct), 29 U.S.C.A. §§ 651–678 (West 1985 & Supp. 1994), in 1970, its primary concerns were twofold—assuring the personal safety and health of workers and reducing lost production and its related increased costs. The OSHAct implements its goals through several interrelated means. First, the Act provides for research into occupational health and safety with the goal of reducing work hazards through the development of appropriate safety and health standards. Second, the Act contains reporting and recordkeeping requirements to make employers accountable and to provide necessary data. Third, the Act establishes and encourages a variety of programs to carry out the goals of the Act. Finally, the Act authorizes an administrative structure that includes regulatory and punitive measures to implement the Act's goals. As with CERCLA, the Act does not create any private right of action for personal injuries arising in the workplace. The OSHAct's entire thrust is toward information dissemination, regulation, and enforcement of workplace health and safety measures.

1. Administrative Structure

The OSHAct establishes a tripartite administrative structure for oversight of safety and health matters related to employment. The most visible agency created under the Act is the Occupational Safety and Health Administration (OSHA), located within the Department of Labor. OSHAct § 5(a)(2), 29 U.S.C.A. § 654(a)(2) (West 1982). OSHA's primary responsibilities are in the areas of standard setting and enforcement. Thus, OSHA is primarily responsible for inspecting workplaces, determining compliance with standards, and proposing appropriate sanctions and remedial action where violations have occurred.

The second agency created under the OSHAct is the National Institute for Occupational Safety and Health (NIOSH). OSHAct § 22, 29 U.S.C.A. § 671 (1976). NIOSH is the research arm that is responsible for providing information to OSHA to be used in the development of health and safety standards. In contrast to OSHA, NIOSH is under the auspices of the Centers for Disease Control (CDC) within the Department of Health and Human Services. Some critics have viewed the bifurcation of the research and rulemaking functions authorized under the OSHAct as problematic. One benefit of the separation is to allow the research function to avoid any biases that might be present in OSHA, where economic interests are considered in addition to the health and safety of employees. But the lack of coordination between the two agencies on occupational health and safety issues has given some reason for concern. *See generally* Stephen A. Bokat & Horace A. Thompson III, Occupational Safety and Health Law 695–710 (1988) (discussing NIOSH's statutory authority, its programs, and court oversight).

The third administrative arm created by the OSHAct is the Occupational Safety and Health Review Commission (OSHRC). OSHAct §§ 10(c) & 12, 29 U.S.C.A. §§ 659(c) & 661 (1982). OSHRC sits as a quasi-judicial review board to oversee cita-

tions that have been issued by OSHA for violations
of OSHA standards. In general, OSHRC becomes
involved when an employer challenges an OSHA
citation. The case is determined by an administrative law judge in the first instance, with subsequent
board determination available. The system also
provides for court review on the record established
below before OSHRC.

2. Occupational Safety and Health Standards

a. *Contents of the Standards*

Section 5(a)(2) of the OSHAct requires that employers comply with any standards promulgated
pursuant to the Act and contained in the Code of
Federal Regulations. Standards exist for individual
substances, including asbestos, lead, and bloodborne
pathogens. The process for promulgation of standards is protracted, and it is not uncommon to have
the courts involved in resolving legal challenges to
proposed standards. These standards establish permissible exposure limits (PELs) for the specific substances. In general, OSHA may only promulgate a
health standard upon a finding that a risk of "material impairment" of employees' health occurs at the
current levels of exposure. Industrial Union Department, AFL–CIO v. American Petroleum Institute (S.Ct.1980).

Typically, a standard includes requirements and
specifications for labels and personal protective
equipment. It also includes requirements for employer monitoring of employee exposure to the des-

ignated substance. Where the standard suggests employee medical examinations or laboratory screening tests, OSHA cannot compel the examination or test for a specific employee, but may require the employer to make testing available. For example, in the lead standard, specifications for monitoring employee blood lead levels are set forth, as well as a medical removal program that enables an employee with excessive blood lead levels to be removed to a non-lead exposure job while the levels recede without being required to take a reduction in pay. *See* 29 C.F.R. § 1910.1025.

b. *Example: Bloodborne Pathogens Rule*

The bloodborne pathogens standard became generally effective in 1992, primarily as a result of concern for the spread of the HIV virus through contact with human blood in the health care workplace. 29 C.F.R. § 1915.1030. The standard requires employers with one or more employees at risk of contracting HIV or hepatitis-B virus (HBV) through workplace exposure to develop and submit a written exposure control plan. The plan must be available to all employees. In implementing the plan, the employer is required to follow universal precautions. This essentially means that all substances regulated under the standard are to be treated as being contaminated with the pathogens, whether or not it is known that the pathogens are present. For example, all needles and sharps used in a hospital are treated as carriers of the viruses, and use and disposal are regulated uniformly and strictly.

To follow universal precautions, employers may implement engineering controls—those that eliminate the hazard altogether—or work practice controls—those that reduce exposure by placing precautions on risky tasks. Thus, needles may no longer be recapped, thereby reducing the risk of exposure by eliminating the risk of skin puncture during that task. The work practice controls mostly address containers, personal protective equipment, and housekeeping, with special attention given to HIV and HBV research laboratories and production facilities.

In addition, the standard makes available to all employees with occupational exposure to HBV a vaccination and to those who have been exposed a post-exposure evaluation. Confidentiality is required of all records kept regarding employees.

The bloodborne pathogens rule provides an example of the kinds of choices OSHA must make in issuing a standard. It also demonstrates some of the important policy issues that must be weighed in the process. Concern for worker privacy is crucial, but identification of routes of exposure and collection of information regarding hazards in the workplace are important in advancing the goals of the OSHAct. Sometimes these various policies can conflict sharply. Workers may be reluctant to report exposures and may be unwilling to participate in any medical monitoring made available by the employer out of fear of discrimination. Federal laws governing discrimination in the workplace may provide some relief, but the law surrounding the application of these laws to specific workplace situations is still evolving. *See generally* Sec. E *infra.*

3. General Duty Clause

Distinct from compliance with the OSHA standards is the employer's obligation pursuant to the general duty clause of OSHAct. Section 5 of the Act provides that an employer must keep the workplace free from "recognized hazards" that cause or are likely to cause death or serious physical injury to the employees. This provision was intended to be a catchall to mandate a duty in situations in which the OSHA standards are not applicable. This section has not been interpreted to establish strict liability, and the short clause is open to interpretation at every turn. Thus, OSHRC has interpreted the clause to require that for liability to exist under the general duty clause, the employer must have been able to avoid the violation. *See* National Realty & Construction Co. v. OSHRC (D.C.Cir. 1973).

For a hazard to be "recognized" within the meaning of the general duty clause, it must be one of which the employer, or at least the employer's industry, had knowledge at the time of the violation. "Hazard" has been interpreted broadly, and includes those exposures that are not apparent to the human senses. Much controversy has ensued over the interpretation of the degree of certainty that must exist for the requisite causation, with the major disagreement being over whether a probability or possibility test was intended.

Finally, the general duty clause was intended to address serious harms—only those that cause or are likely to cause death or serious physical injury. Mandatory penalties per violation are set forth in the OSHAct, but, again, the Act does not provide a remedy for damages for private persons.

4. Hazard Communication Standard

The OSHA Hazard Communication Standard is different from the standards for specific substances discussed above. For one thing, this standard applies to all chemicals and reaches beyond the workplace to the place of manufacture or importing. Moreover, the thrust of the standard is on worker autonomy. The theory behind the Hazard Communication Standard is to provide the workers with sufficient information to make their own choices regarding the hazards that they face in the occupational setting. This recognition of worker autonomy is a move away from the older concept of the paternalistic employer.

The goal of the Hazard Communication Standard (HCS), 29 C.F.R. § 1910.1200, is to provide for the evaluation of chemicals used in the workplace and to provide a comprehensive mechanism for the communication of information regarding the hazards from manufacturers to employers and, ultimately, from employers to employees. The standard applies to hazardous chemicals known to exist in the workplace "in such a manner that employees may be exposed under normal conditions of use or in a foreseeable emergency." 29 C.F.R. § 1910.1200 (b)(2). It applies only to chemicals that are known to pose a health hazard or a physical hazard. 29 C.F.R. § 1910.1200(c). A "health hazard" is determined by "statistically significant evidence based on at least one study conducted in accordance with established scientific principles that acute or chronic health effects may occur in exposed employees." 29 C.F.R. § 1910.1200(c). A "physical hazard," on the other hand, is determined by "scientifically valid evidence" that it is (among other things) combustible, explosive, or reactive. *Id.*

Determination of the existence of a hazard is placed primarily on the manufacturers and importers of the chemicals. The manufacturer or importer is required to develop a material safety data sheet (MSDS) for each hazardous chemical containing specific detailed information regarding the chemical and the hazards it presents. The MSDS travels with the chemical to the employer's place of business. The manufacturer or importer also must properly label the substance. *See* Martin v. American Cyanamid Co. (6th Cir.1993).

The duty of the employer is initially to develop a written hazard communication program designed to identify hazardous chemicals present in the workplace and to formulate a plan for informing employees of the hazards. 29 C.F.R. § 1910.1200(e). The MSDS is an integral part of the hazard communication program, and employers are required to make MSDSs available and obvious to employees while at work. *Id.* § 1910.1200(b). The hazardous chemicals should be properly and clearly labeled. The standard contemplates further information and training on the handling of hazardous substances in specific work operations. Further, the employer is expected to develop methods to determine and manage a release of the hazardous chemical as well as steps employees can take to protect themselves under such circumstances. *Id.* § 1910.1200(h). Finally, the written hazard communication program must be accessible to the employees. *Id.* § 1910.1200(e)(4).

While this explosion of information made available to the worker regarding workplace exposures is certainly salutary, one might well wonder whether the HCS's goal of worker autonomy has been effectively achieved. The threat of latent disease that may or may not manifest itself years or decades later may have little impact on a worker making an employment decision. Rather, the individual worker's personal economic situation—need for a job, need for job advancement, or need for a certain salary level—may trump these speculative health concerns. Furthermore, the wealth of information itself may prove overwhelming for most individuals. Assessing and comprehending one's own true risk of ill health effects is a daunting endeavor, one that professional risk analysts find difficult at best. Nevertheless, on balance, the HCS's requirements of evaluation of chemicals in the workplace and disclosure of known hazards are a step toward achieving the OSHAct's goal of protecting workers' health.

5. OSHA Enforcement

OSHA is responsible for workplace inspections, but any penalties assessed against employers deemed to be in violation of applicable standards are assessed by OSHRC. Civil penalties are available on a per violation basis, with more severe penalties reserved for willful violations of the OSH-Act. The Government's policy toward civil penalties has vacillated, however, depending upon the political inclinations of the Administration. Accordingly, no single clear approach to the use of civil penalties has emerged.

Criminal penalties also are available for willful violations of the OSHAct that result in the death of an employee. They are not available in cases in which an employee is injured but does not die. A corporate officer may be held criminally liable under the OSHAct as an "employer" for company violations where the officer's role in the company was pervasive. United States v. Cusack (D.N.J. 1992). An employee may not be prosecuted under the OSHAct for aiding and abetting an employer, however. United States v. Doig (7th Cir.1991).

In appropriate circumstances, the case would be referred to the Department of Justice for evaluation and a decision whether to prosecute. In reality, the criminal penalties are rarely used. Reformers have attempted to rectify this for several years, however.

Typical bills have called for the OSHAct to be amended to include criminal sanctions for conduct that results in serious bodily injury and to make workplace violations felonies, rather than misdemeanors. *See, e.g.*, OSHA Criminal Penalty Reform Bill, S 445, 102d Cong., 1st Sess. (1991) (introduced by Sen. Howard Metzenbaum).

D. STATE CRIMINAL ENFORCEMENT OF WORKPLACE SAFETY

The OSHAct has been interpreted to permit the states to enact their own criminal laws governing workplace health and safety violations. For example, in People v. Pymm (N.Y.1990), the court held that the OSHAct did not pre-empt state criminal laws applying to workplace health and safety. *Pymm* involved a hidden mercury reclamation operation set up in the basement of a thermometer plant. The court noted that mercury can be highly toxic and exposure at chronic low doses can cause permanent neurological damage. Various OSHA inspections revealed that workers at the plant were not adequately protected from the hazards posed by exposure to mercury. In addition, the employer had failed to reveal the basement operation to the inspectors, despite the inspectors' requests to see all areas operated by the company. Once the basement area was located and inspected, mercury levels tested at five times the permissible level under OSHA. The employers were charged under state law with counts of conspiracy, falsifying business records, and first and second degree assault.

The *Pymm* court held that the OSHAct established a minimum standard of workplace safety and
that the OSHAct penalties therefore acted as a floor
above which the states could act in supplementing
them with their own criminal penalties. The court
relied on the savings clause contained in the OSH-
Act in concluding that state criminal laws governing
the same conduct as that regulated by the OSHAct
were valid as applied. The court stated:

> We do not accept the appellants' argument that
> Congress' foremost purpose in drafting the [OSH]-
> Act was to ensure uniformity of workplace health
> and safety standards and that individual State
> prosecutions stand as an obstacle to the accom-
> plishment of that purpose. The Act's ... provi-
> sions ... indicate to us that Congress was willing
> to accept a multiplicity of regulatory approaches
> provided that the safety and health of workers
> were not compromised....

> ... In fact, criminal prosecutions under State
> criminal law would seem to further the goal of
> ensuring the safety and health of American work-
> ers by deterring future instances of criminally
> culpable employer conduct.

Thus, state criminal law may provide a separate
means of prosecuting employers for certain types of
conduct in providing unsafe working conditions for
their employees. For a critique of the use of the
criminal justice system as a forum for addressing
workplace health and safety, see Thea D. Dunmire,
The Problems With Using Common Law Criminal

*Statutes to Deter Exposure to Chemical Substances
in the Workplace,* 17 N. Ky. L. Rev. 53 (1989).

E. REMEDIES FOR EMPLOYER
DISCRIMINATION

Employees' susceptibility to injuries related to
toxic substances in the workplace could lead to
impermissible employment discrimination by employers. This was the ruling of the United States
Supreme Court in UAW v. Johnson Controls, Inc.
(S.Ct.1991), in which employees of a battery manufacturer alleged that they had been discriminated
against in matters of employment on the basis of an
employee protection policy directed at the exposure
of female workers to lead. There was no dispute
that the employer was in compliance with the
OSHA standard for lead in the workplace. The
employer's policy was concerned with protecting the
developing fetuses of pregnant employees from the
potentially harmful effects of chronic low-level exposure to lead in the mothers' jobs. The case contained an overt gender issue: Did the employer's
enforcement of its policy preventing women of
child-bearing age from working in positions that
would necessitate exposure to lead, a known teratogenic substance, violate Title VII of the federal anti-
discrimination laws? The Court answered with a
resounding "yes." Because the fetal protection policy was discriminatory on its face, the Court applied
the "bona fide occupational qualification" (BFOQ)
test to determine whether the discrimination was
justifiable. The BFOQ test required that to use

gender or pregnancy as a basis for discrimination, the employer must be able to show that gender or pregnancy actually interferes with the employee's ability to perform the job. This test plainly was not met.

The issue that was not completely resolved by *Johnson Controls*, however, was whether in the absence of the discriminatory policy the employer would find itself subject to increased tort liability for birth defects to employees' offspring. If so, arguably the employer would experience substantial cost increases. While the Court stated that such concerns are not a defense to a Title VII discrimination claim, the Court noted that where an employer has not acted negligently—having, presumably, complied with both OSHA and Title VII and given employees appropriate warning regarding the hazards to which they and their developing fetuses may be exposed—imposition of tort liability would be unlikely. *See generally* Widera v. Ettco Wire & Cable Corp. (N.Y. App.Div.1994) (in case not involving discrimination issues, holding appropriate the dismissal of action brought by infant allegedly injured by in utero exposure to workplace chemicals carried into home on parent's work clothes because employer owed no duty to infant). Nevertheless, significant questions remain concerning the possibility and projected impact of increased tort liability. Among the many messages sent by the Supreme Court in *Johnson Controls* are that employer self-protection from tort liability cannot come at the cost of impermissible discrimination and that worker autonomy is to be respected in decisions relating to health and safety in the workplace, provided that all relevant information is made available.

Other discrimination issues have emerged as a result of employee exposure to toxic substances in the workplace. Concerns have been expressed as to whether information obtained by employers through health or genetic screening and monitoring may be used in personnel decisions, with respect to both hiring and retention. Health concerns may involve the extent to which a worker may begin to manifest early signs and symptoms of latent disease related to workplace exposures. Another kind of health concern is the existence of communicable disease in the worker, an issue that has raised much interest because of the AIDS epidemic. Genetic concerns may range from identifying a worker's genetic predisposition to developing certain illnesses to determining whether a worker has a genetically predisposed sensitivity to a particular substance in the workplace. For an overview of the complex subject of genetic screening and monitoring in the workplace, including the legal issues raised, see generally United States Congress, Office of Technology Assessment, Genetic Monitoring and Screening in the Workplace (1990). The identification and use of genetic information is in its infancy now. But as genetic medicine becomes increasingly sophisticated, employers may find genetic screening an attractive mechanism for eliminating applicants who may be genetically susceptible to certain work-related illnesses. Employers may seek to avoid the costs—such as insurance benefits and lost productivity—of ill employees.

Obviously, only some of the potential uses of health and genetic information by employers invoke toxic tort issues. In the broad toxic tort context, questions arise as to the circumstances under which an employer's use of health or genetic information concerning a specific employee would constitute impermissible discrimination.

This area of the law is very problematic, but two major federal statutes exist that may offer relief for employees who claim to have been victims of improper discrimination of this sort. The Federal Rehabilitation Act, 29 U.S.C.A. §§ 701–797a (West 1985 & Supp. 1994), applies to public employees, whereas the more recent Americans With Disabilities Act (ADA), 42 U.S.C.A. §§ 12101–12213 (West Supp. 1994), applies to private employment situations. Both statutes make it illegal to discriminate against an individual otherwise qualified for the job on the basis of a disability. The definition of disability includes communicable illnesses. *See* School Bd. of Nassau County v. Arline (S.Ct.1987) (Rehabilitation Act case involving employee with tuberculosis); Chalk v. U.S. District Court Central Dist. of Calif. (9th Cir.1988) (Rehabilitation Act case involving employee with HIV). In general, an employee must present with symptoms of the disability for the statute to apply. Thus, increased susceptibility to occupational illness, without manifestation of the illness, would not appear to be covered.

Furthermore, employers are required to provide reasonable accommodations for persons within the statute. If the employee declines the employer's offer of a reasonable accommodation, the employer may be justified in discharging the employee. *See* Severino v. North Fort Myers Fire Control Dist. (11th Cir.1991) (upholding employer's right to discharge AIDS-infected fireman who refused reasonable accommodation).

The ADA permits an employer to require a medical examination of "conditional offerees." 42 U.S.C.A. 12112(d)(3). The Equal Employment Opportunity Commission (EEOC) has interpreted this provision to permit an employer to require the conditional offeree, but not mere applicants and not employees, to undergo examination into matters not specifically related to the conditions of the proposed employment. 29 C.F.R. § 1630.14 (1994). This conceivably could provide a means of conducting genetic testing or HIV screening that otherwise would not be permissible for employees. Even though under the ADA the results of such examinations may not be used to discriminate against conditional offerees, the opportunity could be present for employer action that may have a discriminatory effect. Questions involving this particular provision of the ADA are certain to be resolved by future litigation.

CHAPTER FIVE

OTHER SPECIAL DEFENDANTS

A. GOVERNMENTAL ENTITIES

1. Sovereign Immunity Generally

Sometimes injured persons will seek to bring claims against a governmental entity on the basis of the government's conduct. The conduct of which the plaintiff complains may be any kind of activity for which a private party could be liable. In the absence of a statute to the contrary, sovereign immunity generally protects governmental entities from many kinds of actions, including tort actions. Where the government has waived its sovereign immunity, the statutes generally are riddled with exceptions. Other restrictions on suits against the government also exist, either within the waiving statute or elsewhere. The result has been that toxic tort plaintiffs who bring suit against governmental entities may encounter judicial constructions of the exceptions to the government's waiver of sovereign immunity that prevent such actions from going forward.

Kenney v. Scientific, Inc. (N.J.Super. Law Div. 1985), a case construing the New Jersey Tort Claims Act, N.J. Stat. Ann. § 59:1–1 to 1–7 (West 1992), offers an example of the myriad issues that can be raised when a plaintiff sues the government in a toxic tort claim. The New Jersey act illustrates the problems courts have with the exceptions-within-exceptions approach of most tort claims acts. The *Kenney* action was brought by residents in the vicinity of two landfills—one privately owned and one owned and operated by the Township—against the owners and operators of the landfills, numerous generators (including another Township) of waste deposited at the landfills, the transporters of the waste, and the State of New Jersey (for licensing the landfills and failing to properly inspect, regulate, and supervise them). As with most tort claims acts, the New Jersey act retains immunity for strict liability claims; thus, the *Kenney* plaintiffs alleged claims for negligence and nuisance, as well as an assortment of other theories.

The New Jersey Tort Claims Act applies to all public entities, including the State, counties, municipalities, and public agencies. N.J. Stat. Ann. § 59:1–3 (West 1992). While stating a general rule of sovereign immunity, the Act allows a public entity to be liable "for injury proximately caused by an act or omission of a public employee within the scope of his employment" in the same manner that a private person would be liable. *See* N.J. Stat. Ann. § 59:2–2 (West 1992). The Act contains a variety of exceptions to this liability. Among the exceptions are matters that related to the plaintiffs' claims in *Kenney*. First, no public entity may be liable for licensing a landfill or hauler of waste.

Nor may the public entity be liable for improper inspection, regulation, or supervision of the landfill. Thus, neither the State nor the Township could be liable under these theories.

The *Kenney* court was more concerned about a separate limitation that applied to actions arising out of dangerous conditions of public property, which theory clearly formed the basis for the plaintiffs' allegations. Under the Act, the public entity may be held liable upon a showing that (1) the property was in a dangerous condition at the time of the plaintiff's injury, (2) that the condition was the proximate cause of the injury, and (3) that the injury was reasonably foreseeable. In addition, one of the following must be shown: (1) a negligent or wrongful act or omission by a public employee; or (2) actual or constructive notice of the dangerous condition and sufficient time to protect against the injury. Moreover, the entity's measures to protect persons against the condition, or its failure to take measures, would lead to liability only if "palpably unreasonable." N.J. Stat. Ann. § 59:4–2 (West 1992).

With respect to the State, the court dismissed the claims because the allegations did not arise out of a condition on State property. But with respect to the Township, the court found a question of fact on the reasonableness of the Township's activities at its landfill.

Another issue addressed in passing by the *Kenney* court is of some overall significance in actions against governmental entities. States typically have notice of claim provisions for actions against public entities that require the filing of a written notice with the public entity within a certain period of time following accrual of the cause of action. The time period is typically rather short. *See* N.J. Stat. Ann. § 59:8–8 (West 1992) (90 days). Furthermore, shortened statutes of limitations may apply to tort actions against governmental entities. *Compare* N.Y Civ. Prac. L. & R. 214 (McKinney 1990) (3–year limitations period for tort actions) *with* N.Y. Gen. Mun. Law § 50–i(1) (McKinney 1990) (1–year and 90–days limitations period for tort claims against public entities). Determination of when a cause of action accrues for notice of claim purposes will be governed by the case law interpreting the statutes of limitations generally. *See* Kenney v. Scientific, Inc. (N.J.Super. Law Div.1985) (applying discovery rule to accrual for determination of timeliness of notice of claim). *See generally* Chapter 6, Sec. A *infra*.

2. Federal Tort Claims Act

The United States Government has waived its sovereign immunity for tort claims in limited circumstances. The Federal Tort Claims Act, 28 U.S.C.A. § 1346(b) (West 1994), provides that the federal district courts shall have exclusive jurisdiction over claims for money damages against the United States alleging personal injury, wrongful death, or property damage as a result of a negligent act or omission by a Government employee within the scope of employment. Although the case law interpreting the Federal Tort Claims Act generally has developed outside of the context of toxic torts, several significant toxic tort cases have involved interpreting some key exceptions to the Act.

a. Discretionary Function Exception

By far the most sweeping and problematic exception to the United States's waiver of immunity for tort claims is the discretionary function exception. This exception provides that the United States may not be held liable for any claim "based upon the exercise or performance or the failure to exercise or perform a discretionary function or duty on the part of a federal agency or an employee of the Government, whether or not the discretion involved be abused." 28 U.S.C.A. § 2680(a) (West 1994). What constitutes a discretionary function is not easy to ascertain.

In Berkovitz v. United States (S.Ct.1988), the United States Supreme Court demonstrated the depth of analysis that may be required to determine whether the conduct that was alleged was a matter of protected governmental discretion. Berkovitz was an action for personal injuries suffered by an infant allegedly as a result of ingesting a dose of an oral polio vaccine. The plaintiffs claimed that the Division of Biologic Standards (DBS), an agency within the National Institutes of Health, had improperly licensed the vaccine. They claimed further that the Bureau of Biologics of the Food and Drug

Administration had improperly released the specific lot of vaccine from which the child's dose came.

For conduct to fall within the discretionary function exception it must involve judgment or choice on the part of the actor. Dalehite v. United States (S.Ct.1953). Moreover, the conduct must be of the sort that the discretionary function exception was enacted to protect, so as to "prevent judicial 'second-guessing' of legislative and administrative decisions." United States v. Varig Airlines (S.Ct.1984). While these principles may seem somewhat vague, it is clear from the *Berkovitz* decision that the discretionary function exception will *not* apply "when a federal statute, regulation, or policy specifically prescribes a course of action for an employee to follow." The Court also made clear that the discretionary function exception does not apply automatically to all agency activities.

Beyond these general guidelines, close and specific scrutiny must be conducted on the context of the agency conduct forming the basis of the complaint. In *Berkovitz*, the Court first examined the required duties of DBS with respect to licensing vaccines. It concluded that more specificity was needed as to the plaintiffs' claim. If the plaintiffs were claiming that the vaccine had been licensed without DBS first making its required determination as to whether the vaccine complied with regulatory standards, then the claim would not go to a discretionary function, but rather to a mandatory function, and would be actionable. If, on the other hand, the plaintiffs were claiming that DBS had made the determination of compliance incorrectly, and if that determination properly consisted of policy judgments, then the discretionary function exception would shield the conduct.

With respect to the release of the lot of vaccine, the Court conducted a different analysis. First, the Court stated that any claims challenging the Bureau of Biologics' right to determine the appropriate manner of release of vaccine lots would be construed to arise from a discretionary function. Ultimately, however, the *Berkovitz* plaintiffs' claims were held not to fall within the exception because the Bureau had chosen to put into place its own *mandatory* policy for lot release. Because Government employees had no discretion to deviate from the mandatory policy, the conduct could form the basis of an action against the Government. Thus, although the establishment of the policy on lot inspection was discretionary in the first instance, once the Bureau put into effect a mandatory policy that all employees were required to follow, the agency action in releasing the lot of vaccine could not be a protected discretionary function.

Berkovitz is a complex case with important lessons for attorneys. It instructs courts to undertake focused and detailed analysis on each aspect of the conduct alleged in the complaint before ruling on the applicability of the discretionary function exception. The lesson of the Bureau of Biologics' internal policy is that regulatory activity that first appears as discretionary may be transformed into nondiscretionary conduct. After *Berkovitz*, however, agencies may be discouraged from putting into place their own stringent safety policies for fear of opening the door to governmental liability. In C.R.S. by D.B.S. v. United States (D.Minn.1993), a serviceman alleged that he had contracted the AIDS virus as a result of a blood transfusion at a military hospital. The military had followed existing blood guidelines issued by the American Association of Blood Banks and by the FDA. The court held that the Government could not be held liable for failing to develop more stringent guidelines. This result is correct. But *Berkovitz* may inhibit agencies from taking extra safety measures when they have good reason to do so.

b. *Feres Doctrine and Military Service*

Another exception to the Federal Tort Claims Act that has figured prominently in toxic tort litigation, and which has developed in the court opinions, is what is known as the *Feres* doctrine. The *Feres* doctrine played a significant role in the Agent Orange litigation. When Vietnam veterans and their families commenced the federal class action for personal injuries arising from exposure to the herbicide known as "Agent Orange" during the Vietnam war, they named manufacturers of the herbicide as defendants, but not the United States Government. *See generally* Chapter 9, Sec. A(1) *infra.* An important reason for omitting the Government from the suit was the fact that the action fell well within a recognized exception to the Act. In Feres v. United States (S.Ct.1950), the Supreme

Court held that armed forces members cannot bring tort actions against the Government for harms that "arise out of or are in the course of activity incident to service." Policy considerations supported this rule. First, a compensation mechanism for injured members of the armed forces was available through the Veterans' Administration. Second, suits against the Government, if allowed, were seen as detrimental to military discipline.

An issue of law that arose in the Agent Orange litigation related to the fact that the defendants impleaded the Government, claiming that the Government should be liable to the defendants for any damages the defendants may be ordered to pay to the plaintiffs. The court held that under the rule of Stencel Aero Engineering Corp. v. United States (S.Ct.1977), which extended the *Feres* doctrine, the Government could not be required to indemnify defendants in an action in which the plaintiff could not have sued the Government directly. Thus, because the members of the plaintiff class who were members of the armed forces were not allowed to sue the Government directly, *Stencel* prevented the defendants from impleading the Government with respect to those claims. This applied as well to the derivative claims of family members.

With respect to the civilian family members' claims of related miscarriages and fetal deformations, however, neither the rationale behind *Stencel* nor the policies underlying *Feres* applied, and the Government was retained as a third-party defendant. *See* In re "Agent Orange" Prod. Liab. Litig.

(E.D.N.Y.1984). These independent claims of family member ultimately failed on several grounds, including causation. *See* Adams v. United States (2d Cir.1987); In re "Agent Orange" Prod. Liab. Litig. (E.D.N.Y.1985).

B. GOVERNMENT CONTRACTORS

The Agent Orange litigation involved a further issue related to the operation of the Federal Tort Claims Act. The herbicide products manufactured by the defendants were ordered by the Government for military use. Thus, these government contractors argued that because they manufactured the herbicide to Goverment specifications, they should be protected. *See* In re "Agent Orange" Prod. Liab. Litig. (2d Cir.1987) (actions by plaintiffs who opted out of the Agent Orange class action).

Policy reasons favor allowing government contractors to be immune from suits seeking compensation for injuries arising out of contracts with the Government, at least in some circumstances. Liability imposed upon government contractors could impair the military procurement process, which has its own special concerns for military efficiency, avoidance of delay, and cost containment. Because government contractors manufacture their products to Government specifications for uses set by the Government, the Government's control over the product would seem to work in favor of immunity for the contractor. On the other hand, courts demand some assurance that the Government was at least aware of the hazards of the product that gave rise to the plaintiffs' claims against the contractor.

The accepted elements of the government contractor defense, as identified in the Agent Orange litigation, consist of the following:

1. That the government established the specifications for [the product];

2. That the [product] manufactured by the defendant met the government's specifications in all material respects; and

3. That the government knew as much as or more than the defendant about the hazards to people that accompanied use of [the product].

In re "Agent Orange" Prod. Liab. Litig. (E.D.N.Y. 1982) (Pratt, J.). Interestingly, the Second Circuit allowed the defendant contractors to assert the government contractor defense, finding that they met the first two elements and that no hazards existed to be communicated to the Government. In re "Agent Orange" Prod. Liab. Litig. (2d Cir.1987).

In Boyle v. United Technologies Corp. (1988), the Supreme Court developed a federal common law recognizing the government contractor defense. The Court found legislation on the issue lacking and determined that the issues raised by the government contractor defense were unique federal interests warranting creation of federal common law. The Court reasoned that because the Government is insulated from liability for its choice of the design of military products due to the discretionary function exception, allowing the contractors to share the immunity was reasonable. The federal common law adopted by the Court reflected the same three traditional elements of the government contractor defense that were articulated in the Agent Orange opinion and numerous others.

C. SUCCESSOR AND PREDECESSOR CORPORATIONS

1. Successors

Because of the long latency periods for illnesses to manifest themselves following toxic exposures, it is not uncommon for culpable parties to disappear, become insolvent, or change hands. The traditional rule is that successor corporations do not assume the liabilities of their predecessors, including liabilities in tort, unless one of the following is present:

1. express or implied agreement;

2. de facto consolidation or merger of the selling corporation and the purchasing corporation;

3. the purchasing corporation is a mere continuation of the selling corporation; or

4. fraud or other intent to avoid responsibility for the liabilities.

This rather narrow set of rules developed out of concern for commercial creditors and shareholders and to address various tax and contract law issues. Accordingly, these exceptions to the traditional rule of nonliability generally have been applied quite narrowly.

Thus, de facto merger has been interpreted to apply when the stockholders of the selling corporation and those of the purchasing corporation are identical. The "mere continuation" exception requires that the plaintiff be able to show "that there is continuity in management, shareholders, personnel, physical location, assets and general business operation between selling and purchasing corporations following the asset acquisition." Ramirez v. Amsted Industries (N.J.1981). Continuation of the general business of the selling corporation, without these other factors, would not trigger the exception.

In the era of increased product liability actions, the traditional rule has been criticized. *See generally* Ramirez v. Amsted Industries (N.J.1981). Some courts have created a separate exception to the rule of nonliability for continuation of the same product line. If the successor corporation continues to manufacture the same product line using the same design, personnel, and location it may be liable for product liability claims arising out of a specific product that was manufactured by the predecessor. In Ray v. Alad Corp. (Cal.1977), the court characterized the rule as follows: "[A] party which acquires a manufacturing business and continues the output of its line of products under the circumstances here presented assumes strict tort liability for defects in units of the same product line previously manufactured and distributed by the entity from which the business was acquired." Thus, this exception will apply notwithstanding the fact that the successor did not expressly assume the liabilities of its predecessor nor did it actually manufacture the product that caused the plaintiff's injury.

The policy underlying this extension of liability was that in a product line continuation situation, the successor may be credited with the skill and experience of its predecessor and is in a superior position to the consumer to bear costs and assess risks. Defendants have criticized this exception for creating an impediment to business transactions because potential purchasers would be uncertain about the number of potential liabilities that could arise. Nevertheless, courts that have adopted the exception have observed that the unknown, potential liabilities should either be handled as part of the acquisition through price reduction or partial indemnification agreements, or dealt with through insurance. *See* Ramirez v. Amsted Industries (N.J. 1981).

Despite disagreement among courts, similar concepts of successor liability may apply under CERCLA. In Smith Land & Improvement Corp. v. Celotex Corp. (3d Cir.1988), the court held that traditional concepts of successor liability should apply under CERCLA, but used sweeping language to suggest that more expansive successor liability may be appropriate. In United States v. Distler (W.D.Ky.1990), the court recognized a product line exception on the basis of the substantial continuity between the predecessor and successor corporations.

2. Predecessors in Title

A different set of problems arises when a successor corporation attempts to hold a distant predecessor strictly liable for contamination of the property. In T & E Industries, Inc. v. Safety Light Corp. (N.J.1991), the plaintiff, T & E, was the current owner of a site contaminated by radium tailings. Radium was processed at the site for many years by United States Radium Corporation (USRC), which owned the property until 1943. USRC's immediate successor was unaware of the hazards associated with the radium tailings and constructed a portion of the plant over the tailings. The property was subsequently owned by a series of parties and was eventually purchased by T & E, an electronic component manufacturer, in 1974.

In 1979, T & E was ordered to decontaminate or abandon the site, pursuant to a 1978 federal law governing mill tailings. T & E took various measures, but eventually the site was placed on the National Priorities List for cleanup. *See generally* Chapter 3, *supra*. T & E subsequently closed the plant and moved its manufacturing operation, but the property could not be sold until cleanup had occurred. T & E then sought to hold USRC liable on the basis of strict liability for abnormally dangerous activities.

While the traditional rule of caveat emptor usually applied in a situation such as this, the *T & E* court was convinced that this case fell within an exception. The exception, as set forth in the Restatement (Second) of Torts § 353, as well as case law, allows a seller to be liable for affirmative concealment or passive failure to disclose a condition of the property posing an unreasonable risk to persons. The seller is in a position superior to purchasers of the property to assess the risks and prevent future harms, in the court's view. The exception was not intended to prevent sellers and purchasers from entering into real property transactions, provided that the hazards are disclosed and the purchaser voluntarily assumes the risk.

D. LENDERS

In the context of CERCLA cleanup liability, conflict has arisen over the extent to which a lender can be considered an "owner or operator" of property and, therefore, a potentially responsible party. This question is critical in the common situation in which a bank or other lender holds a security interest in the property, typically a mortgage. The definition of owner or operator in Section 101(2)(A) of CERCLA excludes lenders, but only if they have not "participated in the management" of the facility. The split in the case law has involved the kinds of activities that constitute participation in management.

The most discussed decision on CERCLA lender liability has been United States v. Fleet Factors Corp. (11th Cir.1990). In *Fleet Factors*, the court indicated that participation in financial management of the facility may be sufficient to impose liability, even without any actual day-to-day management. The court stated:

> [A] secured creditor may incur [CERCLA] liability, without being an operator, by participating in the financial management of a facility to a degree indicating a capacity to influence the corporation's treatment of hazardous wastes. It is not necessary for the secured creditor actually to involve itself in the day-to-day operations of the facility in order to be liable.

Under the *Fleet Factors* test, a lender need not have foreclosed on the property to expose itself to liability. Not all circuits have agreed with the *Fleet Factors* test, however. *See* In re Bergsoe Metal Corp. (9th Cir.1990) (requiring some actual management of the facility).

In 1992, EPA issued regulations designed to resolve the confusion evidenced by the case law. *See* 40 C.F.R. § 300.1100 (1992). The regulations described the actions lenders could take with regard to the property without becoming liable under CERCLA. Generally, the guidelines protected a greater number of activities than had the *Fleet Factors* test. EPA stated that merely being in the position to influence or control the operation of the facility was not enough to impose liability on the lender. Rather, the lender would be liable if it made decisions regarding the facility's environmental compliance or took responsibility for overall management of the facility.

In 1994, the D.C. Circuit, in Kelley v. EPA (D.C.Cir.1994), vacated EPA's lender liability rule. The court held that in the absence of Congressional intent to the contrary, it was appropriate for the federal district court, and not EPA, to determine the scope of liability under CERCLA. Accordingly, EPA lacked the authority to define the scope of lender liability by regulation, thus causing the court to vacate the lender liability rule. Similarly, the court refused to accord deference to EPA's view of statutory interpretation on this matter. As a result of *Kelley*, confusion remains as to the precise scope of lender liability under CERCLA.

E. INSURERS

Insurance companies are significant participants in toxic tort litigation. As defendants seek to interpret their liability insurance agreements as expansively as possible, so as to be covered for the activities involved in the underlying lawsuit, their insurers seek to both limit coverage and shift liability to other insurers related to the case in some way. Thus, where an asbestos worker suffering from asbestos-related disease files suit against 20 manufacturers of asbestos products, each insurer of a defendant manufacturer will attempt to shift liability for the full amount of damages onto each of the others. Moreover, where a single defendant was insured by different companies, seriatim, over the period of time from first exposure to manifestation of the illness, each insurer will seek to have liability for the full amount of the damages imposed on the others. These issues implicate both the duty to defend the lawsuit and the duty to indemnify.

Insurance issues in toxic torts typically arise as matters of interpreting the provisions of comprehensive (or commercial) general liability (CGL) policies. As a matter of established law, the duty to defend the insured is broader than the duty to indemnify, although courts may become involved in both aspects.

1. Coverage Questions

a. *Occurrence*

Coverage questions have arisen in situations in which an action has been brought against the insured for personal injury or property damage associated with the insured's use or disposal of hazardous substances. The standard CGL policy describes the trigger for coverage in terms of an "occurrence" (changed from the earlier term "accident"). Occurrence is defined to include both isolated accidental releases and continuous exposures. The occurrence must not be expected or intended. For an occurrence to be intended, the harm must have been intentional, not merely the act. Thus, the intentional disposal of hazardous waste at a facility is covered, provided that the insured did not intend that it migrate into the drinking water supply of a nearby community, thus causing the lawsuit for which coverage is sought. But coverage may be precluded where the insured was aware of the likelihood of harm that may result from its activities, as

where the insured had reason to know that the
drinking water supply was contaminated from the
site, yet continued to dispose of wastes at the site.
See American Mutual Liability Insurance Co. v.
Neville Chemical Co. (W.D.Pa.1987).

b. *Latent Illness*

A major coverage issue in toxic tort actions involves identifying the insurer or insurers who are
required to indemnify the insured when a plaintiff
recovers for personal injuries that are manifested
years or decades after exposure. The typical CGL
policy requires that the bodily injury have occurred
within the policy period. Whether a particular insurer will be responsible depends on the trigger of
coverage used. The "trigger" is some event within
the period of time that the policy was in effect that
forms the basis for coverage.

Time of exposure is one such trigger. The theory
underlying this trigger is that in many circumstances it can be assumed that the plaintiff suffered
some form of bodily harm at the time of exposure,
even if the disease did not manifest observable
symptoms until much later. Thus, exposure to
asbestos fibers during the policy period can be
deemed to immediately initiate the disease process,
thus causing the requisite bodily injury at the time
of exposure. Insurance Company of North America
v. Forty–Eight Insulations, Inc. (6th Cir.1981).
There seems to be some difference of interpretation
as to whether the existing scientific literature must
support the presumption of injury at the time of

exposure—as with asbestos—or whether the exposure itself creates the presumption of sub-clinical injury.

In contrast, some courts have applied a discovery trigger. Under this rule, the bodily injury is held to occur at the time the illness manifests itself in objective symptoms. *See* Eagle–Picher Industries, Inc. v. Liberty Mutual Insurance Co. (1st Cir.1987) (asbestos). The discovery rule is consistent with the transformation in statutory limitations periods for personal injury actions arising from toxic exposures. *See* Chapter 6, Sec. A, *infra*. The discovery rule may be more difficult for an insurer to take into account than the exposure rule, as the insured's activities and, thus, the risks that are being insured at the time of manifestation of the disease may not be the same kinds of activities that gave rise to the claim. Thus, predicting potential liabilities becomes more difficult as time goes on.

In Zurich Insurance Co. v. Northbrook Excess & Surplus Insurance Co. (Ill.App.Ct.1986), the court took a compromise position and applied a "split trigger." This test resulted in coverage by both the carrier that insured the loss at the time of exposure and the insurance carrier at the time of discovery of the illness.

The broadest interpretation of the bodily injury requirement, however, is the multiple or continuous trigger, which finds coverage by any policy in effect during the entire time from first exposure to manifestation of disease. *See* Keene Corp. v. Insurance

Company of North America (D.C.Cir.1981). The
theory behind this trigger is that in latent disease
cases the bodily injury is continuous throughout the
period from the initial exposure to the manifestation of illness. This trigger is beneficial to the
insured because it provides the most coverage.
With many insurance carriers often covering the
risk, the insured may seek to be indemnified by as
many as necessary (each up to the policy limits, of
course) to reimburse the loss.

c. Asbestos Abatement

The CGL policy also typically covers property
damage liability, defined as injury to or destruction
of tangible property during the policy period.
Sometimes defining property damage is not so easy.
This was the case with the surge of litigation involving abatement of asbestos in buildings. In
claims brought by building owners for recovery of
the costs of inspecting the buildings and remediat-
ing the conditions of deteriorating asbestos, insurers have argued that no physical injury or destruction of property occurred and that therefore the loss
is not covered. In United States Fidelity & Guar-
anty Co. v. Wilkin Insulation Co. (Ill.1991), the
court held that the presence of asbestos in the
building constituted property damage within the
meaning of the insurance policies. The insurers
argued that any harm was mere intangible economic harm as evidenced by diminished property values.
The court rejected this argument, stating that because the ill health effects of asbestos are known,

and because building owners are required by law to remove the asbestos due to its potential toxic effects, its presence constitutes true property damage.

The trigger of coverage in a property damage case may differ from the trigger in a personal injury case. Courts tend to look at this issue on a case-by-case basis. The result may depend on the continuing nature of the damage. *See generally* Gerald W. Boston & M. Stuart Madden, Law of Environmental and Toxic Torts 529–42 (1994) (discussing various issues of coverage within context of environmental and toxic torts).

2. Payments for Multiple Occurrences

Many toxic torts actions claim injury occurring over a period of time. This is true whether the action arises from a workplace exposure, such as asbestos, a product, such as a prescription drug, or contamination of water or land. Where a policy contains a monetary limit for each occurrence, this issue could become significant. This was the case in American Red Cross v. Travelers Indem. Co. (D.D.C.1993), in which the insured was seeking to be indemnified for claims made against it by covered persons who claimed to have received HIV-contaminated blood products. The insurer argued that all the claims constituted a single occurrence within the contemplation of the policy and were subject to the single occurrence cap. The court held, however, that the claims were separate because separate acts or omissions occurred and the injuries were due to separate causes. Thus, the insured was entitled to multiple payments, rather than one payment. As this case demonstrates, the court will look beyond the absolute number of claims for which the insured seeks to be indemnified and determine whether the overall circumstances and causation constitute a single occurrence or multiple occurrences.

3. Pollution Exclusion Clauses

Pollution exclusion clauses have appeared in CGL policies for several decades. The exclusion has been applied to both land-related liabilities and to product-based liabilities. As a historical matter, the wording of the exclusion has changed over time, apparently to clarify the intent of the clause as a result of substantial litigation throughout the 1970s. Initially, the pollution exclusion clauses exempted releases into land, air, or water of categories of toxic substances, but the exclusion did not apply to "sudden and accidental" releases. These older policy provisions are important for toxic tort litigation because often courts are called upon to construe the provisions of a policy that was in effect at a much earlier date. *See* Section E(1)(b), *supra*, for a discussion of triggers of coverage.

What constitutes a "sudden and accidental" release has occupied much of the case law, with some courts interpreting it to require a single, unexpected incident, and other courts requiring only that the release be unintended. *See, e.g.,* Lumbermens Mutual Casualty Co. v. Belleville Indus., Inc. (1st Cir.1991) (holding that occurrence was not "sudden and accidental" where there was reasonable expectation of release); Claussen v. Aetna Casualty & Surety Co. (11th Cir.1989) (holding that "sudden and accidental" release must be unexpected and unintended). The latter interpretation may allow coverage for gradual releases occurring over a period of time, and this issue has become the subject of some debate. Further, debate has also ensued as to whether the pollution exclusion clause was applicable where the substance released into the environment was a product manufactured by the insured rather than waste.

Revision of the CGL policy in the mid–1980s predictably gave rise to new language for the pollution exclusion clause. The clause excluded bodily injury or property damages "arising out of the actual, alleged or threatened discharge, dispersal, release or escape of pollutants." The new pollution exclusion deleted the "sudden and accidental" exception that had appeared in the older exclusion clause and removed the phrase that required the discharge to be "into the land, the atmosphere or any watercourse or body of water." The exclusion by its terms also applies to governmental cleanup liabilities. Although this exclusion appears to be airtight for insurers, the ultimate interpretation of it by the courts remains to develop. *See* Pipefitters Welfare Educational Fund v. Westchester Fire Insurance Co. (7th Cir.1992) (holding that liability of insured arising from personal injuries due to exposure to PCBs was exempt from coverage). Some courts have begun to interpret the new exclusion much more broadly than the earlier one. *See, e.g.*, Oates v. State of New York (N.Y.Ct.Cl.1993) (excluding discharge within a building from coverage in lead exposure action).

Although the language of the pollution exclusion clause has changed, courts may be called upon to interpret both the old and new versions in the context of toxic tort actions. When the plaintiff alleges latent illness from an exposure that occurred years earlier, several different insurance policies may be implicated, depending upon the trigger of coverage used. Accordingly, the opportunity for numerous complex issues of coverage often presents itself in toxic tort litigation.

F. INDETERMINATE DEFENDANTS

One of the unique characteristics of toxic torts is the frequency with which plaintiffs are unable to identify the precise defendant or defendants that caused their injuries. The realities of toxic causation account for this difficulty. The problem of indeterminacy may arise from a variety of directions. For example, an asbestos plaintiff may have been exposed to numerous asbestos-containing products during the course of employment, but may not be able to identify the precise manufacturers of the products after a lapse of many years. Or, persons claiming injury from groundwater contamination from a local waste disposal site may be unable to determine which specific substance deposited at the site caused their injuries. Moreover, dozens or even hundreds of waste generators may have deposited similar hazardous substances at the site, making precise identification impossible.

The problem of indeterminate defendants has arisen most commonly in the DES cases, however. Diethylstilbestrol (DES) was a prescription medication given to many women during the period of time from 1947 until 1971 to prevent miscarriages and for a variety of other conditions. DES has been associated with development of adenocarcinoma of the vagina and other ailments in offspring who had been exposed to the DES in utero while their mothers were ingesting the drug. The manifestation of the physical problems in the offspring generally have occurred during adolescence and on into early adulthood.

The indeterminacy issue resulted from the set of circumstances surrounding the marketing of the drug during those decades when it was in production. First, DES essentially was produced in "generic" form, with no distinctions made between the products of separate drug companies. Color, shape, and markings on the products were all indistinguishable. The design and formula of the drug were identical among manufacturers. Second, approximately 300 companies participated in the manufacture or marketing of DES during the period. The market has been characterized as a "fluid" one in which companies passed in and out of the market on an irregular basis, making it difficult for a plaintiff to pinpoint the probable group of manufacturers who may have produced the drug ingested by the mother. Finally, because of the lapse in time between exposure and manifestation—in conjunction with the protracted time period during which the drug was developed and eventually marketed—many crucial records on the production of DES have been lost by the companies, making it difficult to determine the type of DES manufactured by them. The plaintiffs' own records often have been incomplete as well. *See generally* Collins v. Eli Lilly Co. (Wis.1984) (describing background circumstances of marketing and FDA approval of DES).

Plaintiffs in DES cases have argued for the application of a variety of legal doctrines to overcome the problems created by the indeterminate defendant problem. In general, however, courts have been reluctant to apply either traditional or innovative theories of liability to relieve the DES plaintiff's burden in this situation. *See generally* Burnside v. Abbott Laboratories (Pa.Super.1985) (stating the standard rule that where plaintiff is unable to identify the defendant or defendants responsible for the injury, action must be dismissed). Thus, most jurisdictions have rejected indeterminate claims for failure to identify the defendant.

1. Alternative Liability

Some DES plaintiffs have argued for the application of the rule of alternative liability established by Summers v. Tice (Cal.1948). *Summers* involved a hunting accident in which two hunters discharged their firearms simultaneously, injuring the plaintiff. The plaintiff was unable to identify which hunter's

bullet caused the injury and named both as defendants in the lawsuit. The court allowed the action
to proceed, announcing the following rule adopting
Section 433B(3) of the Restatement (Second) of
Torts:

> Where the conduct of two or more actors is
> tortious, and it is proved that harm has been
> caused to the plaintiff by only one of them, but
> there is uncertainty as to which one of them has
> caused it, the burden is upon each such actor to
> prove that he has not caused the harm.

Thus, it is incumbent upon a defendant to exculpate
itself by showing that its activities could not have
caused the injury to the plaintiff. The rule of
alternative liability is supported by the fact that the
defendants, even though acting independently, are
in a superior position to sort out the facts and
circumstances of the incident alleged and identify
the specific cause.

In general, courts have rejected application of
alternative liability to DES cases. *See* Collins v. Eli
Lilly Co. (Wis.1984). A primary reason for rejection
of this theory in the context of DES is the fact that
the DES manufacturers were not necessarily in any
better position than the plaintiffs to identify the
specific manufacturer or manufacturers whose DES
caused the injury alleged. A second reason points
to the assumption underlying the alternative liability theory that all negligent parties will be brought
before the court. This is not necessarily the case in

DES litigation, reducing the likelihood that the responsible party will be held liable to the plaintiff.

Nevertheless, at least one court has applied the alternative liability theory in DES litigation. In Abel v. Eli Lilly & Co. (Mich.1984), the court required that the plaintiff bring all potential tortfeasors before the court. Once this was done, the plaintiff was required to prove: (1) that all defendants manufactured or distributed the DES involved; (2) that the plaintiffs' mothers ingested DES; (3) that the DES ingested was marketed in Michigan; and (4) that the drug ingested caused the type of injury suffered by the plaintiffs. A defendant could then exculpate itself by showing that it could not have manufactured or distributed the DES ingested by the plaintiffs' mothers.

2. Concerted Action

DES plaintiffs have attempted unsuccessfully to apply the theory of concerted action in indeterminate defendant cases. Concerted action requires a common plan or design among the defendants, and DES plaintiffs have argued that the collaboration among the various manufacturers of DES to obtain FDA approval for the drug and to subsequently market the drug constituted the requisite common design. See Restatement (Second) of Torts § 876 (1979). Plaintiffs have alleged that there was a tacit understanding among DES manufacturers to improperly test the drug or to warn of its hazards. Courts generally have held that plaintiffs have not adequately proved this alleged tacit understanding.

Although the manufacturers acted in a parallel fashion, their actions did not rise to the level of concerted action. *See generally* Tigue v. E.R. Squibb & Sons, Inc. (N.Y.1987). Moreover, the concerted action theory typically applies to situations in which a single identified culpable party is before the court, but plaintiffs seek to bring additional parties, acting in concert with that party, into the action for additional liability. This approach is not consistent with the DES case profiles. *See* Collins v. Eli Lilly Co. (Wis.1984).

3. Civil Conspiracy

Likewise, a theory of civil conspiracy has been rejected by most courts addressing the indeterminate defendant dilemma in DES actions. The civil conspiracy theory requires the plaintiff to prove that the defendants "combined" to market DES for use in pregnancy knowing that the drug was unsafe. As with concerted action, the parallel behavior of DES manufacturers cannot support the allegation that the defendants conspired. *See* Collins v. Eli Lilly, *supra*.

4. Enterprise Liability

The concept of enterprise liability, also known as industry-wide liability, was enunciated in Hall v. E.I. duPont de Nemours & Co. (E.D.N.Y.1972). *Hall* involved plaintiffs who were injured by blasting caps manufactured by defendants pursuant to safety standards developed by the industry. The court held that because the defendants jointly controlled the risk posed by the blasting caps, liability could be imposed on the basis of the industry's culpable conduct. Thus, each defendant contributing to the development of the industry safety standard could be held liable. In DES cases, however, the industry-wide control over the safety standard was not present. Rather, the FDA was responsible for setting the standard; the manufacturers' participation in the FDA approval process was not tantamount to industry control over safety standards. *See* Collins v. Eli Lilly Co., *supra*. *See generally* Naomi Scheiner, Note, *DES and A Proposed Theory of Enterprise Liability*, 46 Fordham L. Rev. 963 (1978) (proposing enterprise liability as the best solution to causation problems in DES cases).

5. Market Share Liability

As a result of the inadequacy of existing collective liability theories to satisfactorily address concern raised in the DES cases, some courts have turned to a theory of market share liability. The landmark case of market share liability was Sindell v. Abbott Laboratories (Cal.1980). This theory apportions liability among defendants according to the relative participation of each defendant in the marketing of DES. The first requirement of *Sindell* was that the plaintiff join in the lawsuit defendants representing a "substantial share" of the market in the geographical area relevant to the action. If the plaintiff proves a prima facie case, with the exception of identification of the specific defendant causing the injury, the burden then shifts to the defendants. A defendant can only exculpate itself from liability by demonstrating that it could not have manufactured or distributed the DES alleged to have caused the plaintiff's injuries. Those defendants remaining in the lawsuit would be liable for a percentage of the damages that approximates their respective shares of the DES market. The liable defendants will be held severally liable only and defendants may not be held strictly liable. Brown v. Superior Court (Cal. 1988). The rationale behind this approach is that the market share is a reflection of the likelihood that a particular defendant caused the injuries alleged.

While some version of *Sindell* market share liability has been adopted in a few states, it has not found general acceptance in DES actions, primarily due to the numerous problems associated with the approach. First, defining the relevant market and determining the respective market shares has proven problematic, particularly in the context of DES where records of the manufacturers' participation in the market may be scant. Second, some critics cite the inequity of the fact that under a market share theory, a non-negligent major participant in the market could end up bearing a substantial share of the liability. In contrast, a small-share, negligent defendant could escape significant liability. Finally, some have expressed concern that the widespread adoption of market share liability would deter the development of new products. This overdeterrence arises by virtue of the fact that manufacturers participating in the market would be required to pay some share of the judgment regardless of their innocence or degree of culpability.

As a result of such concerns, courts that have adopted market share liability have usually attempted to improve upon it by developing some variation of the approach. Thus, in Collins v. Eli Lilly Co. (Wis.1984), the court applied a risk contribution theory of liability. The *Collins* court devised an approach by which the plaintiff need only name as a defendant one member of the class of defendants who could have caused the injury, rather than a broader share of the market. Of course, the plaintiff who names only one DES manufacturer runs the risk that the defendant will succeed on a defense or will be judgment-proof. As with *Sindell*, the defendant or defendants named could exculpate themselves by showing that the DES they manufactured could not have caused the plaintiff's injury.

The major departure from *Sindell* came with determining the shares of liability. The *Collins* court employed market share as only one factor in a multi-factored consideration focusing on the degree to which the defendant created or participated in the risk that ultimately caused the plaintiff's injury. The factors were: (1) the degree to which the defendant took a role in gaining FDA approval of DES; (2) the defendant's market share; (3) whether the defendant took a leadership role or acted passively; (4) whether the defendant issued warnings on the hazards of DES; (5) whether the defendant continued to produce DES after learning of the hazards; and (6) whether the defendant took any steps to reduce the risk of harm. Thus, the test proposed by the court focused on the level of control that the defendant had over the risk as well as steps that the defendant may have taken to mitigate the hazard.

The New York Court of Appeals took a different approach in adopting market share liability. In Hymowitz v. Eli Lilly & Co. (N.Y.1989), the court allowed the plaintiff to name defendants representing a substantial share of the *national* DES market. Liability was based upon the particular defendant's share of the market. In a significant departure from *Sindell*, the defendants would not be allowed to exculpate themselves unless they did not market DES for use during pregnancy. This variation from *Sindell* is significant because a defendant who marketed DES for use during pregnancy but whose product could not have been ingested by the plaintiff's mother because it was not marketed in the relevant geographical area could still be held liable. Any perceived problems regarding personal jurisdiction over defendant DES manufacturers who never marketed their product in the state were dispensed with in In re DES Cases, Ashley v. Abbott Laboratories (E.D.N.Y.1992), in which the court found personal jurisdiction purely on the basis of the companies' participation in the national DES market, a market whose consequences reached far beyond the immediate locale of the products' sale.

6. Market Share Beyond DES Cases

Market share liability, where adopted, generally has been limited to DES cases because of the unique set of circumstances presented. *See Hymowitz v. Eli Lilly & Co., supra* (expressly limiting market share liability in New York to DES cases). Courts considering other kinds of toxic tort claims have been split on the merits of adopting market share liability. But in general, courts have approached the market share theory circumspectly.

In a major case, Shackil v. Lederle Laboratories (N.J.1989), the court refused to apply market share liability in suits alleging defective DPT vaccines. The court contrasted the DES cases, noting that the generic production of the product that characterized the marketing of DES was not present with respect to DPT vaccine. This was particularly true with respect to the plaintiff's allegation that the particular batch of vaccine from which the plaintiff's dose came was defective. Moreover, the court stated that "the imposition of a theory of collective liability in this case would frustrate overarching public policy and public-health considerations by threatening the continued availability of needed drugs and impairing the prospects of the development of safer vaccines." *But cf.* Morris v. Parke, Davis & Co. (C.D.Cal.1987) (applying market share liability where manufacturing defects were alleged to be characteristic of entire industry).

Likewise, most courts that have addressed the issue have rejected market share in asbestos personal injury cases. For example, Celotex Corp. v. Copeland (Fla.1985) presented the not uncommon situation in which a worker was able to identify some, but not all, of the manufacturers of the asbestos-containing products to which he had been exposed. Rejecting market share liability, the court found that the types, amounts, and relative toxicity of the asbestos in different products vary, thus distinguishing the products from the generic DES. Due to the magnitude of asbestos litigation, it may well be that any application of a collective liability theory would best be left to the legislature.

In a major development, however, a California appellate court has applied the market share liability theory in an asbestos case arising out of a plaintiff's exposure to asbestos fibers in brake pads. In Wheeler v. Raybestos–Manhattan (Cal.Ct.App. 1992), the court held that market share liability may be applied where the products of the manufacturers were not fungible. In *Wheeler*, the asbestos-containing brake pads of the manufacturers were not "absolutely interchangeable." The court stated, however, that for the purpose of applying *Sindell*, it was sufficient that the brake pads contained "roughly comparable quantities of the single asbestos fiber, chrysotile." *But see* Goldman v. Johns–Manville Sales Corp. (Ohio 1987) (holding that market share liability theory was not appropriate because the products were not interchangeable due to varying asbestos contents in the products of the various manufacturers).

Some acceptance of the market share theory has appeared in cases alleging HIV-contaminated blood products. In Ray v. Cutter Laboratories (M.D.Fla. 1991), the court held that market share liability applied to negligence claims brought by hemophiliacs who contracted the virus from a blood clotting product derived from the plasma of thousands of blood donors. The plaintiffs had been unable to identify which batch or batches of the blood product caused their diseases. The latency period between exposure to the blood and discovery of the illness aggravated the situation. Thus, the court held that market share liability was appropriate.

In Smith v. Cutter Biological, Inc. (Haw. 1991), another case involving a blood clotting product, the court not only adopted market share liability, but applied the national market approach of *Hymowitz*. The court noted that the clotting product was not generic in the sense of DES; that is, the clotting product was only as safe as the blood of the individual donors that comprised a particular batch. Accordingly, the blood clotting product "is only harmful if the donor was infected; DES is inherently harmful." Nevertheless, the court found that fairness dictated application of market share liability. Exculpation was allowed only if the defendant could prove none of its product was on the market at the time of the alleged injury.

In the clotting factor cases, it is clear that the plaintiffs were in no position to sort out the complex donation and manufacturing scheme that characterized the production of the clotting factor products. Thus, the defendants were in a better position to determine the circumstances under which the product became contaminated and to control the situation in the first instance. This may help to account for the courts' willingness to allow market

share liability in these cases. The clotting factor
cases present an example of courts' efforts to find a
solution to this troubling problem in toxic torts.
But for the most part, courts have been reluctant to
shake the traditional tort tree to fashion remedies
for the indeterminate defendant problem.

CHAPTER SIX

DEFENSES

The earlier chapters have addressed defenses only insofar as they relate directly to substantively negating a specific cause of action that the plaintiff has alleged (e.g. state-of-the-art defense in failure to warn product liability claims) or to limit claims against a particular defendant (e.g. sovereign immunity). This chapter discusses other defenses that may be asserted to bar a claim.

A. STATUTES OF LIMITATIONS

It is axiomatic that a statute of limitations will bar a cause of action that is commenced after a designated period of time. The rationale for this is to protect defendants from stale claims and to impose some finality on the litigation. The period of time within which the plaintiff may bring the claim typically runs from the time of accrual of the claim. In many toxic tort actions, the traditional concept of a statute of limitations has proved to be inadequate. When does the action accrue for the purpose of triggering the running of the statutory period? In cases of latent illness, when does the injury actually occur? At the time of exposure, or at the time when the illness manifests itself? Legislatures and courts have struggled with this issue and have taken a variety of approaches.

1. Exposure Rule

The typical statutory period for the commencement of an unintentional tort claim is between two and four years from the time of injury. For latent illness claims, the traditional approach was that the action accrued at the time of last exposure. Thus, if a person's illness was not manifested until many years following the last exposure—as was the case in many asbestos-related disease cases—the plaintiff's claim would be time-barred. *See* Bassham v. Owens–Corning Fiber Glass Corp. (D.N.M.1971) (decided on other grounds). As a result of the inequity of such a result, and considering that under traditional concepts of injury the plaintiffs would not have the basis for a claim until manifestation of the illness, courts and legislatures acted to modify the rules governing statutory periods to accommodate toxic injuries.

2. Judicial Discovery Rule

By now, virtually every jurisdiction has remedied the problems inherent in the exposure rule, whether by statutory mandate or by judicial ruling, for most latent illness claims arising from exposure to drugs, chemicals, and asbestos. An early United States Supreme Court case, Urie v. Thompson (S.Ct.1949), articulated the equitable reasons for applying a discovery rule to latent illness claims. In that case, which derived from a compensation claim for work-related silicosis under the Federal Employers' Liability Act, the Court emphasized the unfairness of interpreting accrual to preclude a claim before the plaintiff has reason to know of the illness.

This rationale has been accepted by the states. In Louisville Trust Company v. Johns–Manville Products Corp. (Ky.1979), an asbestos case not unlike *Bassham*, the court ruled that the date of accrual of the cause of action was not the time of last exposure, but rather was when the plaintiff knew or should have known of the injury. The court observed that "[a]n action accrues only at the time the plaintiff suffers an actionable wrong," and an actionable wrong is evidenced by some loss or damage. The court applied the discovery rule to actions based on either negligence or product liability theories. Such discovery rules are adaptations of discovery rules that had been employed in many jurisdictions for other kinds of troublesome claims, such as fraud and foreign-object medical malpractice claims.

An important issue that arises in applying the discovery rule is the interpretation of "knew or should have known." In general, the date of accrual will be when the plaintiff was aware of the injury *and* of the potential cause. But what of the situation in which the plaintiff becomes ill, but is unaware of the precise cause of the illness? To what extent is the plaintiff required to investigate the possible causes of the illness by seeking opinions of physicians or other experts so as to preserve the cause of action? In Evenson v. Osmose Wood Preserving Company of America, Inc. (7th Cir.1990), the plaintiff was treated for nasal polyps and allergic rhinitis for more than three years before being advised by a physician that the condition was related to a workplace chemical. He then filed suit. During the early years of treatment, the other physicians had suspected the workplace connection, but upon performing clinical tests, had concluded that the chemical was not the cause. If the initial symptoms and suspicions triggered the running of the applicable two-year statute, the plaintiff's claim would have been time-barred.

The *Evenson* court, refusing to apply a bright line test, held that the running of the statute was triggered by the knowledge of the plaintiff of a "reasonable possibility" that the particular exposure was the cause of the symptoms. Under the facts of *Evenson*, the court stated that "[a] reasonable possibility, while less than a probability, requires more than the mere suspicion possessed by [the plaintiff], a layperson without technical or medical knowledge." Thus, the plaintiff was not aware of a "reasonable" possibility of the workplace cause until after the last physician expressed that opinion.

Often, the determination of the accrual trigger is a close call, and courts have reached different results on similar sets of facts. In Kullman v. Owens–Corning Fiberglas Corp. (6th Cir.1991), the court held that the plaintiff should have known that he had an actionable claim when he suspected that the dust he breathed in the workplace might have caused the breathing problems from which he suffered, even though he was not diagnosed with asbestosis until several years later. His action was time-barred. In contrast, in Joseph v. Hess Oil (3d Cir.1989), the court held that the plaintiff's illness, coupled with his knowledge of his exposure to asbestos and an awareness of the hazards of asbestos, was insufficient to satisfy the "knew or should have known" test.

3. Statutory Discovery Rule

Some state legislatures have enacted statutory discovery rules that have attempted to address the major issues that arise in toxic tort litigation. A statutory discovery rule does not eliminate the need for judicial input, however. A major, broad statutory discovery rule was enacted in New York, effective in 1986, governing claims for personal injury or property damage "caused by the latent effects of exposure to any substance or combination of substances, in any form, upon or within the body or upon or within property." N.Y. Civ. Prac. L. & R. 214–c(2) (McKinney 1990). The statute provides that the three-year tort limitations period begins to run at the time of discovery of the injury or when the injury should have been discovered through "the exercise of reasonable diligence." This language seems to require some investigative action by the plaintiff after becoming suspicious of a connection between the illness and an earlier exposure.

The statutory language is vague concerning which substances fall within its discovery rule. It refers merely to "substance" and defines "exposure" as "direct or indirect exposure by absorption, contact, ingestion, inhalation or injection." *See* N.Y. Civ. Prac. L. & R. 214–c(1) (McKinney 1990). In Prego v. City of New York (N.Y.App.Div.1989), the court held that Section 214–c applied to an action brought by a plaintiff claiming that she contracted the AIDS virus from a puncture by a negligently discarded contaminated needle in a hospital setting. The defendant argued that the action should be time-barred because the HIV virus was not within the contemplation of the statute. The court disagreed, holding that "biological transmitters of latent diseases" met the statutory definition. Moreover, the court believed that because the legislature was aware of the nature of transmission of HIV at the time the statute was enacted, it would have expressly excluded it or other biological organisms if it had so intended.

The New York statute places a limit on the time that the plaintiff has for learning the cause of the illness. The statute builds in a tiered system that allows reasonable time for discovery of the cause, but requires that as a certain amount of time passes the plaintiff must show that scientific knowledge of causation was not available at a more timely date. Ultimately, however, if the plaintiff has not discovered the cause of the illness within five years from discovering the illness the claim will be barred.

In conjunction with the discovery statute, the New York legislature authorized the revival of certain categories of claims that had been dismissed as

time-barred. The revived claims were those based
on exposure to any of a handful of enumerated
substances, including asbestos and DES. 1986 N.Y.
Laws 682 §§ 4–5. The revival statute has with-
stood constitutional challenge. *See* Hymowitz v. Eli
Lilly & Co. (N.Y.1989). Recently, the revival of
silicone gel breast implant claims also has been
permitted. 1993 N.Y. Laws ch. 419.

4. Property Damage Claims

In some states, the discovery limitations period
applies to both actions for personal injuries and
actions for property damages. *See, e.g.*, N.Y. Civ.
Prac. L. & R. 214–c (McKinney 1990). This is not
the case in all jurisdictions, however. For example,
the court in Corporation of Mercer University v.
National Gypsum Co. (11th Cir.1989), after certifying the question to the Georgia Supreme Court,
held that property damage claims against asbestos
manufacturers for abatement of asbestos in buildings were not subject to the discovery statute of
limitations that applied to personal injury claims.

A separate question has arisen in the context of
nuisance claims. Courts sometimes apply a rather
technical distinction between a permanent nuisance
and a continuing nuisance. A permanent nuisance
is one that cannot be discontinued and will continue
indefinitely; presumably, all damages associated
with the permanent nuisance occur at one time and
could be assessed in a single determination. Therefore, a permanent nuisance would be subject to a
fixed statute of limitations running from the time of

the creation of the nuisance. *See* Phillips v. City of
Pasadena (Cal.1945). In contrast, a continuing nuisance is of a more sporadic or discontinuous nature.
Plaintiffs claiming a continuing nuisance may bring
successive actions. For an explanation of this distinction and discussion of the case law, see Gerald
W. Boston & M. Stuart Madden, Law of Environmental and Toxic Torts 574–80 (1994).

B. STATUTES OF REPOSE

Statutes of repose operate in a manner different
from statutes of limitations. They operate in conjunction with statutes of limitations to give defendants maximum protection from stale claims. A
statute of repose bars an action brought beyond a
certain period of time after a designated action.
This is most clearly seen in product liability claims.

In Braswell v. Flintkote Mines, Ltd. (7th Cir.
1983), an asbestos case, the court examined the
Indiana Product Liability Act, which established a
two-year statute of limitations with an outside limit
of ten years from the date of delivery of the product.
See Ind. Code Ann. § 33–1–1.5–5(b) (Burns 1992).
Thus, if the ten-year repose statute had run, the
claim was barred notwithstanding the possibility
that the statute of limitations may not have ex-
pired. The court found the Indiana statute to be
consistent with the goals of repose statutes, stating
that "although affording plaintiffs ... a reasonable
time to present their claims, they protect defendants and the courts from having to deal with cases

in which the search for truth may be seriously impaired by the loss of evidence." *Braswell*, at 530. The court upheld the statute, rejecting the plaintiffs' argument that it violated the due process and equal protection clauses of the U.S. Constitution. The distinction made between product liability defendants and other kinds of defendants for the purpose of the statutory limitation period was not fundamentally unfair and was reasonably related to the governmental goals sought. This was so even though the statute served to bar some claims before the injury actually occurred.

While the challenges to statutes of repose on federal constitutional grounds have been uniformly rejected, some different results may occur when the challenge is based upon the state constitution. Thus, in Alabama, the courts have accepted an argument challenging the statute of repose based upon the interpretation of an "open courts" provision in the state constitution that assured all persons in the State a remedy. *See* Jackson v. Mannesmann Demag Corp. (Ala.1983) (holding statute of repose unconstitutional where it bars an action before action accrued); *accord* Perkins v. Northeastern Log Homes (Ky.1991). Some courts have ruled to the contrary, however, construing their own constitutional provisions. *See, e.g.*, Sealey v. Hicks (Or.1990).

Statutes of repose have not been enacted solely for product liability claims. Often, such statutes appear in reference to conditions of real property, limiting claims related to a condition to a certain period of time after any improvement on the property. *See, e.g.*, Md. Code Ann., Cts. & Jud. Proc. § 5–108 (1989).

C. RES JUDICATA

Res judicata, or claim preclusion, often presents a dilemma for plaintiffs and courts in toxic tort actions. This is because toxic injury does not present itself in the manner of traditional injuries. Take the example of asbestos-related disease. An asbestos worker, knowing he has been exposed to the substance and learning of the hazards associated with it, may first believe that he has a claim for fear of contracting asbestos-related disease or a claim for increased risk of contracting the disease, two types of claims discussed in Chapter Eight. The worker then may manifest asymptomatic pleural placques in the lungs, a condition associated with exposure to asbestos. Subsequently, the worker suffers from asbestosis, and ultimately, perhaps, suffers from mesothelioma, a form of lung cancer that is found in high rates in asbestos workers. If the worker chooses to bring an action when he suffers from asbestosis, but not yet from mesothelioma, will a subsequent claim for mesothelioma be barred by the doctrine of claim preclusion?

Res judicata generally allows a claimant only one bite of the litigation apple. When a valid and final judgment has been taken on a particular claim, res judicata prevents a subsequent action on the same claim, with the exception of an action on the judg-

ment if the plaintiff was successful in the first
action. This is the general rule against claim-
splitting. To determine what constitutes a claim,
the modern approach is a transactional one. Most
courts follow the rule in Section 24 of the Restatement (Second) of Judgments:

> [T]he claim extinguished includes all rights of the
> plaintiff to remedies against the defendant with
> respect to all or any part of the transaction, or
> series of connected transactions, out of which the
> action arose.... [A transaction is] to be deter-
> mined pragmatically, giving weight to such con-
> siderations as whether the facts are related in
> time, space, origin, or motivation, whether they
> form a convenient trial unit, and whether their
> treatment as a unit conforms to the parties' ex-
> pectations or business understanding or usage.

Thus, the transactional analysis test encompasses
different evidence, theories, injuries, or remedies.

Although some exceptions to claim preclusion exist, the main issue with respect to toxic tort actions
such as the asbestos situation is identification of the
scope of the transaction, i.e. the scope of the claim
that is extinguished. To what degree should claim-
splitting be allowed? This issue is intimately con-
nected to the accrual question in statutes of limitations. Assuming the relevant jurisdiction has a
discovery statute, and forbids claim-splitting, a
plaintiff's entire claim (including illnesses related to
the exposure that develop at a later date) would
accrue at the time of discovery of the first injury.

Effectively, a plaintiff could be barred from bringing a claim before the plaintiff even knew of it. This is similar to the dilemma faced by courts addressing challenges to statutes of repose. As a result of the close connection between the claim preclusion issues and statutes of limitations, most of the case law on this question has arisen within the context of the statutes of limitations. While it is not directly controlling on the claim preclusion issue, it is safe to assume that courts prefer to read the accrual rules and the claim preclusion rules compatibly.

The traditional res judicata approach—and a strict application of claim preclusion rules—would bar any accrued action arising out of the same circumstances as a claim previously adjudicated. *See* Gideon v. Johns–Manville Sales Corp. (5th Cir. 1985). An emerging trend, however, allows a plaintiff to split the claim under some circumstances.

In Wilson v. Johns–Manville Sales Corp. (D.C.Cir. 1982), the court examined the rationales behind accrual rules, particularly the concern for disappearance of witnesses and evidence over the passage of time. The court said that latent disease cases demand "narrower delineation of the dimensions of a claim." The court was closely attuned to the special concerns of toxic tort litigation: "Key issues to be litigated in a latent disease case are the existence of the disease, its proximate cause, and the resultant damage. Evidence relating to these issues tends to develop, rather than disappear, as time passes."

The *Wilson* court looked at another dimension of claim-splitting as well. The traditional rule allows a plaintiff to recover for all damages, past, present, and future, flowing from the actionable conduct of the defendant. The court noted that traditionally, future damages must be reasonably certain, however, to be recoverable. The difficulty toxic tort plaintiffs would have in proving the reasonable certainty of a future illness influenced the court in preferring a rule allowing claim-splitting.

As the *Wilson* case demonstrated, these res judicata issues are also closely tied to the question of whether courts should recognize present claims for increased risk of contracting illness in the future. There has been vigorous reaction to plaintiffs' attempts to bring such claims, with considerable concern for their speculative nature. The allowance of such claims, if the court is amenable to them at all, will be closely dependent upon the claim-splitting rule and the accrual rules in the relevant jurisdiction. A discussion of increased risk claims appears in Chapter Eight, Sec. B.

D. PLAINTIFF'S CULPABLE CONDUCT

With the tort reform movement that brought comparative negligence, contributory negligence has become far less of a concern for plaintiffs, as generally a finding of contributory negligence will not absolutely bar a plaintiff's claim, but will reduce the plaintiff's overall recovery by the percentage of fault attributable to the plaintiff's conduct. Some states, however, retain some form of bar, but only if the plaintiff's culpable conduct reaches a certain level. *See, e.g.*, Minn. Stat. Ann. § 604.01 (West 1988) (providing that plaintiff who is more than 50% at fault may not recover).

With respect to product liability claims, the Restatement makes clear that contributory negligence is not a defense to a strict product liability claim. Assumption of the risk of a known danger, where voluntarily and unreasonably undertaken, will provide a defense to such claims, however. *See* Restatement (Second) of Torts, § 402A, comment n (1965). In toxic tort actions, it may be difficult for a defendant to show either that the danger was known or that the plaintiff encountered it unreasonably.

With respect to nuisance claims, the plaintiff's culpable conduct can be relevant as well. To determine whether contributory negligence will be available as a defense, it is necessary to look to the underlying conduct alleged—negligent, intentional, reckless, or abnormally dangerous. According to the Restatement, contributory negligence is not available as a defense in nuisance actions based upon intentional or reckless conduct. Restatement (Second) of Torts, § 840B(2) (1977). It may be a defense when negligent conduct is alleged, to the extent that it is available in any other negligence action within the jurisdiction. *Id*. § 840B(1). With respect to nuisance claims based upon strict liability, "contributory negligence is a defense only if the plaintiff has voluntarily and unreasonably subjected himself to the risk of harm." *Id*. § 840B(3). Assumption of the risk is a defense to nuisance claims where the defendant can show that the plaintiff had knowledge of the hazard, appreciated the magnitude of the hazard, and voluntarily encountered it. *Id*. § 840C.

Coming to the nuisance may be raised by defendants when a plaintiff has taken possession of the property after the nuisance has been created. The Restatement characterizes coming to the nuisance not as an absolute defense, but as one factor in determining whether an actionable nuisance claim exists. *See id*. § 840D. A majority of courts tend to discredit this defense, however, and reject it as an absolute defense.

E. PRE-EMPTION

The interface between private law and public law is one of the fundamental characteristics of toxic torts. Much of the conduct alleged in private toxic tort actions is regulated to some degree by public law mechanisms, embodied in statutes or regulations. To a great extent, private rights of action exist independently from the regulatory schemes. But occasionally, and increasingly, there is overlap between duties defined by public law and those defined by the common law. When this overlap is contradictory or creates sufficiently ambiguous obligations, the defendant may be able to assert a defense that the public law obligation pre-empts the operation of the common law.

Quite often, public law obligations are minimum standards, whereas the common law imposes more stringent obligations. When the pre-emption defense is asserted, the court is called upon to determine whether the legislature intended to allow the common law to operate in the same area of the law, or whether incompatible common law standards are precluded. Where the statute in question contains a pre-emption provision that addresses this issue, the determination may be easy. Where the statute is ambiguous or silent, however, the court must construe the statutory language or infer the legislative intent, a task that is much more difficult.

Accordingly, courts have taken two basic approaches to pre-emption—express pre-emption and implied pre-emption. As a general rule, there is a presumption against pre-emption. Express pre-emption derives from language contained directly in the statute that evidences the legislature's intent to pre-empt the common law. Sometimes statutes will contain savings clauses that expressly retain all rights under the common law, and the court's task will be relatively simple. *See, e.g.*, CERCLA § 310(h) (providing that CERCLA "does not affect or otherwise impair the rights of any person under Federal, State, or common law" except under limited circumstances). Where the express language of the statute indicates an intent to pre-empt private remedies, the language may be ambiguous or unclear as to the scope of the pre-emption. Where the statute is silent, the court must determine whether (1) the legislature intended to "occupy the field" with legislation that was so sweeping that no room was left for the common law or (2) the common law actually conflicts with the statutory scheme. A court may find an "actual conflict" where it is impossible to comply with both the common law and the statutory requirements or where the common law acts as an obstacle to the fulfillment of the statutory objectives.

1. Federal Environmental Cases

Several important cases have addressed the existence of private rights of action in areas that overlapped with statutory provisions of the federal environmental laws. The United States Supreme Court has read the federal environmental statutes expansively to pre-empt such claims. Thus, in Milwaukee v. Illinois (S.Ct.1981), the Court held that the plaintiff-respondent, the State of Illinois, had no claim under the federal common law against the City of Milwaukee and other public entities for endangering the health of its citizens through improper treatment and disposal of sewage into Lake Michigan. Rather, the Federal Water Pollution Control Act (Clean Water Act) provisions covering discharge permits pre-empted the pre-existing federal common law providing a cause of action for abatement of the nuisance. The Court found that Congress, in enacting the Clean Water Act, 33 U.S.C.A. §§ 1251–1387 (West 1986 & Supp. 1994), occupied the field with a comprehensive program of water pollution regulation. *See also* Middlesex County Sewage Authority v. National Sea Clammers Association (S.Ct.

1981) (pre-emption of federal common law of nuisance by comprehensive provisions of Clean Water Act and Marine Protection, Research, and Sanctuaries Act of 1972).

The *Milwaukee* Court left open the issue of whether actions under state law survived. In International Paper Co. v. Ouellette (S.Ct.1987), the Court held that a state-law claim involving interstate water pollution was expressly preserved by the Clean Water Act's savings clauses. Furthermore, the Court held that the applicable state law in an interstate pollution case was the law of the state where the discharge was located, not the state where the effects of the discharge were felt. Because the choice of law was not explicitly addressed in the savings clauses, the Court reached this conclusion by an implied pre-emption analysis, determining that application of the affected state's law would frustrate the implementation of the goals of the Clean Water Act.

2. Cigarette Cases

In a significant and far-reaching decision, the Supreme Court employed a detailed pre-emption analysis in Cipollone v. Liggett Group, Inc. (S.Ct. 1992). The *Cipollone* case involved a decedent whose representatives claimed that she developed lung cancer as a result of smoking cigarettes manufactured by the defendant-respondent companies. She began smoking in 1942 and smoked until her death in 1984. The action stated claims based upon strict product liability, negligence, express warranty, and fraudulent misrepresentation, all under state law. The respondents raised the pre-emption defense, arguing that the petitioners' claims were precluded by the Federal Cigarette Labeling and Advertising Act.

The Court found that the Act contained an express pre-emption provision, and that interpreting the provision required examination of the history of the Act and its subsequent amendments to discern Congress's intent. The Court rejected the Third Circuit's analysis based on implied pre-emption, holding that "[w]hen Congress ... has included in the enacted legislation a provision explicitly addressing [pre-emption], and when that provision provides a 'reliable indicium of congressional intent with respect to state authority, ... there is no need to infer congressional intent to pre-empt....'" (quoting Malone v. White Motor Corp. (S.Ct.1978)).

The Cigarette Labeling Act had passed through several incarnations. One of the requirements of the original 1965 Act was that all packages of cigarettes bear the label "CAUTION: CIGARETTE SMOKING MAY BE HAZARDOUS TO YOUR HEALTH." The Act contained an express pre-emption provision prohibiting other state cigarette labeling requirements, but not affecting state common-law actions: "No statement relating to smoking and health shall be required in the advertising of cigarettes." In 1969, however, both the warning and the pre-emption provision changed. Congress modified the label requirement to state "WARNING: THE SURGEON GENERAL HAS DETER-

MINED THAT CIGARETTE SMOKING IS DAN-
GEROUS TO YOUR HEALTH." The pre-emption
provision changed from a prohibition of "state-
ments" to a proscription of any "requirements or
prohibitions imposed under state law with respect
to the advertising or promotion" of cigarettes. The
Supreme Court interpreted this provision to encompass obligations imposed under the common law in
addition to any regulations or labeling requirements
under state statutes.

The next issue was the effect that this pre-emption provision had on the petitioners' specific
claims. Timing was significant in this case, as the
decedent began smoking well before the Act was
enacted, but continued smoking thereafter. The
Court examined each claim individually. First, the
Court held pre-empted any failure to warn claims
with respect to the period *after 1969*, the date when
the language of the pre-emption provision changed.
In a significant distinction, the Court stated that
pre-emption would not apply to claims that derive
solely from the manufacturers' testing or research
or other such activities unrelated to the advertising
or promotion of cigarettes.

Second, the claims for express warranty were not
pre-empted. The Court characterized express warranties as requirements imposed by a private party,
and not requirements imposed under state law.
Accordingly, any express warranties would not fit
within the language of the pre-emption provision of
either the 1965 Act or the 1969 Act. It mattered
not that the express warranties claimed may have

been based on advertising rather than made in documentary form.

Third, the Court held that some of the fraudulent misrepresentation claims were pre-empted, while some survived. The Court held pre-empted any claims that the manufacturers advertised the cigarettes in a manner so as to neutralize the health warnings because it viewed such claims as an aspect of failure to warn. In contrast, however, the petitioners' allegations that the manufacturers concealed material information regarding the health effects of their cigarettes generally were not pre-empted. The Court reasoned that the relevant duty here was a general duty not to deceive rather than any duty associated solely with smoking and health, thus taking the claims outside of the pre-emption provision.

Finally, the Court held that the claims for conspiracy to misrepresent or to conceal material facts were not pre-empted. The basis for these claims was the same as for the intentional fraud claims; thus, they should be treated the same for pre-emption purposes.

Both the plaintiffs' bar and cigarette manufacturers claimed victory in the *Cipollone* case. Future litigation will define the parameters of claims that survive the *Cipollone* decision. In a major class action based upon claims of smoking addiction, Castano v. American Tobacco Co. (E.D.La.1994), the federal court has held that the numerous claims alleged were not pre-empted. The claims were for

fraud, negligent misrepresentation, intentional infliction of emotional distress, strict liability, breach
of warranty, and violation of state consumer protection statutes, and were fashioned to avoid *Cipollone*'s pre-emption of warning claims. The major
thrust of the lawsuit was the allegation that the
cigarette manufacturers' knowledge of the hazards
of smoking extended back over a period of decades,
and that they deliberately withheld the information
from the public.

The *Castano* court's analysis focused upon information that had been learned during Congressional
hearings from the contents of certain industry documents relating to the industry's testing and research practices. The court found that the majority
of the claims alleged related to those industry practices and not to matters involving the promotion
and advertising of cigarettes. Even the claims for
negligence and strict liability survived because they
arose from charges that the cigarettes were defectively designed because they contained nicotine in
addictive levels; they did not arise from warning
claims.

Thus, in the cigarette cases—and predictably in
other kinds of cases as well—the survival of plaintiffs' claims will be closely tied to the details of the
allegations in the complaint. By its terms, *Cipollone* saved cigarette warning claims predating 1969,
express warranty claims, and most claims based in
fraud or deceit. *Castano* demonstrates that *Cipollone* leaves ample room for product liability claims

focused on tobacco industry conduct in researching and developing its products.

3. Pesticide Cases

The Court's approach in *Cipollone* has been applied to claims related to statutes other than the Cigarette Labeling Act. Claims against pesticide manufacturers were affected dramatically by the Supreme Court's decision in *Cipollone*. The labeling and packaging of pesticides and other substances is regulated by the Federal Insecticide, Fungicide, and Rodenticide Act (FIFRA), 7 U.S.C.A. § 136 (West 1980 & Supp. 1994). Section 136v(b) of FIFRA contains an express pre-emption provision that pre-empts state law claims that constitute "requirements for labeling or packaging in addition to or different from" those imposed under FIFRA. Several courts have had occasion to interpret this provision in light of *Cipollone*.

In Papas v. Upjohn Co. (11th Cir.1993) (Papas II), the court examined the plaintiffs' claims of negligence, strict liability, and breach of implied warranties arising out of exposure to a substance regulated under FIFRA. Essentially, the claims alleged the defendant manufacturer's failure to warn consumers of hazardous chemicals contained in the product and failure to advise of precautions to be taken to prevent harm. The court found that the claims, however characterized, would nevertheless require the factfinder to decide whether the defendant had adequately labeled and packaged the product according to state law standards. The court held that this contravened the express pre-emption provision of FIFRA. Further, the court rejected the plaintiffs' argument that their implied warranty claims should survive based upon the *Cipollone* Court's analysis allowing express warranty claims. In contrast to express warranty claims, which exist through private representations by the seller, the court found that implied warranty claims exist by operation of state law. Thus, the plaintiffs' implied warranty claims also were pre-empted.

A majority of courts addressing the FIFRA pre-emption issue have reached the same conclusion regarding claims that have a basis in warnings. *See, e.g.*, King v. E.I. duPont de Nemours & Co. (1st Cir.1993); Worm v. American Cyanamid Co. (4th Cir.1993) (distinguishing negligent testing claims); MacDonald v. Monsanto Co. (5th Cir.1994).

Following the emerging pattern in cigarette cases applying *Cipollone*, case law interpreting the FIFRA pre-emption provision is holding that some kinds of claims will survive the pre-emption analysis. For example, in Higgins v. Monsanto Co. (N.D.N.Y. 1994), the court allowed claims for negligent testing, strict liability for defective design, and breach of express warranty. The court emphasized the mandate to read pre-emption provisions narrowly and rejected the defense argument that the claims should be pre-empted because imposition of common-law testing standards could result in a change in labeling.

4. Medical Device Cases

Various pre-emption rulings have also appeared on claims involving products regulated under the Medical Device Amendments (MDA) to the Food, Drug, and Cosmetic Act. The MDA established three classes of medical devices, classed according to the invasive nature of the device and regulated with increasing rigor. The pre-emption provision states that "no State ... may establish ... with respect to a device intended for human use any requirement— (1) Which is different from, or in addition to, any requirement applicable under [the MDA], and (2) which relates to the safety or effectiveness of the device ...." 21 U.S.C.A. § 360k (West Supp. 1994). The scope of the MDA pre-emption provision is somewhat broader than the analogous provision in either the Cigarette Labeling Act or FIFRA because the FDA seeks to regulate not just the labeling, but also the design of the product. This is reflected in the language of the pre-emption provision.

A number of appellate courts have found claims to be pre-empted. See Mendes v. Medtronic Corp. (1st Cir.1994) (pacemaker); King v. Collagen Corp. (1st Cir.1993) (collagen injection); Gile v. Optical Radiation Corp. (3d Cir.1994) (intraocular lens); Stamps v. Collagen Corp. (5th Cir.1993) (collagen injection); Slater v. Optical Radiation Corp. (7th Cir.1992) (intraocular lens); Duncan v. Iolab Corp. (11th Cir.1994) (intraocular lens). The Eighth Circuit, however, in National Bank of Commerce of El Dorado v. Kimberly–Clark Corp. (8th Cir.1994),

held that where the complaint alleged that the
manufacturer did not comply with the FDA's regulations on the product's warning label, the claim
could stand. *National Bank of Commerce* involved
a claim for toxic shock syndrome allegedly arising
out of the use of the defendant's tampons, classified
as a Class II medical device and subject to an
intermediate degree of regulation. The plaintiff
agreed that the content of the warning was as
prescribed by regulation, but claimed that the format of the warning was inadequate. Finding that
FDA marketing approval of the device did not constitute approval of the specific format of the warning label, the court held that the claim could be
maintained. The court was careful to say, however,
that pre-emption would apply to any claim that
sought to impose a warning that conflicted with the
FDA regulation.

In a decision that was close to the reasoning of
Cipollone, the court in Ministry of Health, Ontario
v. Shiley Inc. (C.D.Cal.1994), held that the MDA did
not pre-empt all claims brought against the manufacturer of a heart valve. While the court held that
strict liability, negligence, failure to warn, and mis-
branding claims were pre-empted, it ruled that
claims for breach of warranty, fraud, and misrepresentation survived.

In Mulligan v. Pfizer Inc. (S.D. Ohio 1994), the
court closely examined the pre-emption provision of
the MDA in conjunction with other provisions, including FDA implementing regulations, *see* 21
C.F.R. § 808.1(d)(1) (1994), and concluded that any

state or local requirements of "general applicability"—applying to other products in addition to devices—were not pre-empted. *Mulligan* involved a prosthetic knee device that malfunctioned, and the court held that the plaintiff's claim was not pre-empted. *See also* Elbert v. Howmedica, Inc. (D.Hawaii 1993) (holding no pre-emption on different grounds for claim based upon same prosthetic knee device). *Mulligan* is noteworthy because of its intense scrutiny of the language of the pre-emption provision in light of the implementing regulations and other statutory provisions. The extent to which other courts will adopt a similar analysis remains to be seen.

As the pre-emption cases under the MDA, as well as those under FIFRA, demonstrate, *Cipollone* demands that courts confronted with pre-emption issues examine closely the focus of the statute in question as well as the precise language of the pre-emption provision. Further, the court must analyze the basis for the plaintiff's claims in the light of the statutory provisions. Only through this kind of detailed scrutiny will the court be assured of reaching an accurate result on pre-emption issues.

CHAPTER SEVEN

CAUSATION

A. INTRODUCTION TO THE TOXIC CAUSATION PROBLEM

1. The Cause–in–Fact Problem

Legal causation traditionally has included two components—cause-in-fact and proximate cause. Typically, the cause-in-fact requirement is viewed as the easier of the two to satisfy because it requires merely the identification of the series of factual events leading up to an injury. Proximate cause, in contrast, is based in policy, rather than fact. The policy basis of causation directs the court to identify which factual events will be recognized as legal causes of the injury. Toxic torts challenge traditional causation analysis on all fronts.

The most troublesome reality in toxic torts actions is that the plaintiff usually cannot draw a direct factual connection between the defendant's activity or product and the injury alleged. Latent disease that characterizes toxic injury is vastly different from traumatic or acute injury that is typical of the traditional tort claim, such as a motor vehicle accident. Consider the example presented by Allen v. United States (D.Utah 1984), in which the court was confronted with claims of leukemia and other illnesses alleged to have been caused by exposure to radiation during the atomic testing program conducted by the United States Government. The court distinguished the toxic causation presented in the action from the standard tort causation issue:

> In most cases, the factual connection between defendant's conduct and plaintiff's injury is not genuinely in dispute. Often, the cause-and-effect relationship is obvious: A's vehicle strikes B, injuring him; a bottle of A's product explodes, injuring B; water impounded on A's property flows onto B's land, causing immediate damage.

> In this case, the factual connection singling out the defendant as the source of the plaintiffs' injuries and deaths is very much in genuine dispute. Determination of the cause-in-fact, or factual connection, issue is complicated by the nature of the injuries suffered ... , the nature of the causation mechanism ... , the extraordinary time factors and other variables ....

One complicating factor in *Allen* was the latency period between the time of the exposures and the manifestation of the illnesses. Because the connection between the exposure and the illness was not immediately apparent, questions arose as to the possibility of intervening events—instead of the initial exposure alleged—that may have caused or contributed to the injury.

A second complicating factor in *Allen* was the fact that the cancers alleged were of a "non-specific nature," appearing not just in the population of persons exposed to radiation during the testing program, but also in the general population in what is referred to as background levels. No clinical distinction could be drawn between the cancers in the plaintiffs and the cancers in the general population. Moreover, although exposure to radiation was known to be associated with the illnesses alleged by the plaintiffs, other exposures and sources were also known to be associated with those illnesses. Therefore, there was no certainty as to which exposure actually did cause the injury.

A related problem is the inability of the scientific community to determine the precise cause of many illnesses. Scientific research has not reached conclusive and comprehensive results on carcinogenesis, mutagenesis, or teratogenesis in humans. Additionally, hard clinical evidence of the causal connection, from the plaintiff's treating physician or other medical specialists, often is lacking. This reality impedes the plaintiff in proving the necessary elements of the claim. The relationship between the scientific study of the causes of illness and the legal proof of causation has generated close analysis of the standard for admissibility of scientific evidence, discussed in Section B, *infra*.

2. General Causation and Specific Causation

Every causation analysis, implicitly if not explicitly, makes a determination of both general causation and specific causation. General causation (sometimes referred to in the case law as "generic causation") refers to the determination that the particular exposure was *capable* of causing the kind of injury that the plaintiff has alleged under the circumstances alleged. The next step is specific causation, which demonstrates that the exposure *actually* caused the injury in the plaintiff. *See generally* Sterling v. Velsicol Chemical Corp. (6th Cir.1988) (bifurcating trial of causation issues between general causation, to be decided for group of plaintiffs, and specific causation, to be decided later on individual basis). This dual analysis is generally compressed in the traditional tort action. Thus, for example, a blow on the head such as the one suffered by a plaintiff who struck the windshield during a motor vehicle accident, was *capable* of causing a concussion such as the one suffered by the plaintiff. That the motor vehicle accident *actually* caused the plaintiff's concussion is substantiated by the logical progression of events and supporting evidence, showing that the plaintiff's head hit the windshield with a certain force and that symptoms consistent with a concussion injury were manifested immediately thereafter.

The analysis is attenuated and bifurcated in the toxic tort action. Asbestos exposure provides an example of the "easier" kind of toxic causation analysis. Scientific studies have shown that exposure to asbestos fibers is capable of causing a degenerative disease of the lungs called asbestosis. Following a latency period of years or decades, the disease eventually manifests itself in objective symptoms. How can the injured person show that the exposure so many years earlier actually caused this particular occurrence of the disease? Asbestosis is considered a "signature disease" of exposure to asbestos fibers because clinical tests can show with some measure of certainty that asbestos exposure was the causal trigger for the illness. Thus, the precise diagnosis of asbestosis in the plaintiff provides the necessary proof of specific causation. The asbestos plaintiff has an easier task than plaintiffs with other kinds of illnesses because of the existence of the diagnosable "signature disease."

Most illnesses alleged to be caused by toxic exposures cannot be shown to be so closely related to a particular level of exposure as in the "signature disease" situation, however. Returning to the claims in *Allen*, cancers that are indistinguishable from background cancers in the general population make a showing of specific causation virtually impossible. At best, the plaintiff would be able to show that the exposure was capable of producing the illness—in other words, general causation.

As a general rule, the standard for proving causation in civil actions is by a preponderance of the evidence. The inability to show specific causation may be an insurmountable obstacle for toxic tort plaintiffs in proving their claims. The viability of the claims may be dependent upon the degree to which the court is willing to entertain evidence based upon the probability, rather than the legal certainty, that the defendant's activities or product caused the plaintiffs' injury.

3. Probabilistic Evidence

The goal of most toxic tort plaintiffs, therefore, is to prove that the *probability* that the exposure caused the injury was sufficiently high as to compensate for the lack of cause-in-fact. Probabilistic evidence such as statistical studies and published medical data is the most common form of evidence that toxic tort plaintiffs will seek to introduce in support of their causation cases. This contrasts with the heavy reliance in traditional tort actions on direct medical evidence of the plaintiff's condition. Although courts have been amenable to circumstantial evidence of all sorts in traditional tort actions, probabilistic evidence has been viewed with disfavor and even disdain.

Professor Troyen Brennan has observed that when science moved from the fixed certainty of the Newtonian universe to the variable reality of quantum physics and relativity theory, the law of toxic causation was left behind. *See* Troyen Brennan, *Causal Chains and Statistical Links: The Role of Scientific Uncertainty in Hazardous–Substance Litigation*, 73 Cornell L. Rev. 469 (1988). *See generally* Laurence H. Tribe, *The Curvature of Constitutional Space: What Lawyers Can Learn from Modern Physics*, 103 Harv. L. Rev. 1 (1989) (developing an important analysis of the relationship between science and the law). Professor Brennan stated:

The scientific association between a toxic substance and injury to a person relies on probabilistic evidence: epidemiological studies and statistical associations. Philosophers of science readily accept such evidence and, indeed, acknowledge that probabilistic reasoning dominates much of physics and medicine.... [In contrast,] [c]orrective justice aspects of tort law assume the existence of traceable causal chains leading from actor to harm....

. . .

[C]ommon law courts ... cling to conceptions of individual responsibility that coincide neatly with eighteenth century science's notions of causation.

Brennan, *supra*. An example of a court demanding the "traceable causal chains" cited by Brennan occurred in the Agent Orange litigation. *See* In re "Agent Orange" Prod. Liab. Litig. (E.D.N.Y.1984) (fairness opinion approving settlement of class action). Judge Weinstein noted the deficiencies in the probabilistic evidence submitted by the plaintiffs, finding that "[t]he probability of specific cause would necessarily be less than 50% based upon the evidence submitted." The court's assessment of the plaintiffs' poor likelihood of success in proving causation was one factor in the court's conclusion that the settlement was fair.

Another example of judicial resistance to probabilistic evidence is reflected in the reaction to the market share liability cases. *See, e.g.*, Sindell v. Abbott Laboratories (Cal.1980) (allowing plaintiff to join a substantial share of the relevant market and, where valid claim proved, to recover from each defendant proportionate share of judgment reflecting its share of market). Even when limited exclusively to the unique circumstances of DES, courts generally have refused to apply some form of collective liability where the plaintiff is unable to identify the specific defendant or defendants who manufactured the product that caused the injury. *See generally* Chapter Five, *supra*. Market share liability is grounded on statistical percentage shares in the DES market; at least theoretically, the share reflects the probability that the defendant actually manufactured the DES ingested by the plaintiff's mother. *Hymowitz* market share liability, based upon a national market with virtually no exculpation allowed, is a more extreme example. *See* Hymowitz v. Eli Lilly & Co. (N.Y.1989). What critics dislike so much about market share liability, and about all uses of probabilistic evidence, is the possibility that the defendant who is held to be liable for the plaintiff's injury may not, in fact, have caused the injury.

4. Legal Certainty Versus Scientific Certainty

Courts and juries are accustomed to applying the preponderance of the evidence standard to causation in civil actions. Scientific evidence complicates this endeavor because scientific certainty and legal certainty are not identical. To the contrary, they are two entirely distinct concepts. Scientists will refrain from pronouncing a causal connection between an exposure and a disease unless the probability of causation is in the vicinity of 95 percent.

The legal standard of proof is set at 51 percent. The real problem is not in the difference between these two numbers, however. Rather, the problem is in translating the scientific standard into a legal standard. There is not a direct correlation between scientific certainty and legal certainty. Thus, a single study concluding that an association exists between a chemical and an illness may not satisfy the legal standard, notwithstanding the significance of the results. Consequently, the legal system has been reluctant to allow a finding of causation in the absence of scientific consensus. The relationship between scientific and legal certainty has provoked much debate over the appropriate evidentiary standard for scientific evidence.

5. "Lone Pine" Orders

Recognizing the importance of proof of causation to plaintiffs' cases, and also recognizing the difficulty plaintiffs will have in supplying the necessary proof, defendants' counsel have sought to require plaintiffs to provide their proof in the pretrial phase of the litigation. Defendants then can use the information supplied as the basis for a summary judgment motion seeking dismissal of the action. The orders requiring production of such proof are called "Lone Pine" orders, taking their name from Lore v. Lone Pine Corp. (N.J.Law Div.1986), in which the court ordered the plaintiffs to produce documentation of causation, including the facts of each of their exposures and reports of treating physicians and any other experts on the issue of causation. "Lone Pine" orders need not appear exactly as the one in the namesake case so long as they require some proof of causal connection. A dismissal sanction may be built into the order for failure to comply with its requirements.

Such orders appeal to courts so that judicial resources will not be wasted on frivolous lawsuits. Plaintiffs complain that these orders serve the defendants' purposes of keeping the issues from the jury, thus divesting the plaintiffs of their right to jury trial, and placing excessive emphasis on causation over culpability. *See generally* Allan Kanner, Environmental and Toxic Tort Trials § 8.02, at 184–86 (1991).

B. SCIENTIFIC EVIDENCE

One explanation for judicial resistance to probabilistic evidence may be the unusual nature of the evidence itself. The scientific and statistical studies that typically accompany a toxic tort plaintiff's claim require specialized knowledge and expertise to interpret. The scientific questions raised by the litigation are often subject to several interpretations, and it is not uncommon to have scientific studies reaching contradictory conclusions. Moreover, the validity of the scientific studies presents a significant evidentiary challenge for the courts.

The claims of the plaintiff may rest on novel issues of science. Thus, scientific inquiry on the issues may be in its initial stages. The scientific community may not have reached a consensus on the degree of probability that the exposure may have caused the injury suffered by the plaintiff. Indeed, the very existence of early litigation on a particular subject often encourages study of the relationship between exposure to a substance and a particular disease. This inevitably means that early plaintiffs of this sort will be undercompensated. As the body of scientific evidence develops, a more direct causal connection may emerge, with eventual consensus among experts. Under this scenario, later plaintiffs would be adequately compensated. Of course, the possibility exists that no clear causal connection will ever be found. This dilemma has sparked debate over the proper treatment of novel scientific theories in toxic tort actions. Such theories often rely heavily on probabilistic evidence.

A movement has arisen that characterizes many novel scientific theories as "junk science" and advocates a ban on novel scientific evidence in the courtroom. *See generally* Peter W. Huber, Galileo's Revenge: Junk Science in the Courtroom (1991). The "junk science" commentators have argued for strict scrutiny of all scientific evidence with an emphasis on scientific consensus. The high visibility of the advocates of this view has generated strong responses from both supporters and critics. *Compare* Lee Loevinger, *Science and Legal Rules of Evidence: A Review of Galileo's Revenge: Junk Science in the Courtroom*, 32 Jurimetrics J. 487 (1992) (supporting views of "junk science" commentators) *with* Jeff L. Lewin, *Calabresi's Revenge? Junk Science in the Work of Peter Huber*, 21 Hofstra

L. Rev. 183 (1992) (critiquing level of scrutiny advocated by "junk science" commentators).

1. Procedural Approach

Courts may scrutinize scientific evidence at two distinct procedural stages of the litigation. The first stage is the admissibility stage. While the most common form of challenge to the admissibility of evidence is at trial, by objections made by counsel opposing the introduction of the evidence in question, in toxic tort actions a wholesale challenge to the admissibility of the plaintiff's causation evidence typically occurs in a motion in limine at the outset of the action.

The court's decision on the admissibility of the scientific evidence is not necessarily dispositive of the ultimate issues to which the evidence relates, however. Typically, the defendant brings a summary judgment motion seeking to have the action dismissed on the ground that no question of fact exists. This is the sufficiency stage. If the plaintiff's scientific evidence—which is usually the most probative evidence of causation—is ruled inadmissible, usually the case will be dismissed. Conceivably, evidence could survive the admissibility inquiry, but the action could be dismissed nonetheless because the plaintiff's causation evidence, although admissible, is insufficient as a matter of law. *See, e.g.*, Brock v. Merrell Dow Pharmaceuticals, Inc. (5th Cir.1989) (dismissing Bendectin action for insufficiency of evidence of causation).

2. Epidemiological Studies

Because direct human experimentation is uncommon, except in the limited area of clinical drug trials, and is generally unacceptable for ethical reasons, plaintiffs have had to seek support for their causation claims in epidemiological studies. Epidemiology is a methodology that employs surveys and statistics to determine the probability of an association between a specified exposure and the occurrence of disease. It examines the frequency and distribution of diseases and studies the factors that may influence their occurrence. Epidemiology does not determine the occurrence of a disease in a specific person. Rather, it looks at groups of persons and draws inferences regarding the causes of illness in each of the groups. Thus, epidemiological studies are probabilistic evidence because they cannot, nor do they purport to, identify actual causes. They determine the level of risk of contracting a disease that affects the identified group. *See generally* Bert Black & David E. Lilienfeld, *Epidemiologic Proof in Toxic Tort Litigation*, 52 Fordham L. Rev. 732 (1984).

Epidemiological studies often begin with demographic surveys of large segments of the population, looking for the rates of occurrence of certain diseases. Such basic studies may result in a figure that represents the "baseline" level, or essentially background level, of an illness in the general population. Sometimes, an illness clusters within a certain geographic area (e.g. residents in the vicinity of a hazardous waste site), occupation (e.g. mesothelioma among asbestos workers), or other activity (e.g. smokers and lung cancer). This basic information can form the basis of further surveys and statistical studies.

Researchers undertake several different kinds of epidemiological studies when seeking to discover disease/exposure associations. The epidemiological studies most commonly discussed in toxic tort litigation are the cohort study and the case-control study.

a. Cohort Studies

Cohort studies are prospective studies that follow a group of individuals exposed to a particular substance over a period of time to determine whether they contract a particular illness. Statistical studies may then calculate whether the group has demonstrated an increased risk of developing the illness over members of the nonexposed population. If the relative risk of contracting the illness is greater in the exposed group than in the nonexposed population, the information is examined to determine whether a causal connection may exist. Epidemiologists do this by calculating the "attributable risk" and then undertaking a more subjective analysis of the biological plausibility of the proposed causal connection. These criteria are designed to verify the assumptions made in translating a statistical association into a biological inference of causation.

b. Case-Control Studies

The case-control study is retrospective in nature, as it begins by identifying a group of persons who have contracted a certain illness ("case" group) and a group who has not contracted the illness ("control" group), then surveys the two groups to determine whether the members of the case group have any characteristics in common that may be associated with the disease. An example of such a study might be to look at persons with mesothelioma compared to persons without the illness. The study might reflect that a certain percentage of persons with mesothelioma worked in the asbestos industry for a period of time, while the control group contained a much smaller percentage of asbestos workers.

Critics of case-control studies point out that they are susceptible to bias in the design, where a researcher begins with a certain predisposition toward finding a particular causal connection and designs the study around that. A further problem could be the recall bias of the participants in the study, as the study may seek information over a period of decades. Case-control studies are preferable to cohort studies when time is of the essence, however, as cohort studies could take years before any meaningful data are collected.

c. Drawbacks of Epidemiological Studies

In addition to problems of bias in the design of a study, epidemiological studies may yield questionable results for several reasons. First, the researcher must study a sufficiently large sample size to obtain significant statistical results. For results to be distinguishable from background levels, an appropriately sized sample must be used for subtle distinctions to be accurately assessed. Second, due to the long latency period associated with some diseases, a study may not follow the subjects for a sufficiently long time so as to accurately reveal the rate of disease in the group studied. Third, some diseases may be caused by a combination of factors or by alternative factors. Fourth, a correct analysis of the data may be masked by confounding factors. For example, cigarette smoking, in addition to the exposure under study, may be a confounding factor in studies of certain illnesses.

3. Toxicological Studies

Toxicological studies are laboratory studies that may be conducted either in vivo (on animal tissue) or in vitro (on cultures in a laboratory container). They have some clear advantages over epidemiological studies. The carefully controlled manner in which these tests are properly conducted allows researchers to obtain reasonably accurate information in all respects, including exposure (dose). Toxicological studies are more problematic than epidemiological studies, however, as any conclusions require extrapolation from the laboratory data to humans.

a. *Animal Studies*

Animal laboratory studies have been widely criticized for the assumptions that researchers make in extrapolating to humans from the animal data. This task is referred to as species-to-species extrapolation. One such criticism is that human systems are sufficiently different from animal systems—metabolically and in other ways—to render any extrapolated data misleading. Another major criticism is that dose-response data—i.e. the manner in which the animals' system responds to exposure at different doses—does not accurately predict human responses at analogous doses. Thus, critics argue, if a laboratory rat manifests a liver tumor at a certain dosage of a chemical, it is not necessarily correct that a human would develop liver cancer, or any cancer at all, from being exposed to an estimated analogous amount of the same chemical.

Further, the large doses of chemicals that researchers often use in animal studies to achieve results in a relatively speedy time frame, when translated into human doses may result in amounts far in excess of any exposure that humans could realistically anticipate. Researchers commonly extrapolate down from large doses to estimate the effect at lower doses. Critics find this kind of extrapolation very problematic, and there is much disagreement over the method of extrapolation for estimating carcinogenicity at low doses.

Notwithstanding these criticisms, animal studies have proven useful in suggesting a relationship between an exposure and illness in humans. Courts have approached animal studies with reservation and prefer to see some corroborating epidemiological or clinical evidence in conjunction with the animal studies when offered for proof of causation. *See* Longmore v. Merrell Dow Pharmaceuticals, Inc. (D.Idaho 1990). *See generally* Jack L. Landau & W. Hugh O'Riordan, *Of Mice and Men: The Admissibility of Animal Studies to Prove Causation in Toxic Tort Litigation*, 25 Idaho L. Rev. 521 (1988–89).

b. *Short-Term Tests*

These tests are highly problematic, and their use in toxic tort litigation to prove causation has been so vehemently questioned as to effectively minimize their utility in that context. Nevertheless, such studies may accompany and corroborate other types of scientific evidence introduced on the issue of causation. The best-known short-term test, referred to as the Ames test, generally studies the mutagenic effect of a suspected toxic substance on bacteria cultured in a laboratory container. Because the bacteria reproduce rapidly, many generations may be examined during the course of the study. Although the test directly tests mutagenicity, a meaningful correlation exists between mutagenicity and carcinogenicity, so the test is also used to suggest a carcinogenic effect.

The short-term tests are subject to some of the same criticisms as animal studies, but to an even greater degree. The Ames test has been sharply criticized by its founder for certain conclusions regarding the relationship between chemicals and cancer that have been drawn from the test data. Moreover, the test has been known to yield a high percentage of false positives, perhaps skewing results. All of these problems combine to render the short-term test of limited value in proving causation in toxic tort actions.

C. ADMISSIBILITY OF SCIENTIFIC EVIDENCE IN THE COURTS

Evidentiary challenges of plaintiffs' causation evidence are becoming standard in toxic tort actions. This can be the most significant aspect of the lawsuit because exclusion of even some of the plaintiff's expert testimony on causation can be fatal to the case. The admissibility issues relate to the evidence of both plaintiffs and defendants. As a practical matter, because plaintiffs bear the burden of proof, admissibility is generally viewed as a more dispositive issue for plaintiffs than for defendants.

1. Traditional Admissibility Standard

Prior to the United States Supreme Court's decision in Daubert v. Merrell Dow Pharmaceuticals, Inc. (S.Ct.1993), the standard for admissibility of scientific evidence in the federal courts was established initially by a federal appellate court in Frye v. United States (App.D.C.1923). *Frye* served as the standard for state rulings on the admissibility of scientific evidence as well. *Frye* pre-dated the Federal Rules of Evidence by half a century. But even after the promulgation of the Federal Rules, the influence of the *Frye* doctrine continued to dominate the federal cases. Today, many states still adhere to the *Frye* doctrine and have not changed their admissibility rules to reflect the impact of *Daubert*.

a. The Frye Doctrine

Frye v. United States (App.D.C.1923), was a criminal case involving the admissibility of blood pressure deception measurements to prove the defendant's guilt. The court stated: "[W]hile courts will go a long way in admitting expert testimony deduced from a well-recognized scientific principle or discovery, the thing from which the deduction is made must be sufficiently established to have gained general acceptance in the particular field in which it belongs." This test apparently was intended to exclude all novel or developing scientific theories. Following the promulgation of the Federal Rules of Evidence in 1975, courts reached different conclusions as to whether the *Frye* requirement of "general acceptance" survived or whether it was supplanted by the relevant Federal Rules. Because the Federal Rules were silent on the *Frye* issue, courts were left to speculate on the impact of the Rules on the *Frye* doctrine.

b. Rules of Evidence

Several provisions in the Federal Rules of Evidence are applicable to a court's decision whether to admit scientific evidence as proof of causation. State evidentiary rules have analogous, if not always identical, provisions.

Rule 402 of the Federal Rules makes all relevant evidence admissible. It is limited by Rule 403, which provides that relevant evidence "may be excluded if its probative value is substantially outweighed by the danger of unfair prejudice, confusion of the issues, or misleading the jury, or by considerations of undue delay, waste of time, or needless presentation of cumulative evidence." Defendants argue that some kinds of scientific evidence are too speculative and have the effect of confusing the jury, who might grant such evidence the same weight as more definitive evidence, either because the expert makes a highly credible and persuasive presentation or because the distinctions between various pieces of evidence are too complex and technical to be fully understood by laypersons.

Two federal rules directly address expert testimony. Rule 702 provides:

If scientific, technical, or other specialized knowledge will assist the trier of fact to understand the evidence or to determine a fact in issue, a witness qualified as an expert by knowledge, skill, experience, training, or education, may testify thereto in the form of an opinion or otherwise.

Rule 703 addresses the basis of the expert's opinion:

The facts or data in the particular case upon which an expert bases an opinion or inference may be those perceived by or made known to the expert at or before the hearing. If of a type reasonably relied upon by experts in the particular field in forming opinions or inferences upon the subject, the facts or data need not be admissible in evidence.

Of course, the party offering the expert testimony must qualify the person as an expert qualified to give the opinion. Rule 703 makes clear that a medical expert need not actually have examined the plaintiff, as experts may base their opinions on information (e.g. clinical test results and reports of examinations) reviewed by them. Moreover, it is irrelevant that the underlying information may be inadmissible hearsay, provided that it is "of a type reasonably relied upon by experts in the particular field."

The Federal Rules remained silent on whether the general acceptance rule of *Frye* was intended to be incorporated into them. Courts have reached widely diverging opinions on the role of general acceptance under the Federal Rules. *Compare* Christophersen v. Allied–Signal Corp. (5th Cir.1991) (incorporating *Frye* into broad Federal Rule analysis); United States v. Smith (7th Cir.1989) (adopting *Frye* doctrine virtually unchanged) *with* United States v. Downing (3d Cir.1985) (rejecting a pure *Frye* standard and developing its own reliability inquiry that included general acceptance as one element); Ferebee v. Chevron Chemical Co. (D.C.Cir.1984) (rejecting *Frye* in case involving novel scientific theory).

2. The Rule of Daubert v. Merrell Dow Pharmaceuticals, Inc.

a. The Bendectin Litigation

Bendectin was a drug prescribed to alleviate the symptoms of "morning sickness" during pregnancy. Plaintiffs brought actions against the manufacturer of the drug for damages for limb deformities in children allegedly caused by first trimester, in utero exposure to Bendectin. More than thirty epidemiological studies were conducted on the effects of Bendectin, but no study found the drug to be teratogenic in humans. In most cases, the defendant's experts convincingly showed that maternal use of Bendectin during the first trimester of pregnancy had not been shown to be a risk factor for the deformities alleged. Consequently, Bendectin plaintiffs employed less traditional scientific evidence to support their cases.

The Bendectin plaintiffs have relied upon several different kinds of studies. First, they proffered both in vivo and in vitro laboratory studies that showed a connection between Bendectin and certain defects. They also employed pharmacological studies that analyzed the chemical structure of Bendectin and identified similarities between it and other substances known to cause birth defects. The most controversial evidence proffered by the plaintiffs was a reanalysis of published epidemiological studies on Bendectin. The reanalysis studies recalculated data from the earlier studies that had found no connection between Bendectin and birth defects. Upon reanalysis, plaintiffs' experts were of the opinion that a causal connection did in fact exist. The reanalysis studies had not been published or otherwise offered for peer review. Among the cases in which the plaintiffs relied upon this evidence were Brock v. Merrell Dow Pharmaceuticals, Inc. (5th Cir.1989) (holding that the evidence was insufficient as a matter of law) and Richardson v. Richardson–Merrell, Inc. (D.C.Cir.1988).

Historically, defendants have been overwhelmingly successful in the Bendectin cases, often on summary judgment motions. *See generally* Joseph Sanders, *The Bendectin Litigation: A Study in the Life Cycle of Mass Torts*, 43 Hastings L.J. 301 (1992). Yet, in many cases that actually went to trial, the juries found for the plaintiffs. *See generally* Joseph Sanders, *From Science to Evidence: The Testimony on Causation in the Bendectin Cases*, 46 Stan. L. Rev. 1 (1993). This has added some fuel to the arguments of defendants that when juries are allowed to consider scientific evidence, they are likely to reach the wrong result. The Bendectin litigation has served as a central focus of the debate over the admissibility of scientific evidence in the courtroom.

b. *Daubert v. Merrell Dow Pharmaceuticals, Inc.*

The Supreme Court's decision in Daubert v. Merrell Dow Pharmaceuticals, Inc. (S.Ct.1993), settled the dispute among the federal courts over the applicability of *Frye* to the Federal Rules. In a unanimous opinion on this point, Justice Blackmun wrote that the general acceptance test of *Frye* was replaced by the Federal Rules of Evidence. The Court stated that "under the Rules, the trial judge must ensure that any and all scientific testimony or evidence admitted is not only relevant, but reliable." The reliability analysis derives from Rule

702 in conjunction with several other Rules, including Rules 403, 703, and 706.

A majority of the Court went on to further delineate the inquiry that the trial court is required to make when presented with scientific evidence. The Court interpreted Rule 702 to require "a valid scientific connection to the pertinent inquiry as a precondition to admissibility." The Court was especially concerned about the relationship between science and the law:

> The adjective "scientific" implies a grounding in the methods and procedures of science. Similarly, the word "knowledge" connotes more than subjective belief or unsupported speculation.... Proposed testimony must be supported by appropriate validation .... In short, the requirement that an expert's testimony pertain to "scientific knowledge" establishes a standard of evidentiary reliability.

The Court acknowledged that "arguably, there are no certainties in science," because scientific knowledge is constantly evolving. But certainty is required in the law—at least, a measure of certainty at the time a decision is rendered in a particular lawsuit. Thus, the Court acknowledged the difficulty of the problem presented by novel scientific evidence: the scientific knowledge is in an initial or developing stage, but the law requires a decision.

The Court vacated the decision of the appellate court and remanded the case for further proceedings. The Court offered some "general observations" to assist courts in performing their gatekeeping role and conducting the reliability analysis. In essence, the observations amount to a multi-factored test. Initially, the Court made clear that pursuant to Federal Rule 104(a), trial courts are expected to undertake a preliminary inquiry on admissibility, most commonly by motion in limine, to determine whether the proposed expert testimony constitutes *scientific knowledge* and whether that knowledge will assist the factfinder in determining a fact in issue. Thus, the "fit" between the expert's opinion and the precise issue to be decided in the case is crucial.

The factors established by the Court as essential considerations in the trial court's reliability analysis were: (1) whether the scientific technique or theory has been tested; (2) whether the study has been published or has undergone some other form of peer review; (3) the rate of error associated with the scientific technique used; and (4) whether the theory is generally accepted in the relevant scientific *(Frye)* community. The Court was careful to note that no single factor is necessarily determinative of admissibility. Thus, if the theory does not have general acceptance in the relevant community, testimony based on the theory may still be admissible if other indicia of reliability are present. The Court also emphasized that the trial court's inquiry must focus only on the "principles and methodology" of the scientific evidence. The trial court may not subject the conclusion of the expert to the analysis. This last point is particularly important when the court considers the general acceptance factor. So long as the methodology of the study is a generally accepted technique, it should be irrelevant whether the conclusions offered by the expert, who is relying on the study, are generally accepted.

The *Daubert* Court also expressed confidence in the ability of the traditional mechanisms of the jury system, such as cross-examination, to assure that appropriate evaluations of scientific evidence are made. This faith in the jury system was consistent with an apparent rejection by the Court of the position of the "junk science" commentators.

c. *Impact of Daubert*

Daubert could be interpreted to represent a more liberal approach to the admissibility of scientific evidence than the *Frye* doctrine. While this appears true from the language of the opinion, *Daubert* does not appear to have had the effect of opening the courtroom doors wide to scientific evidence, as some had feared. Certainly, with respect to Bendectin cases, *Daubert* has made no difference at all. *See, e.g.*, DeLuca v. Merrell Dow Pharmaceuticals, Inc. (3d Cir.1993) (affirming, in light of *Daubert* decision, district court's holding that plaintiff's scientific evidence was inadmissible). Arguably, the decision has made little, if any, difference in the determination of the admissibility of scientific evidence in other kinds of cases as well. *See generally* Jonathan M. Hoffman, *A Briefcase and an Opinion: Post-"Daubert" Expert Testimony—A Major Shift*, 22 Prod. Safety & Liab. Rptr 379 (1994) (surveying post-*Daubert* cases). In any event, the federal courts are now scrutinizing the evidence under several criteria, not solely the general acceptance standard. Such close attention could result in greater exclusion of evidence because each of the various factors considered offers an opportunity for the court to find evidentiary deficiencies in the proffered evidence.

Although the Court rejected strict application of *Frye*, the general acceptance test survived as one factor. Courts in circuits accustomed to applying *Frye* will likely give maximum weight to general acceptance. Moreover, the Court's approach to scientific evidence treats novel theories in the same manner as more established theories. One message that *Daubert* gives to litigants is that theories that are too speculative or unfounded in scientific methodology will not be tolerated. *See, e.g.,* O'Conner v. Commonwealth Edison Co. (7th Cir.1994) (excluding evidence of radiation as cause of plaintiff's cataracts because merely subjective opinion); Chikovsky v. Ortho Pharmaceutical Corp. (S.D.Fla. 1993) (excluding causation testimony relying on study of substance similar, but not identical, to medication to which plaintiff exposed).

D. REFORMS IN JUDICIAL MANAGEMENT OF SCIENTIFIC EVIDENCE

In 1993, the Carnegie Commission on Science, Technology, and Government issued an important report on the uses of scientific and technological evidence in the courtroom. *See* Carnegie Comm'n on Science, Technology, & Government, Science and Technology in Judicial Decision Making: Creating Opportunities and Meeting Challenges (1993). The Commission identified epidemiological and toxicological evidence as challenging the judicial system in unprecedented ways. The report examined the role of the judiciary in addressing questions involving scientific evidence and recommended means of enhancing judicial understanding and decisionmaking. The Commission emphasized its belief that existing procedural mechanisms, including the Federal Rules of Civil Procedure and the Federal Rules of Evidence, provide courts with sufficient means for addressing complex issues of science and technology (S & T) in litigation.

The report made several recommendations for maximizing the utility of those procedural mechanisms in S & T litigation. The Commission initially made several threshold findings to guide its proposals. First, it acknowledged the need for an active role for the trial judge, who should focus on resolving S & T issues prior to trial so as to encourage early disposition of actions. Second, the Commission expressed the need to facilitate jury understanding of scientific evidence to reduce the risk of erroneous results. Third, the report focused most of its attention on the need for education—both of the judiciary and the scientific community—to facilitate the exchange of information. The more the legal community and the scientific community understand about each other's methodologies and fundamental modes of operation, the more useful the exchange of substantive information can be.

The Commission proposed:

Judges should engage in the active management of complex S & T issues throughout the stages of litigation whenever appropriate.

Judicial education should include S & T issues, both in programs of a general nature and in focused S & T programs.

Institutional linkages should be forged between the judicial and scientific communities.

A Science and Justice Council consisting of lawyers, scientists, and others outside the judiciary should be established to initiate and monitor developments and to suggest future reforms with respect to the judicial system's treatment of scientific and technological issues.

The purpose of the Science and Justice Council would be to act as a neutral forum for the consideration of institutional reforms. The Commission envisioned that ultimately the Council would extend its knowledge and expertise beyond the judicial system to colleges and law schools.

The Federal Judicial Center is implementing the proposals set forth in the report. Its initial effort has produced a pilot program and a reference manual for judges on science and technology. Eventually, the Center will develop protocols for judicial analysis of expert scientific evidence in specific kinds of cases.

E. THE PROBLEM OF INDETERMINATE PLAINTIFFS

The problems involving indeterminate *defendants* have been discussed elsewhere. *See* Chapter Five, Sec. F, *supra*. That situation focused upon the problems inherent in the DES litigation rendering plaintiffs unable to identify the precise defendant whose product cause the injuries alleged. While the unique circumstances of the DES litigation created significant causation problems for the plaintiffs, some courts have managed those problems by allowing the "indeterminate defendants" to be treated under special rules of collective liability, including market share liability. *See, e.g.*, Sindell v. Abbott Laboratories (Cal.1980).

The problem of indeterminacy also occurs with respect to plaintiffs. The indeterminate plaintiff situation arises in toxic torts in two ways. First, some persons who have been exposed to a particular substance and have become ill may actually have contracted the illness from another cause. Assuming the absence of a "signature disease," and due to the inability of toxic tort plaintiffs to show cause-in-fact, the precise cause of their illness may never be known. A second kind of indeterminate plaintiff is the future claimant. This situation arises because latency periods for the development of disease are unequal from individual to individual. Not everyone who has been exposed to a particular substance over the same period of time gets sick at the same time. Thus, all liability of a defendant for the

injuries resulting from a single course of conduct
cannot be resolved simultaneously, nor even sometimes within the same decade. The future claimant
issue is addressed in Chapter Nine, Sec. D(2), *infra*.

The first kind of plaintiff indeterminacy has generated judicial and scholarly interest because of the
issue of causal indeterminacy. Some courts and
commentators have struggled to find a means to
resolve all claims arising out of exposure to the
defendants' product or to hazardous substances for
which the defendants are responsible in a single
proceeding. The notion of collective recovery mechanisms has met with some resistance, however. In
contrast to the *indeterminate defendant* situation,
in which collective liability was imposed upon the
defendants so as to advance the policy goals of
deterrence, loss shifting, and loss spreading, collective recovery in the *indeterminate plaintiff* situation
would likely result in overcompensation of some
persons, most notably those whose illness was not
actually caused by the alleged exposure.

This was one of the general issues discussed by
the court in Allen v. United States (D.Utah 1984).
The court proposed a relaxation of the cause-in-fact
requirement in the situation presented. The court
noted that the leukemias and other conditions alleged by the plaintiffs to have been caused by exposure to ionizing radiation released during the United States Government's atomic testing program
were identical to the same illnesses existing in the
general population without such an exposure. Nevertheless, the court held that sufficient statistical

evidence existed to demonstrate a close association between low-level exposure to radiation and the cancers alleged by the plaintiffs. The court stated that where the defendant has acted negligently in putting the plaintiffs at risk and the statistical evidence consistently shows "substantial, appropriate, persuasive, and connecting factors" associating the exposure with the injuries alleged, the factfinder could reasonably make a finding of causation. The court also required an analysis of a variety of factors applicable to individual plaintiffs—including exposures to other substance and personal variables such as the type of cancer alleged—for a determination of consistency with the known scientific data. At that point, the burden would shift to the defendants to disprove the causal connection.

A different approach to the indeterminate plaintiff problem has been proposed by Professor Richard Delgado. In an important piece, Professor Delgado proposed a collective, or class solution to the indeterminate plaintiff problem. *See* Richard Delgado, *Beyond Sindell: Relaxation of Cause–In–Fact Rules for Indeterminate Plaintiffs*, 70 Calif. L. Rev. 881, 899–902 (1982). The proposal consisted of the following:

The "prima facie case" that plaintiff must satisfy ... consists of the following elements: (i) that plaintiffs have suffered an injury; (ii) that the injury be one that could have resulted from either natural or human causes, acting separately and without synergy; (iii) that the injuries be causally indeterminate—that is, not identifiable as hu-

manly or naturally caused; (iv) that the defendant is the only possible human cause; and (v)
that the population injured, mode of risk, and
other variables be uniform and stable enough to
permit calculation of the increased number of
victims. Once the plaintiff has established the
prima facie case, the burden of proof shifts to the
defendant to prove noncausation with respect to
each injury. If he or she fails to do so, liability
will be imposed for the number of unproved victims.

Recovery would be collective, not individualized.
Thus, Professor Delgado proposes: "The plaintiff
class, if successful, would recover an amount corresponding to its combined losses attributed to defendant's actions. This amount would be allocated
among the members pro rata, after subtracting
litigation costs." The advantage of this approach is
that it is designed to reflect the measure of harm
created by the defendant. While Professor Delgado
acknowledges that this proposal creates a certain
amount of overcompensation (compensating persons
for being "within the zone of risk"), he finds the
result acceptable because of the deterrent effect of
holding defendants accountable for the risks they
create.

Judge Weinstein endorsed a class-wide approach
in the Agent Orange litigation. There, Judge Weinstein was responsible for examining the fairness of
a proposed settlement of the over two million personal injury claims arising from the United States
Government's use of the defoliant known as Agent

Orange during the Vietnam War. For a discussion of the various aspects of managing the Agent Orange class action, see Chapter Nine, Sec. A(1) & passim, *infra*. In approving the $180 million settlement, Judge Weinstein rejected an individualized assessment of causation in favor of a collective approach. He advocated a class-wide assessment of overall harm to the plaintiffs and holding the defendants liable to each plaintiff for a pro rata share of damages. *See* In re "Agent Orange" Prod. Liab. Litig. (E.D.N.Y.1984).

Most judicial efforts to settle mass toxic tort litigation have logged a considerable amount of time contemplating the appropriate treatment of indeterminate plaintiffs. Further, the use of aggregative procedures to resolve mass toxic tort litigation reflects the tension between the desire for individualized resolution of causation and the efficiency of collective resolution. These procedures are discussed in Chapter Nine, Secs. A & B, *infra*.

CHAPTER EIGHT

INJURIES AND DAMAGES

A. EMOTIONAL DISTRESS

As a general rule, a plaintiff who recovers on a claim for personal injury is entitled to compensation for all damages for injury past, present, and future arising out of the circumstances giving rise to the action. W. Page Keeton et al., Prosser and Keeton on Torts § 12 (5th ed. 1984). Thus, a plaintiff who proves a claim for physical injury resulting from exposure to chemicals from a hazardous waste site may recover for both the physical illness and any emotional distress associated with it.

Many potential toxic tort plaintiffs claim emotional distress without any accompanying illness or other physical injury, however. These claims are sometimes referred to as "fear of cancer" claims or as the misnomer "cancerphobia." The law has had considerable difficulty recognizing such claims without some objective proof of their validity. Concern for imagined claims or fraudulent and frivolous lawsuits has prevented most jurisdictions from recognizing emotional distress claims without some additional corroboration. Moreover, courts have expressed concern that emotional distress may be so fleeting and short-lived that it should not properly be compensated.

1. Outrageous Conduct

If the conduct of which the plaintiff complains is extreme and outrageous courts will probably allow a claim for intentional or reckless infliction of emotional distress absent a physical injury. Because of the outrageous nature of the conduct, juries may reasonably infer that the plaintiff suffered emotional distress. *See* Restatement (Second) of Torts, § 46 (1965) (recognizing tort of outrageous conduct causing severe emotional distress). For example, in Capital Holding Corp. v. Bailey (Ky.1994), the plaintiff alleged, among other claims, a claim of outrageous conduct causing severe emotional distress. He alleged that he had contracted with the defendant building owner to remove pipes and ducts from the basement of a building, but had not been told that those items were contaminated with asbestos. He stated further that the owner knew of the asbestos contamination before hiring him, but did not inform him of the hazard. Upon learning of the contamination approximately two years later, he underwent medical diagnostic tests that revealed no present illness. He was told, however, that he had an increased risk of developing asbestosis and mesothelioma. The court allowed the outrageous conduct claim to stand, finding that the record showed that for several months the plaintiff had been "knowingly and recklessly exposed" to the asbestos.

2. Negligent Infliction of Emotional Distress
a. Physical Injury Requirement

The allegation of negligent conduct is more problematic, however, and most courts require that for such a claim to be viable the plaintiff must allege physical harm. Section 436A of the Restatement (Second) of Torts sets forth the general rule under these circumstances: "If the actor's conduct is negligent as creating an unreasonable risk of causing either bodily harm or emotional disturbance to another, and it results in such emotional disturbance alone, without bodily harm or other compensable damage, the actor is not liable for such emotional disturbance." The physical harm may be—but is not required to be—caused by the defendant's conduct; physical harm that results from the emotional distress is sufficient to satisfy the requirement.

In Payton v. Abbott Labs (Mass.1982), the court applied this rule on certification from federal court in a class-action case brought by persons who were exposed to DES. The court discussed the concept of reasonable foreseeability of injury that has traditionally been a requirement in the law of negligence. In the court's opinion, this requirement could be satisfied in appropriate cases either where emotional distress is caused by or causes physical injury. The court applied the following test:

> [The plaintiff] must allege and prove she suffered physical harm as a result of the conduct which caused the emotional distress.... [F]urther, ... a plaintiff's physical harm must either cause or

be caused by the emotional distress alleged, and
... the physical harm must be manifested by
objective symptomatology and substantiated by
expert testimony. Finally, the emotional distress
for which compensation is sought must be reasonably foreseeable ....

In applying the test, the plaintiff's compensation
will be for an amount of emotional distress that a
reasonable person would have suffered under the
circumstances.

A version of this test has been applied by many
courts. For example, in Ayers v. Township of Jackson (N.J.1987), plaintiffs whose well water was contaminated by toxic chemicals that leached into the
aquifer from a Township landfill brought several
claims against the Township, including one for emotional distress. The emotional distress claim was
based upon the plaintiffs' knowledge that they had
ingested polluted water. None of the plaintiffs
claimed any disease or other physical injury as a
result of the ingestion of the contaminated water,
however. Although the plaintiffs' expert witness, a
clinical psychologist, had testified that the plaintiffs
were suffering depression, worry, and stress, the
court rejected the emotional distress claim because
the plaintiffs were not exhibiting any physical
symptoms.

In Anderson v. W.R. Grace & Co. (D.Mass.1986),
a case directly controlled by *Payton*, the court expanded on the concept of physical injury. The
plaintiffs sought damages for emotional distress

that they had suffered on account of the defendants' conduct and also as a result of witnessing the death by cancer of family members. The plaintiffs, who claimed that their family members' injuries were caused by exposure to toxic chemicals that had migrated into the drinking water supply, had not themselves suffered any physical injuries. With respect to the claims of emotional distress directly tied to the defendants' conduct, the court held that any claims meeting the physical injury requirement would stand. Physical harm based upon subcellular injury (e.g. chromosomal damage) may meet this requirement, the court noted. The plaintiffs' responses to the defendants' interrogatories included a statement that they suffered from increased susceptibility to disease as a result of drinking the contaminated water. The court found this to be a sufficient allegation of physical harm to meet the *Payton* standard to withstand dismissal.

With respect to the emotional distress claim for witnessing the death of a family member, the court analyzed this claim under the rule of bystander recovery. Cases involving bystander recovery typically involved a parent witnessing a child being struck by a motor vehicle. The Restatement (Second) of Torts § 436(3) (1965) allowed bystander recovery if an immediate family member (the plaintiff) had been within the zone of danger created by the defendant's negligence. *See* Dillon v. Legg (Cal. 1968). The *Anderson* court did not allow recovery on this theory because the emotional distress did not occur sufficiently close in time to the alleged negligent conduct of the defendant to meet the requirements of the "zone of danger" element. Thus, the court limited the bystander rule to traumatic injury.

b. Relinquishment of Physical Injury Requirement

In a recent groundbreaking case, the California Supreme Court took the controversial step of allowing a claim for negligent infliction of emotional distress in the absence of physical injury. In Potter v. Firestone Tire and Rubber Company (Cal.1993), the court addressed the claims of several landowners who claimed to have been exposed to toxic substances due to the proximity of an adjacent landfill containing toxic waste. None of the plaintiffs was suffering from any disease or other physical condition. They did allege, however, that they were subject to an increased, but unquantified, risk of contracting cancer in the future. In rejecting the physical injury requirement in this case, the court stated:

> [T]he physical injury requirement is a hopelessly imprecise screening device—it would allow recovery for fear of cancer whenever such distress accompanies or results in any physical injury, no matter how trivial, yet would disallow recovery in all cases where the fear is both serious and genuine but no physical injury has yet manifested itself.

Nevertheless, the *Potter* court did place some limitations on a plaintiff's recovery for emotional distress.

The court stated that the plaintiff can only recover for emotional distress that is reasonable and serious. Reasonableness is not established merely by the fact of exposure, however. The court required that the plaintiff show that the emotional distress was based upon a knowledge that the likelihood of developing cancer is more likely than not.

For a plaintiff to meet this test, the plaintiff must present reliable medical or scientific testimony quantifying the risk of developing cancer. The court acknowledged that in some cases it may be difficult for the risk to be quantified, but noted that in other types of cases involving the risk of developing a disease plaintiffs had been able to acquire the requisite expert opinion. The court believed that applying the quantification of risk requirement best served the policy considerations of keeping litigation within manageable limits and assuring that persons who recover for emotional distress are those with legitimate claims.

Potter is remarkable for abandoning the physical injury requirement and replacing it with notions of risk. In doing so, the court implicitly recognized that risk alone may be as concrete an injury as physical injury. It is important to remember that in emotional distress claims the compensation is for *fear* of developing a disease for which there is an increased risk. Claims based on fear have some tradition in the law that allows courts to have a certain comfort level with the developing doctrines in the latent disease context. In contrast, claims that seek compensation for the increased risk itself, for which there is very little legal context, have caused courts to manifest considerable discomfort. *See* Section B, *infra*.

c. *Fear of AIDS*

In Kerins v. Hartley (Cal.App.1994), a California court had the opportunity to apply *Potter* to a case in which the plaintiff sought damages for fear of contracting the AIDS virus. The plaintiff commenced the action after learning that the surgeon who had performed her surgery was infected with HIV. The surgeon stated that no exposure occurred during the surgery, and the plaintiff offered no evidence to the contrary. Because, at best, the plaintiff could demonstrate only a small possibility of her becoming infected with HIV, the court held that the claim did not meet the standard of *Potter*. The likelihood of the plaintiff developing AIDS did not constitute a significant probability and, accordingly, did not meet the preponderance of the evidence standard.

In Johnson v. West Virginia University Hospitals, Inc. (W.Va.1991), the court, applying West Virginia law, took a somewhat less harsh approach. The trial court did not accept the defendant's request for an instruction that there be a demonstrated increased risk of developing AIDS from which the emotional distress flowed. Rather, the plaintiff was only required to prove a reasonable fear of contracting AIDS. This case involved a bite received by a hospital employee from a patient suffering from

AIDS, so the court assumed that an exposure had occurred.

When the actual exposure is not verified, courts may display reticence toward entertaining a fear of AIDS case. In Doe v. Surgicare of Joliet, Inc. (Ill.App.1994), the plaintiff was a hospital patient on whom a medical procedure was performed. The employee performing the procedure had stuck him- or herself with the needle that was eventually used in the procedure. The patient sought to have the employee tested for the AIDS virus, but the employee refused. The plaintiff later tested negative for the virus. The court rejected the plaintiff's claim, even though some "physical impact" had occurred, thus technically satisfying the Illinois basis for a negligent infliction of emotional distress claim. The court found that no exposure had occurred, despite the impact. Absent the exposure, no reasonable fear could be legally recognized because there was no increased risk that the plaintiff would contract the illness.

The fear of AIDS cases demonstrate some ambivalence toward allowing emotional distress claims in that class of cases. Most likely because of a concern for unverifiable claims, the courts tend to scrutinize the exposure element closely. The exposure/non-exposure line is a convenient objective criterion that permits courts to avoid analyzing more subjective criteria, such as the degree of distress.

B. INCREASED RISK OF DISEASE

Claims for increased risk of disease—sometimes called enhanced risk—seek compensation for the risk of developing the disease, whether or not the person ever becomes ill. This is a separate claim from fear of developing the disease; rather, if allowed, it compensates purely for the risk. The typical plaintiff asserting an increased risk claim has been exposed to a toxic substance known to be associated with latent disease, but either has no physical symptoms of illness or has a condition that is known to be a precursor to a more serious illness. Thus, a person exposed to toxic chemicals in the drinking water supply, but who has not manifested symptoms of illness may seek to bring an increased risk claim. Similarly, an asbestos worker with pleural thickening, which has been associated with exposure to asbestos, may seek compensation for the increased risk of developing lung cancer.

Increased risk claims are the most problematic claims that courts confront in the toxic tort context. One reason is that these claims do not comport with traditional notions of what constitutes an injury. Under traditional concepts of standing, courts are accustomed to seeing civil cases that seek redress for an injury. A claim that has not accrued usually will not be entertained. Claims for increased risk do not dispute that the ultimate claim for the disease has not yet accrued. The question that these claims beg is whether they should be recognized as independent claims: because the risk is present and continuing, is not the claim for risk legally cognizable? This conceptual question is not the entire problem, however. If courts do entertain such claims, what are the parameters?

Another reason for the difficulty that courts have with increased risk claims is that they implicate several traditional doctrines and ask the court to apply them in a novel manner. One fundamental concept is that the tort plaintiff may recover all damages arising form the defendant's conduct, past, present, and future. This traditional rule, however, assumed some present injury to person or property, which is absent in the increased risk claims. The second doctrine is res judicata. The prohibition against claim splitting requires that once a cause of action accrues and a plaintiff brings an action, the plaintiff must include all claims arising from the same transaction or series of transactions. *See* Restatement (Second) of Judgments, § 24 (1982). Subsequent claims arising from the same transaction will be barred. *See generally* Chapter 6, Sec. C, *supra.* If initial increased risk claims are allowed, the logical extension of this doctrine would be to bar any subsequent claim for actual injury based upon the same conduct. If compensation for the increased risk is considered to be full compensation for all injuries that might arise in the future, the result will be overcompensation for some (i.e. those who never develop the disease) and undercompensation for others (i.e. those who do develop the disease and suffer injuries in excess of the predicted amount previously compensated).

If, on the other hand, some form of claim-splitting is allowed under these circumstances, different problems arises. If the plaintiff is compensated early for the risk of developing disease, and recovers on a later claim after becoming ill, concern arises over the extent to which the plaintiff may be obtaining a double recovery. Indeed, if claim-splitting is allowed, the increased risk claim may be superfluous, as it will be subsumed into the later illness claim. This would avoid the problems of overcompensating plaintiffs who do not later develop the disease. If, on the other hand, the plaintiff is presently suffering from some lesser exposure-related condition, claim-splitting would be more effective. The plaintiff could bring an early claim for damages related to the first condition, if it constituted a recognized injury, and a subsequent claim for the later illness after it developed. The increased risk claim would again be subsumed into the later action.

Regardless of the approach taken to claim-splitting, there is some crucial interrelationship between the res judicata rule and the rules of accrual for statutes of limitations. A claim cannot be actionable unless recognized by the applicable rules as having accrued. If a claim has accrued, the statutory period will begin to run—and eventually run out. Thus, some coordination must exist between the applicable accrual rule for statute of limitations purposes and the rule on claim-splitting in the same jurisdiction.

1. Cases Relying on Present Injury

Some cases require, explicitly or implicitly, a present physical injury to provide some objective basis for the increased risk claim. A relatively early case, not arising in the toxic tort context, recognized a claim for decreased chance of survival based upon statistical percentages. In Herskovits v. Group Health Cooperative (Wash.1983), the court held that the plaintiff's decedent's decreased chance of survival resulting from a physician's negligence in misdiagnosing lung cancer presented a cognizable claim. The plaintiff alleged that at the time the decedent first saw the physician for lung symptoms, he was not diagnosed with lung cancer. The complaint alleged that had he been properly diagnosed and treated at that time, he would have had a 39 percent five-year survival possibility. At the time he was actually diagnosed, his chance of survival after five years was reduced to 25 percent. This represented a 36 percent reduction in his overall chance of survival after five years. He died approximately two years after the diagnosis of cancer.

The court ruled that these allegations were sufficient to take the case to the jury for a determination of proximate cause between the increased risk and the decedent's death. It was not necessary for the plaintiff to show that it was certain that the decedent would have lived had he been properly diagnosed in the first place.

Herskovits, while relying on risk as the primary element of the claim, nevertheless involved an undisputed physical injury—the course of the decedent's lung cancer and his eventual death. Similarly, in Petriello v. Kalman (Conn.1990), another medical malpractice case, the plaintiff alleged that during a routine D & C, the physician perforated her uterus and suctioned portions of her small intestine, then made an improper incision while attempting to repair the intestine. The court allowed a claim for increased risk of bowel obstruction at some future time.

In the toxic tort context, the court in Brafford v. Susquehanna Corp. (D.Colo.1984), allowed an increased risk claim upon a showing of present physical injury. The *Brafford* plaintiffs alleged that they had experienced an increased risk of future disease as a consequence of exposure to radiation from a uranium tailing pile at the defendant's mining facility. The court defined present physical injury as "immediate, present damage to ... cellular and subcellular structures, incurred proportionately to the amount and duration of the radiation exposure." This rather broad definition of physical injury would accommodate many toxic tort plaintiffs' claims of increased risk of illness.

2. Claims Based Upon Risk Only

In Ayers v. Township of Jackson (N.J.1987), the court addressed a variety of claims brought by persons arising out of the contamination of their drinking water supply. None of the plaintiffs claimed to be suffering from any illness associated with the toxic chemicals. The court held that for a plaintiff to recover on a claim of increased risk, the likelihood of the plaintiff developing the disease must be reasonably certain. This meant that the risk must be quantified. In *Ayers*, the plaintiffs' expert expressly stated that although the plaintiffs had an increased risk of cancer, he was unable to quantify the extent of the increased risk because of a lack of scientific information on the interaction of the various chemicals to which they were exposed. Thus, the court refused to recognize their increased risk claims.

The *Ayers* court's rationales in requiring a quantified risk were several. First, the court expressed concern about large numbers of unsubstantiated claims of increased risk, with many of the plaintiffs never developing the disease for which they were compensated. Second, allowing claims for unquantified risk of illness would require judges and juries to make a determination of whether the disease was reasonably certain without any clear guidance from the scientific community, which is best suited to make such a determination. Third, the court speculated that without some clear restrictions on the availability of increased risk claims, defendants' insurance rates would rise substantially to provide coverage for the many new claims of increased risk that would be brought.

The *Ayers* court also addressed the res judicata impact of increased risk claims. Although this matter was not directly at issue in the case, the court stated that under New Jersey law, plaintiffs who bring increased risk claims—or claims based upon

any other early injury—would not be barred by
either the statute of limitations or the rules of claim
preclusion from bringing a later claim after an
illness has manifested itself. Analyzing this issue
within the context of New Jersey's discovery statute
of limitations, the court noted that the cause of
action for the later disease would not accrue until
the symptoms of the disease appeared and the
plaintiff was aware of the likely cause. The court
also said that the rule against claim-splitting would
not apply:

> [The rule] cannot sensibly be applied to a toxic-
> tort claim filed when disease is manifested years
> after the exposure .... In such a case, the rule
> is literally inapplicable since ... the second cause
> of action does not accrue until the disease is
> manifested; hence, it could not have been joined
> with the earlier claims.

One issue that arises when claim-splitting is allowed in the manner described by the New Jersey
court in *Ayers* is whether claim-splitting renders
increased risk claims unnecessary. If a plaintiff
who later develops an illness related to a prior
exposure is allowed to bring the claim after the
illness has manifested, what purpose does an earlier
increased risk claim serve? Such issues must be
addressed in future litigation before any clear assessment of the viability of increased risk claims
can be made. In any event, any jurisdiction that
recognizes increased risk claims must not fail to
analyze both the res judicata impact and the accrual
issues to assure that the increased risk claims will

not run afoul of other important policies. *See also* Anderson v. W.R. Grace & Co. (D.Mass.1986) (stating that whether claim preclusion applies to later claims depends upon whether the later illness is part of same disease process as subcellular immune system suppression alleged in increased risk claim).

3. What Constitutes Reasonable Certainty of Risk?

Ayers is representative of decisions recognizing the validity of some claims for increased risk of future disease. Because the plaintiffs' claims were unquantified in that case, the court was not in a position to determine what degree of risk was necessary to reach the reasonable certainty standard. In Hagerty v. L & L Marine Services, Inc. (5th Cir.1986), the court established a standard that "the toxic exposure more probably than not *will* lead to cancer." *See also* Potter v. Firestone Tire & Rubber Company (Cal.1993) (stating that more likely than not standard is best measure of existence of cognizable risk of future disease). In Sterling v. Velsicol Chemical Corp. (6th Cir.1988), the court stated that it was not necessary to use the term "reasonable medical certainty," but indicated that the degree of certainty must be greater than "possibly" or "could have." This hedging leaves open the possibility that a risk quantified at less than 51 percent could suffice to provide the basis for recovery.

Petriello v. Kalman (Conn.1990), one of the medical malpractice cases previously discussed, departed

from the more-likely-than-not standard of many of
the other cases. The court held that proof of a
present quantified risk was sufficient, even though
the risk was less than 51 percent. In this case, the
risk of future bowel obstruction was quantified at
between 8 and 16 percent. The court stated: "[A]
plaintiff who has established a breach of duty that
was a substantial factor in causing a present injury
which has resulted in an increased risk of future
harm is entitled to compensation to the extent that
the future harm is likely to occur." Thus, the
probability percentage was to be applied to the total
amount of damages that would be reasonable if the
plaintiff were to develop a bowel obstruction in the
future. The court did not address the res judicata
impact of its decision, but presumably it was fashioned so as to account for the plaintiff bringing an
action on the future injury after it occurred and
being able to recover the full amount of her damages less the percentage previously paid on the
increased risk claim.

C. MEDICAL MONITORING

Courts have been more receptive to claims for
medical monitoring, or medical surveillance, than
claims for increased risk. Generally, the medical
monitoring plaintiffs exhibit the same characteristics as those who bring increased risk claims—
showing some significant exposure, but often mani-
festing no physical symptoms of disease. The claim
for medical monitoring is for costs associated with

periodic medical examinations and diagnostic tests to detect the onset of disease at the earliest possible stage. It is prospective in nature. But it does not seek to compensate for any damages associated with the likelihood of contracting the disease in the future, nor does it compensate in any way for the plaintiff's fear of becoming ill. What it does have in common with increased risk claims, however, is that the basis for recovery is risk.

The focus of the court's inquiry in determining whether a claim for medical monitoring should be allowed is the necessity of the monitoring itself. Consequently, the level of risk that will form the basis of a medical monitoring award is a lesser level than required for most increased risk claims. Courts have used different terminology in articulating the test, but seem to agree that the plaintiff must show that the medical monitoring is reasonably necessary to diagnose the onset of disease. *See, e.g,* In re Paoli Railroad Yard PCB Litigation (3d Cir.1990) (predicting Pennsylvania law) (stating that medical monitoring must be necessary to a reasonable medical certainty); Ayers v. Township of Jackson (N.J.1987) (stating that medical monitoring must be reasonably necessary); Askey v. Occidental Chemical Corp. (N.Y.App.Div.1984) (stating that plaintiffs must establish to reasonable degree of medical certainty that expenditures for medical monitoring are reasonably anticipated to be incurred as a result of exposure).

Courts tend to agree on the elements of a case for medical monitoring expenses. While their language may differ, the same basic requirements are present. In re Paoli Railroad Yard PCB Litigation (3d Cir.1990) is representative of the approach taken by most courts. The court set forth the elements that the plaintiff must prove as follows:

1. Plaintiff was significantly exposed to a proven hazardous substance through the negligent actions of the defendant.

2. As a proximate result of exposure, plaintiff suffers a significantly increased risk of contracting a serious latent disease.

3. That increased risk makes periodic diagnostic medical examinations reasonably necessary.

4. Monitoring and testing procedures exist which make the early detection and treatment of the disease possible and beneficial.

Cf. Merry v. Westinghouse Electric Corp. (M.D.Pa. 1988) (providing that the three elements of medical monitoring claim are exposure to hazardous substance, "potential for injury," and need for early detection and treatment). The plaintiff need not show any present symptoms of illness. But in at least one jurisdiction, the plaintiff must have been *directly* exposed to the hazardous substance. *See* Theer v. Philip Carey Co. (N.J.1993) (holding that wife of asbestos worker, who was exposed to asbestos through washing husband's clothes, was an indirect exposure that did not qualify for medical monitoring damages). The elements of the claim must be proven through expert testimony.

There are several reasons behind the courts' receptivity to medical monitoring claims. First, courts dismissing various claims of toxic tort plaintiffs often express regret that the law provides no remedy for a particular claim. Medical monitoring claims provide some assistance to plaintiffs with significant exposures but who would not otherwise be able to maintain a present claim. Second, courts view medical monitoring as a much less costly alternative to increased risk claims, and one without the disadvantage of overcompensation to persons who ultimately never become ill. Third, the medical monitoring claims may deter defendants from engaging in negligent conduct. The initiation of some financial obligation on the part of the defendant soon after the release or other conduct that caused the exposure will apply more pressure to defendants than allowing them to be free of responsibility until the plaintiffs' illnesses become manifested. Finally, when exposed persons seek early diagnosis and treatment, many may be cured, thus advancing public health interests and reducing the overall future costs of claims.

How should the award for medical monitoring be paid? In *Ayers*, the court used its equitable powers to establish a court-supervised fund to administer the payments. The court noted the difficulty in awarding a lump-sum payment, because of the inability to predict the amounts that will be needed for the monitoring. A court-supervised fund, on the other hand, would limit payment to amounts actually spent. Further, payments typically are ordered to be made only for those extraordinary monitoring expenses that are associated with the defendant's conduct, and not for those medical tests and examinations that reasonable persons would be expected to undergo as a matter of course. *See* Potter v. Firestone Tire & Rubber Co. (Cal.1993).

Medical monitoring also has become an issue within the context of CERCLA. CERCLA provides that private parties may recover the "necessary costs of response" (i.e. cleanup) of a site. There has been a split among the decisions as to whether "necessary costs" include the medical monitoring expenses of private persons who were exposed to hazardous substances from the site. This split is another example of the tension between public law remedies and private law remedies in the law of toxic torts.

The court in Werlein v. United States (D.Minn. 1990) conducted a detailed analysis of the text of CERCLA in concluding that medical monitoring expenses were not recoverable by private parties as necessary costs of response. The *Werlein* court pointed to the fact that the definitional sections encompassing removal and remediation did not refer to medical monitoring expenses. The relevant sections do, however, make reference to steps that may be taken to prevent or mitigate damage to the public health. The court found that Congress did not intend that medical monitoring expenses be included in such steps because Congress had expressly included them in a completely different provision that was not applicable to the plaintiffs' claim. Section 104(i)(1) establishes the Agency for Toxic Substances and Disease Registry, which is authorized in cases of "public health emergencies" to provide medical care and testing to exposed persons. The court concluded that the express reference to medical testing in Section 104(i)(1), and the absence of such a reference in the sections defining response costs, indicated that Congress intended medical monitoring expenses to be excluded from recoverable costs of response. *See also* Woodman v. United States (M.D.Fla.1991) (holding that medical monitoring expenses were matters of private citizens' health and not "public health" matters under response costs provision of CERCLA).

Other courts have reached a different conclusion. In Brewer v. Ravan (M.D.Tenn.1988), the court found medical monitoring expenses necessary to "monitor, assess, and evaluate a release." Thus, such expenses were within the definition of "removal" pursuant to Section 101(23) of CERCLA and therefore an element of response costs. The court distinguished between those medical costs necessary to "assess the effect of the release or discharge on public health or to identify potential public health problems presented by the release," which were recoverable, and costs of treatment of personal injuries or disease caused by the release, which were not recoverable.

D. QUALITY OF LIFE

The Restatement (Second) of Torts § 929 (1979) states that one of the types of damages recoverable for invasions of an interest in property is damage for "discomfort and annoyance." Courts have held that diminution in the quality of life is recoverable as part of the damages for nuisance. In *Ayers, supra,* the plaintiffs complained that as a result of the contamination of their drinking water supply they suffered intolerable conditions from being cut off from their drinking water supplies and left without running drinking water for almost two years. Their complaints included general inconvenience, plus specific problems with obtaining drinking water from barrels supplied to them as a replacement for their usual supply. The court held that the plaintiffs' claims for diminished quality of life were associated with the interference with the use and enjoyment of their property.

The court in Sterling v. Velsicol Chemical Corp. (6th Cir.1988), in allowing a reduced quality of life claim, stated that even though nuisance is a property action, its basis is interference with the lives and well-being of the plaintiffs. The treatment of this type of injury as an aspect of nuisance implies that for damages for diminished quality of life to be recoverable, the plaintiff must demonstrate the elements of a claim for nuisance.

E.   PUNITIVE DAMAGES

Punitive damages are distinct from compensatory damages and are focused on the conduct of the defendant. They are viewed as a kind of quasi-criminal penalty within the civil justice system because of their punitive nature. There have been some challenges to the imposition of punitive damages in strict product liability cases on the basis that the conduct-based proof that is essential to a punitive damages claim is contradictory to the no-fault basis of strict liability. Such challenges have been rebuffed. *See, e.g.*, Jackson v. Johns–Manville Sales Corp. (5th Cir.1986).

Punitive damages claims generally require a showing of egregious conduct on the part of the defendant. Typically, this requirement is satisfied by intentional or reckless conduct, but it may also be satisfied by malicious or grossly negligent conduct. Moreover, a fair number of states have enacted laws that establish a standard of clear and convincing evidence for proof of a punitive damages claim. *See, e.g.*, Alaska Stat. § 09.17.020 (1994); Cal. Civ. Code § 3294 (West 1970 & Supp. 1995); Ky. Rev. Stat. Ann. § 411.184 (Baldwin 1994).

After a determination is made that the standard for an award of punitive damages has been met, the jury then sets the amount of the punitive damages. The standard used by the jury in setting the amount is based upon a determination of the amount necessary to both punish and deter the defendant. The defendant may introduce evidence of its financial worth in mitigation of the damages. The goal of punitive damages is not to drive the defendant company out of business, although many defendants have complained that punitive damages do have that effect, particularly in the context of mass tort litigation.

In Johns–Manville Sales Corp. v. Janssens (Fla. Dist.Ct.App.1984), the court enumerated the following factors typically to be considered in deciding the punitive damages award: (1) the plaintiffs' litigation expenses; (2) the degree of hazard to the public posed by the defendant's conduct; (3) the extent to which the defendant profited from its misconduct; (4) the general attitude and course of conduct of the defendant; (5) the status and number of personnel involved in the conduct giving rise to the punitive damages award; (6) the extent of the conduct and whether the defendant engaged in a coverup; (7) the financial worth of the defendant; and (8) any other sources of punishment for the same conduct.

1. Punitive Damages and Toxic Torts

Some defendants have raised objections to awards of punitive damages in toxic tort actions on the ground that their allowance is fundamentally unfair. In Fischer v. Johns–Manville Corp. (N.J. 1986), a case brought by an asbestos worker, the court rejected several of these arguments. First, the defendants argued that the latent nature of the illness associated with exposure to hazardous substances such as asbestos meant that by the time a punitive award is imposed many years may have passed. This passage of time may result in the defendant's earlier conduct being punished in light of later-learned information about the hazards of that conduct. The *Fischer* court rejected this "changing social values" argument. The plaintiff in *Fischer* alleged that the defendant asbestos manufacturers knew of the hazards associated with exposure to asbestos when he worked in the industry during the 1940s, but that they failed to provide any warnings or safety instructions. The court found that the defendant had knowledge of the hazards of asbestos by the mid–1930s. The court stated: "We cannot imagine that the conduct proven in this case would have been viewed as any less egregious in the 1940's, when the exposure commenced, than it is today."

Second, the defendant argued that because different corporate personnel were in place at the time of the conduct than at the time of the lawsuit, a punitive damages award would not punish the true offenders. The court discounted this argument by pointing to the fact that a corporation is a distinct legal entity, independent of the persons acting within it, and by punishing the corporation the goal of general deterrence would be achieved. *See also* Johns–Manville Sales Corp. v. Janssens (Fla.Dist. Ct.App.1984). Nor would shareholders be wrongly punish by the imposition of punitive damages on the corporation. The court noted that the sales of a harmful product by the corporation would benefit the shareholders; thus, if they can participate in the profits, so too should they be required to participate in the penalties.

2. Judicial Review of Punitive Damages Awards

In a series of opinions over several terms, the United States Supreme Court addressed constitu-

tional challenges to the propriety of awards of punitive damages. In the first case, Browning–Ferris
Industries of Vermont, Inc. v. Kelco Disposal, Inc.
(S.Ct.1989), the Court held that the Excessive Fines
Clause of the Eighth Amendment to the U.S. Constitution did not apply to punitive damages claims
between private parties. The Court stated that the
Clause "was intended to limit only those fines directly imposed by, and payable to, the government."

The other decisions focused on due process challenges to punitive damages awards. In an important watershed opinion, the Court established the
due process standard for review of an award of
punitive damages. Pacific Mutual Life Insurance
Company v. Haslip (S.Ct.1991) arose from a claim
of fraud by an insurance agent in the collecting and
processing of insurance premiums. The plaintiffs'
health insurance coverage was terminated as a result of misappropriation of the premiums by the
agent. The Court approved the Alabama process
for review of punitive damages and upheld the
punitive damages award. The Court stated that
there is no bright line between an award that is
constitutionally acceptable and one that is not.
Rather, a general standard of reasonableness should
apply.

The Court first found the Alabama trial court's
jury instructions to be reasonable. The instructions required the jury to determine an amount that
was sufficient to punish and deter, considering the
character and degree of the wrongful conduct and
the need to deter similar conduct. Next, the Court

examined the Alabama post-trial procedures for scrutinizing punitive damages awards. The procedure was two-tiered: first, the trial court reviewed the jury's award for excessiveness, and then, the appellate court conducted its own independent review. In *Haslip*, the Court held that this review process satisfactorily assured that the punitive damages award was not excessively disproportionate to the reprehensible character of the defendant's conduct.

One of the questions that arose after *Haslip* was whether a state's punitive damages review procedure must be identical to—or more protective of defendants than—the Alabama provisions. In general, however, most state review procedures have been upheld in the wake of *Haslip*. The punitive damages award in *Haslip* was roughly four times the amount of the compensatory award. The Court commented that this ratio "may be close to the line" of due process, but found that it "did not lack objective criteria." In light of this, some courts have found punitive awards that exceeded that ratio to be excessive. *See, e.g.*, Alexander & Alexander Inc. v. B. Dixon Evander & Assoc., Inc. (Md.Ct.Spec. App.1991) (holding that punitive award approximately 50 times compensatory award is excessive).

In TXO Productions Corp. v. Alliance Resources Corp. (S.Ct.1993), the Supreme Court addressed the question of the relationship between compensatory damages and punitive damages. The case involved certain oil and gas rights in West Virginia. The compensatory award of $19,000 was in favor of the defendant on a counterclaim. The jury also award the defendant $10 million in punitive damages—526 times the compensatory award. In holding that the award did not violate due process, the Supreme Court found it appropriate to consider the broad effect of potential harm that could be caused by the defendant's conduct. The Court stated: "[W]e do not consider the dramatic disparity between the actual damages and the punitive award controlling in a case of this character." Further, the Court found it "appropriate to consider the magnitude of the potential harm that the defendant's conduct would have caused to its intended victim if the wrongful plan had succeeded, as well as the possible harm to other victims that might have resulted if similar future behavior were not deterred."

TXO is of particular interest for toxic tort cases. If juries are permitted to consider the potential for further harm that might have arisen from the defendant's conduct, then it would seem that the potential for punitive damages liability for some toxic tort defendants could be virtually endless. In any event, in *TXO*, the Court again refused to draw any bright line for due process purposes. An award of punitive damages must be reviewed under all the appropriate factors to determine its fairness. No specific ratio will be the magic formula. If no compensatory damages are awarded, however, an award of punitive damages will probably not be appropriate. *See* Oliver v. Raymark Industries (3d Cir.1986) (applying New Jersey law).

In yet another decision exploring the due process scope of punitive damages, the Supreme Court this time invalidated a state procedure governing review of punitive damages awards. In Honda Motor Co. v. Oberg (S.Ct.1994), a product liability case, the Court took to task an Oregon procedure that virtually eliminated post-verdict review of the amount of a punitive damages award. The Court noted that "if the defendant's only basis for relief is the amount of punitive damages the jury awarded, Oregon provides no procedure for reducing or setting aside that award." The only review that Oregon required was a determination that at least some evidence support a punitive damages award. Beyond that, no judicial review occurred. The Oregon courts had interpreted *Haslip* as not requiring post-verdict review as a component of due process, particularly in light of the fact that other procedural safeguards were built into the system. The Supreme Court emphasized the need for judicial review of an award of punitive damages as "a safeguard against excessive verdicts" under the common law and held that the Oregon scheme violated due process.

3. Multiple Punitive Awards for the Same Conduct

Notwithstanding the intense attention given by the Supreme Court to the due process parameters of punitive damages awards, the Court has not yet addressed one of the thorniest issues in the toxic tort context. This issue is the due process propri-

ety of multiple punitive damages awards against the
same defendant for the same conduct. The classic
example is that of the asbestos industry. Repeated
punitive damages awards have been assessed
against the same asbestos manufacturers in cases
brought by different plaintiffs, all arising out of the
same general course of conduct in failing to make
known the hazards of asbestos at a time when the
industry first became aware of the danger and in
failing to provide instructions for safe handling of
the asbestos-containing materials. The asbestos
manufacturers' objections to such multiple awards
were not merely grounded in the fairness question.
The manufacturers also faced the prospect of insol-
vency if forced to pay a continuing series of punitive
awards of the magnitude of the awards already
made.

An early case that voiced concern for multiple
awards for a single course of conduct was Roginsky
v. Richardson–Merrell, Inc. (2d Cir.1967). That
case involved claims against the manufacturer of an
anti-cholesterol drug known as MER/29. The court
dismissed the punitive damages claim, but expressed concern about the possibility of punitive
damages "overkill" when multiple plaintiffs sue a
single defendant for the same conduct. The court
was concerned that if awards in future actions were
for similar amounts to the few MER/29 cases that
had already reached verdict, the aggregate effect
would be excessive. In addition, the court saw the
multiple punitive award system as unfair, providing
a windfall for early plaintiffs who might obtain

large awards, but perhaps causing courts to cut off future punitive awards at some point.

Other courts have expressed concern over the due process implications of multiple punitive awards for the same conduct. In the Agent Orange litigation, Judge Weinstein stated that as a matter of both due process requirements and public policy, some limit should be placed upon the number of times a defendant may be punished for the same conduct. In re "Agent Orange" Prod. Liab. Litig. (E.D.N.Y 1983). Cf. In re Northern Dist. of California, "Dalkon Shield" IUD Prods. Liab. Litig. (9th Cir.1982) (noting district court's attempt to ensure that defendant would be punished only once, but stating that class action is not the only way to protect defendant).

Due process challenges to multiple awards generally have met with resistance in the courts. In Leonen v. Johns–Manville Corp. (D.N.J.1989), an asbestos case decided before *Haslip*, the court held that it was not a violation of due process to award multiple punitive damages for the same conduct. The court accepted the need to impose some due process limits on the amounts of punitive damages awards. But the court was concerned that if punitive damages are limited to a single award, the first plaintiff to the courthouse arbitrarily becomes the one to benefit from the award. The court also emphasized the deterrence value of multiple awards. *See also* Dunn v. HOVIC (3d Cir.1993); W.R. Grace & Co. v. Waters (Fla.1994); Kochan v. Owens–Corning Fiberglass Corp. (Ill.Ct.App.1993).

In McBride v. General Motors Corp. (M.D.Ga.1990), a non-toxic tort product liability case, the court also expressed concern about the windfall to the first plaintiff. In _McBride_, the court held unconstitutional a Georgia statute that limited punitive damages to a single award. Among other things, the court held that the statute violated equal protection by discriminating between first plaintiffs and all others.

Not all courts have so unconditionally upheld multiple punitive awards, however. In fact, in another asbestos case decided shortly before _Leonen_, Juzwin v. Amtorg Trading Corp. (D.N.J.1989), the same court, by a different judge, held that the due process clause of the Constitution required that punitive damages be limited to one award per course of conduct. Upon reconsideration, however, the court vacated its decision, while reaffirming its general holding that multiple awards violated due process. The court felt that it was unfair to preclude the current plaintiffs from receiving punitive damages without prior notice. Moreover, the court stated that limitation of punitive damages to a single award would be impracticable until uniform laws were in place to assure that due process was consistent from jurisdiction to jurisdiction. The court noted that some states already limit punitive damages in some fashion—e.g. by caps or by requiring a certain ratio between compensatory damages and punitive damages. A single award in those states may not be intended to fully punish and deter; thus, a subsequent punitive damages award may not violate due process in those jurisdictions. The court reasoned that because asbestos litigation against the same defendants tends to occur across many different jurisdictions, lack of uniformity in the law of punitive damages is an impediment to implementing due process restrictions on awards.

Accordingly, the court proposed a series of factors for use in subsequent proceedings to determine whether punitive damages should be limited to the earlier award. First, the prior proceeding must have considered all evidence concerning the conduct of the defendant. Second, there must have been an opportunity for similarly situated plaintiffs to participate in the punitive damages portion of the proceeding. Third, the court must have instructed the jury that the award in that proceeding would be the only award allowed. In addition, anything else that would assure a full evaluation of all relevant evidence must have been considered. Recognizing that this is a tall order, the court acknowledged that these criteria had probably not been met in any prior proceeding and admitted that it was "powerless to fashion a remedy" under the circumstances.

The *Juzwin* court's exercise in frustration points out the complexity of the issues involved in a due process challenge to multiple punitive damages awards. Courts recognize the inequity in allowing multiple awards, but are powerless to enforce an alternative. Moreover, the available alternatives carry their own problems.

Some remedial proposals have been floated in addition to limiting punitive damages to a single award. To be effective, however, many of these proposals require uniformity among the states, an accomplishment that is widely acknowledged as unlikely to occur. One such proposal is to set an individual cap on the punitive damages allowed for each plaintiff. *See* Fischer v. Johns–Manville Corp. (N.J.1986) (stating that such a cap would be ineffective unless applied uniformly). An aggregate cap is another suggestion, but this solution would create the same race to the courthouse as the single-award solution. Efforts to limit punitive damages to an amount that reflects the harm to the *particular* plaintiff would be difficult to enforce, as the jury would probably need to hear all evidence relevant to the scope of the defendant's conduct in any event. Most observers agree that some means to aggregate all punitive damages claims in one proceeding is the best approach. *See* Chapter Nine, Sec. A(4)(c), *infra*.

4. Legislative Punitive Damages Reform

Substantial legislative activity has occurred at the state level with respect to punitive damages. These reforms have taken several approaches. First, states have enacted various provisions directed at tightening the circumstances under which punitive damages will be available. For example, several states have elevated the standard for proving a punitive damages claim to that of "clear and convincing" evidence. *See, e.g.*, Cal. Civ. Code § 3294

(West 1970 & Supp. 1995); Ky. Rev. Stat. Ann. § 09.17.020 (Baldwin 1994). In addition, a few states have codified a type of "government standards" defense, according to which, in certain kinds of cases, the defendant's compliance with government regulatory standards will operate as a defense to punitive damages claims. *See, e.g.*, Ariz. Rev. Stat. Ann. § 12–701(A) (1992) (FDA approval of drugs); Utah Code Ann. § 78–18–2(1)(a) (1992) (FDA approval).

Second, states have also enacted provisions to limit awards once a determination is made that punitive damages are appropriate. In Colorado, for example, the legislature has enacted a provision limiting a punitive damages award to the equivalent of the amount of the compensatory damages recovered by the particular plaintiff. Colo. Rev. Stat. § 13–21–102(1) (1989). States have also imposed absolute monetary caps on punitive damages awards. *See, e.g.*, Ala. Code § 6–11–21 (1993) ($250,000 per case); Tex. Civ. Prac. & Rem. Code Ann. § 41.007 (West Supp. 1995) (greater of four times compensatory damages or $200,000). Some states have established more creative reforms. In Kansas, the legislature has capped punitive damages at the amount of the defendant's annual gross income or $5 million, whichever is less. Kan. Stat. Ann. § 60–3701(e) (Supp. 1993). In some states, a portion of the punitive damages award will go to a state fund or to a designated public project. *See, e.g.*, Iowa Code Ann. § 668A.1(2)(b) (West 1987) (75% of punitive damages award must go to State

Civil Reparations Trust Fund). In New Hampshire, punitive damages are no longer allowed. N.H. Rev. Stat. Ann. § 507:16 (Supp. 1994).

Third, some states have enacted other procedural requirements for the handling of punitive damages claims. Thus, some states have enacted provisions for bifurcated trials to allow for the separate trial of punitive damages. *See, e.g.,* N.J. Stat. Ann. § 2A:58C–5 (West 1987). In Ohio, the judge has the authority to set the amount of punitive damages. Ohio Rev. Code Ann. § 2307.80(B) (Anderson 1991).

At least one state has addressed the due process question of the propriety of multiple punitive awards against the same defendant arising out of the same conduct. In Georgia, the legislature has enacted a requirement limiting punitive damages to one award per defendant per product. Ga. Code Ann. § 51–12–5.1(e)(1) (Michie Supp. 1994).

In addition to state legislative reforms, punitive damages have been targeted by those who seek federal reforms of product liability law. Various bills introduced in Congress have contained caps on punitive damages awards as well as other restrictions. While federal action would have the advantage of creating uniformity, many have not been persuaded by the merits of the individual proposals. There is every reason to believe that supporters of punitive damages reform will continue to propose measures for Congressional consideration.

CHAPTER NINE

MASS TOXIC TORTS

Toxic substance litigation has transformed the legal system. Professors Marcus and Sherman have identified three characteristics of modern complex litigation, all of which are particularly descriptive of mass toxic torts. First, they observe that the courts, and more frequently the federal courts, are being used to resolve disputes involving multi-faceted, problematic substantive issues, such as those of science and technology. This has inevitably led to the creation of new types of actions. Second, the numbers of parties have multiplied, creating new procedural issues and challenging case management. Third, the monetary stakes in litigation are much higher now, particularly with the increase in punitive damages awards. Richard L. Marcus & Edward F. Sherman, Complex Litigation: Cases and Materials on Advanced Civil Procedure 1–2 (2d ed. 1992).

Mass toxic torts reflect these characteristics. The problems of latent disease claims create challenges in the use of scientific evidence and the application of traditional causes of action to novel circumstances. The monetary stakes in mass toxic tort litigation are not just reflected in the amounts of jury awards. Attorney fees, expert witness fees, and other costs of litigation also can be enormous. The vast numbers of parties in actions such as asbestos claims make it necessary to fashion mechanisms for processing these claims, while avoiding duplicative efforts and maintaining due process.

It has become a matter of consensus that in much mass toxic tort litigation, some form of aggregative procedure is essential to achieve the goals of efficiency and consistency. It is crucial to the effective operation of the judicial system, however, that individualized justice not be totally abandoned in an effort to achieve judicial economy. As the court in Malcolm v. National Gypsum Co. (2d Cir.1993), stated in reversing the district court's consolidation of 600 asbestos cases: "The systemic urge to aggregate litigation must not be allowed to trump our dedication to individual justice, and we must take care that each individual plaintiff's—and defendant's—cause not be lost in the shadow of a towering mass litigation."

While the class action device often tends to be the most high profile aggregative procedure, it is by no means the only one. Multidistrict litigation transfer and consolidation have been used very effectively in some mass torts. This chapter begins with a look at these aggregative procedures in the mass toxic tort context. A pivotal issue in the decision to aggregate involves a determination of whether the parties' interests in individualized adjudication outweigh the system's interest in aggregation.

A. CLASS ACTIONS

When the Advisory Committee to the 1966 amendments to Rule 23 of the Federal Rules of Civil Procedure stated that the class action device was not appropriate for mass torts, the Committee was contemplating a completely different type of mass tort. The mass accidents of the 1960s, confined in space and time, were very different from the latent disease claims of the 1990s. Now, it is generally agreed that the class action device may be an appropriate method of managing certain kinds of mass tort litigation. Class actions not only serve the goals of efficiency and conservation of resources, but they also provide a means of representation for a class of persons who may not otherwise pursue their legal claims. In a class action, the class may consist of plaintiffs or defendants. Because most toxic tort claims for which class certification is sought involve plaintiff classes, this section will focus exclusively on the plaintiff class. In a class action, one or several persons bring the action on behalf of the class. These persons are called the class representatives, and they and their attorneys determine the course of the litigation, the result of which becomes binding on all class members (sometimes referred to as absent class members) who have not chosen to opt out of the class action (where opting out is available).

Although procedures for certifying class actions exist under both federal and state law, this chapter employs the federal class action device, as set forth in Rule 23 of the Federal Rules of Civil Procedure, as a model for understanding the procedural requirements and issues inherent in the mechanism. The Agent Orange litigation provides a well-documented example of the use of the class action device in mass toxic tort litigation in federal court. It serves as a perfect example of the problems and advantages of managing mass toxic torts in a class action. To best understand the procedural and substantive issues that made this litigation so challenging, it is useful to examine the factual context that gave rise to the class's claims as well as the history of the litigation.

1. Agent Orange Litigation

Between 1962 and 1970, approximately five million acres in Vietnam were sprayed with the herbicide 2,4,5–trichlorophenoxyacetic acid, commonly referred to as 2,4,5–T or "Agent Orange." The aerosol was used in United States military operations for aerial defoliation of large areas of land to improve visibility of Vietcong forces and to facilitate the movement of refugees away from areas in Communist control. In 1966, studies began to show that the herbicide was contaminated with dioxin, a highly toxic byproduct of the manufacturing process. Studies further indicated that Agent Orange was associated with birth defects in laboratory animals. In 1970, American armed forces ceased using Agent Orange in Vietnam operations, although the compound continued to be used, with restrictions, in residential areas and on farms in the United

States. *See* Thomas Whiteside, The Pendulum and the Toxic Cloud (1979) (discussing the uses and hazards of Agent Orange and related herbicides). Substantial scientific debate has continued over the extent of the hazard posed by Agent Orange and dioxin.

In 1979, a class action lawsuit was filed on behalf of Vietnam veterans and their families. The plaintiffs described the class as "all those so unfortunate as to have been and now to be situated at risk, not only during this generation but during generations to come." The action named Dow Chemical Company, Monsanto, and several other chemical manufacturers as defendants. Ultimately, the class encompassed 2.4 million Vietnam veterans, plus their families. The complaint presented straightforward product liability claims, but the case created numerous problems involving use of the class action device, judicial management of complex toxic tort litigation, settlement, and other legal issues. During its history, the case went through two federal judges and cost the veterans' lawyers untold amounts of time and money in an extremely risky endeavor. The best history of the Agent Orange litigation is presented in Peter H. Schuck, Agent Orange on Trial: Mass Toxic Disasters in the Courts (1986).

The defendant chemical companies had been under contract with the United States Government to manufacture the Agent Orange used in the Vietnam military operations. The United States was not named as a defendant, mostly because of the *Feres* doctrine exception to the Federal Torts Claims Act. *See generally* Chapter Five, Sec. A(2)(b), *supra*. The veterans also needed the cooperation of the Government in their suit against the manufacturers, and naming the Government as a defendant would have created an adversarial relationship that would have rendered cooperation impossible. *See generally* Peter H. Schuck, *supra*.

Originally, Judge Pratt rendered a decision that a class should be certified. *See* In re "Agent Orange" Prod. Liab. Litig. (E.D.N.Y.1980). In so holding, he examined the policies supporting the use of the class action device in the case. First, he determined that at least at the early stage of the litigation, the class members' interests in individually controlling their separate claims were minimal. Second, the class action device would serve the goal of judicial economy. Third, any problems associated with judicial management of the class action were outweighed by the problems of using any other management device.

When Judge Weinstein assumed control of the Agent Orange case, he noted that no formal certification order had been entered pursuant to Judge Pratt's certification decision. Accordingly, Judge Weinstein revisited the class certification issue and certified the class. *See* In re "Agent Orange" Prod. Liab. Litig. (E.D.N.Y.1983).

In 1984, the action settled for $180 million, due primarily to the managerial efforts of the Honorable Jack B. Weinstein of the United States District

Court for the Eastern District of New York, the judge then assigned to the case. In approving the settlement, Judge Weinstein expressed the opinion that the plaintiff class's foreseeable problems in proving causation made it likely that they would lose at trial. Accordingly, the settlement was deemed to be fair to the class. Veterans have objected to the settlement, but no legal challenge has been found valid. *See* In re "Agent Orange" Prod. Liab. Litig. (E.D.N.Y.1984). Moreover, those veterans who had chosen to opt out of the class action during the period allowed for opting out and who have pursued independent legal claims against the chemical manufacturers have not met with any success. One reason for this was that Judge Weinstein retained jurisdiction over the opt-out claims which he has routinely dismissed for lack of causation, among other issues. *See* In re "Agent Orange" Prod. Liab. Litig. (E.D.N.Y.1985).

More recent events have continued to raise questions about the use of Agent Orange. Charges that the chemical companies produced biased studies regarding the safety of the herbicide led to a Congressional investigation of the circumstances surrounding the manufacture of the herbicide for the Government. In addition, some more recent medical studies have renewed the suggestion of a causal connection between exposure to Agent Orange and the illnesses from which the veterans have suffered. The Veterans Administration, which is charged with providing administrative compensation to veterans suffering injuries related to military service,

had steadfastly refused to consider any claims for
injuries from exposure to Agent Orange with the
exception of those for chloracne (an inflammatory
skin condition) and one other ailment. In recent
years, however, and in response to more recent
medical studies, the V.A. has agreed to compensate
veterans administratively for certain other designated—and serious—illnesses.

2. Certification Requirement

A case cannot proceed as a class action in federal
court unless expressly certified as one by the court.
Rule 23(c)(1) requires that "[a]s soon as practicable
after the commencement of an action brought as a
class action, the court shall determine by order
whether it is to be so maintained." When a federal
court has issued a class certification decision, the
process of handling the litigation as a class action is
intended to be a flexible one. Rule 23(c)(1) provides that a class certification order "may be conditional, and may be altered or amended before the
decision on the merits." This permits the court to
shape the procedural mechanisms to respond to the
unique issues of a particular class action.

3. Prerequisites to a Class Action

By definition, class actions challenge due process.
They are capable of binding absent class members
to whatever judgment is reached, without complete
individualized resolution of their claims. Accordingly, Rule 23 contains a series of prerequisites
designed to ensure that the action is appropriate for
class adjudication. In addition, a further, implicit,

requirement is that an appropriately defined class be identified.

a. Identifying the Class

Rule 23 presupposes that an appropriate class is available. In toxic tort actions, the definition of the class may pose certain problems. This is especially true because tort law tends to be a creature of state law, but mass toxic torts often have a nationwide effect. Despite problems relating to causation as well as the vast numbers of class members, the Agent Orange litigation was certified as a class action. *See* In re "Agent Orange" Prod. Liab. Litig. (E.D.N.Y.1983). Judge Weinstein defined the class as those members of the United States, New Zealand, and Australia armed forces in or near Vietnam between 1961 and 1972 who were injured by exposure to Agent Orange or other phenoxy herbicides. The class was defined as those who claimed injury, rather than the broader category of those who were exposed.

The issue of whether the class can encompass claims of persons who were exposed to a particular substance, but do not claim present injury, was addressed in McElhaney v. Eli Lilly & Co. (D.S.D. 1982). In that case, the class proposed by the plaintiffs was defined as persons exposed to DES "who presently reside in South Dakota." The court expressed concern that the class sought to be certified was only described as those who were *exposed*, and that only some of that group of persons would have manifested injury. The court stated: "It is highly likely that a substantial number of persons in the proposed class would not know whether they were members of such a class, since they do not suffer from any apparent injury, and do not know whether their mothers took DES while pregnant." A second concern voiced by the court was that the proposed class was to encompass exposed persons *born* in South Dakota. The court speculated that these persons' mothers—the persons who ingested the DES—likely were all over the United States and may not be able to be located.

The *McElhaney* court held that the class was not adequately defined, thus rendering class certification inappropriate. The court's true concerns went beyond matters of geography to matters inherent in the nature of toxic torts. The court was bothered by the fact that many of the class members were not suffering from current physical illnesses. The court couched this in terms of "standing," finding that as a result, many of the class members would not have standing to sue. One might argue that the court was inappropriately pre-judging the validity of the plaintiffs' claims at this early stage. But if the class is defined to include only those who currently manifest illness, the defendant may eventually be subject to many future claims, thus diminishing the benefits of having a class action in the first place.

b. *Numerosity*

The first explicit prerequisite of a federal class action is numerosity of the class. *See* Fed. R. Civ.

P. 23(a). The class must be so numerous that use of traditional joinder devices would be impracticable. Judge Pratt determined that this was the case in the Agent Orange litigation, which involved a class of more than two million persons. There is no bright line identifying when numerosity exists. And it is not necessary for the plaintiffs to identify the class members. Indeed, inability to identify the specific class members makes the class action device preferable because joinder would be impracticable under those circumstances. *See* Doe v. Charleston Area Medical Center, Inc. (4th Cir.1975).

c. *Commonality*

The second prerequisite to a class action identified in Rule 23(a) is commonality. Commonality requires that questions of law or fact common to the class are presented by the action. This is just a general screening requirement, and at this stage there is no mandate that the common questions predominate over individual questions. It merely suffices that some common questions of law or fact exist.

In the Agent Orange litigation, the court identified questions of both law and fact that were suitable for a collective decision. These included the government contractor defense, general causation, and the determination whether Agent Orange was a defective product. *See* In re "Agent Orange" Prod. Liab. Litig. (E.D.N.Y.1980). In general, the court believed that most of the affirmative defenses could be handled on a class-wide basis.

d. Typicality

The typicality requirement of Rule 23(a) assures that the representative plaintiffs' claims are typical of the claims held by the class members. Differences among the claims of the class members will not necessarily render class treatment impossible. Rule 23(c)(4) makes clear that a class action may proceed on particular issues or that the class may be divided into subclasses, with each subclass being subject to the provisions of Rule 23 for class actions generally. In the Agent Orange litigation, Judge Pratt rendered his decision on this prerequisite before the class representatives had been named. He expressed confidence, however, that out of the vast number of class members, representatives with claims typical of the various injuries could easily be found.

e. Adequacy of Representation

This prerequisite is intended to assure that the class representatives "will fairly and adequately protect the interests of the class." Fed.R.Civ.P. 23(a)(4). This prerequisite necessarily generates concern about the attorneys who represent the class. The court will be concerned that the representatives' attorneys have an interest in representing the class members and that they have the skill and resources to adequately do so. The court will want to be assured that the class representatives will fully pursue claims and appeals in which the class has an interest and that no conflict of interest exists between the representatives and the class.

Adequacy of representation is especially subject to re-evaluation later in the litigation when the circumstances of the parties may change. In the Agent Orange litigation, Judge Weinstein noted the causation problem and ordered the plaintiffs' counsel to choose a representative claimant for each type of injury alleged. Moreover, the court identified appropriate counsel that it believed had the requisite experience and expertise to adequately represent the interests of the class.

4. Types of Class Actions

Rule 23(b) sets forth descriptions of several kinds of class actions that may be certified following the court's finding that the 23(a) prerequisites have been met. The action must fit into one of the 23(b) categories to be maintainable as a federal class action. In toxic tort litigation, the 23(b)(1)(B) and 23(b)(3) class actions have received the most attention. This section will describe all four categories, with emphasis on the foregoing two types.

a. *General Provisions*

Rule 23(b) provides that a class action may be certified where:

(1) the prosecution of separate actions by or against individual members of the class would create a risk of

    (A) inconsistent or varying adjudications with respect to individual members of the class which would establish incompatible standards of conduct for the party opposing the class, or

 (B) adjudications with respect to individual members of the class which would as a practical matter be dispositive of the interests of the other members not parties to the adjudications or substantially impair or impede their ability to protect their interests; or

(2) the party opposing the class has acted or refused to act on grounds generally applicable to the class, thereby making appropriate final injunctive relief or corresponding declaratory relief with respect to the class as a whole; or

(3) the court finds that the questions of law or fact common to the members of the class predominate over any questions affecting only individual members, and that a class action is superior to other available methods for the fair and efficient adjudication of the controversy.

The class actions described in sections (b)(1) and (b)(2) are mandatory class actions, i.e. actions in which all class members are bound and none is permitted to be excluded from the judgment. A 23(b)(3) class action permits class members to opt out of the action, within a certain period of time after certification as set by the court, and to proceed with an individual action.

b. *Rule 23(b)(1)(A) Class Actions*

The types of actions set forth in 23(b)(1) address some of the difficulties that arise if individual actions by members of the class go forward. Thus, 23(b)(1)(A) is concerned that the party opposing the class action (the defendant, for the present purposes) not be held to conflicting standards of conduct by incompatible results of individual lawsuits. Although this would appear to fit with mass tort actions, the Advisory Committee seems to have had a different type of action in mind. Some examples given in the Advisory Committee notes are "[s]eparate actions by individuals against a municipality to declare a bond issue invalid ... [or] to prevent or limit the making of a particular appropriation or to compel or invalidate an assessment .... " Fed. R. Civ. P. 23, adv. comm. note. Rule 23(b)(1)(A) actions may not be appropriate in actions for money damages. *See* La Mar v. H & B Novelty & Loan Co. (9th Cir.1973) (stating that "the defendants in [money damages actions] can continue the conduct of which the plaintiffs complain even if the plaintiffs are successful ... in their individual actions" and plaintiffs' success "does not fix the rights and duties owed by the defendants to others").

In a mass accident case arising out of the collapse of skywalks in the lobby of the Hyatt Regency Hotel in Kansas City, the district court initially certified a 23(b)(1)(A) class action, finding that a mass tort action fit the requirements of the rule. The decision was later vacated. *See* In re Federal Skywalk Cases (W.D.Mo.1982). Some have suggested that if

23(b)(1)(A) were intended to apply to actions such as the *Hyatt Regency* litigation, the rule would necessarily encompass all money damages actions that involved multiple plaintiffs—a result undoubtedly not contemplated by the rulemakers. *See* Richard L. Marcus & Edward F. Sherman, Complex Litigation: Cases and Materials on Advanced Civil Procedure 353 (2d ed. 1992). The court in the Agent Orange litigation expressed this view. Judge Pratt stated that 23(b)(1)(B) was "*not* meant to apply ... where the risk of inconsistent results in individual actions is merely the possibility that the defendants will prevail in some cases and not in others, thereby paying damages to some claimants and not others." In re "Agent Orange" Prod. Liab. Litig. (E.D.N.Y.1980). Judge Weinstein endorsed this view, noting that if the rule were applied in such a manner, virtually every class action could be a 23(b)(1)(A) class action, a result clearly not intended.

The permissible uses, if any, of 23(b)(1)(A) class actions for toxic tort litigation must await further definition. For the time being, however, courts are taking a conservative approach toward this type of class action, as evidenced by the Agent Orange litigation.

c. *Rule 23(b)(1)(B) Class Actions*

The interests sought to be protected in a 23(b)(1)(B) class action differ from the interests in a 23(b)(1)(A) class action. This kind of class action acknowledges that in some instances, if an action proceeds on an individual basis, later claimants may be prejudiced by an inability to collect on their judgments against the defendants. This is called a "limited fund" class action because it is sometimes invoked in situations in which judgments in favor of early claimants could deplete the defendant's resources, thus leaving later claimants unable to obtain compensation for their injuries. *See* Fed. R. Civ. P. 23, adv. comm. note.

The 23(b)(1)(B) class action has found a use in mass toxic tort litigation, particularly for punitive damages claims. The Dalkon Shield litigation and the Agent Orange litigation show two different attitudes toward its use.

In In re Northern District of California "Dalkon Shield" IUD Prods. Liab. Litig. (9th Cir.1982), the court found error in the district court's certification of a (b)(1)(B) class for punitive damages. The litigation arose out of the use of the Dalkon Shield intrauterine device by women who later claimed an assortment of serious injuries associated with its use. Taking note of the fact that over one thousand lawsuits had already been filed against the device's manufacturer, A.H. Robins, the district court conditionally certified a nationwide punitive damages class under 23(b)(1)(B), as well as a statewide class action on the issue of Robins's liability under 23(b)(3).

On interlocutory appeal from the district court's denial of a motion by some of the plaintiffs to decertify the punitive damages class, the Ninth Circuit held that class certification had been improper. The Ninth Circuit was especially concerned with the lack of documentation as to whether later claims would in fact be impaired if the actions were allowed to proceed individually. The district court had certified the "limited fund" class action without having before it sufficient information regarding the finances, including insurance coverage, of Robins. Moreover, the record was silent on the number of Dalkon Shield claims against Robins that had already been paid. The court stated: "Rule 23(b)(1)(B) certification is proper only when separate punitive damage claims necessarily will affect later claims. The district court erred by ordering certification without sufficient evidence of, or even a preliminary fact-finding inquiry concerning Robins' actual assets, insurance, settlement experience and continuing exposure." Several other federal courts have denied certification of 23(b)(1)(B) class actions for essentially the same reasons. *See* In re Bendectin Prods. Liab. Litig. (6th Cir.1984); In re "Agent Orange" Prod. Liab. Litig. (E.D.N.Y.1980) (in which Judge Pratt originally refused to certify a 23(b)(1)(B) class action).

In the Agent Orange litigation, Judge Weinstein ultimately certified a 23(b)(1)(B) class action for punitive damages. Judge Weinstein disagreed with the standard set forth by the Ninth Circuit in the Dalkon Shield case. Whereas the Ninth Circuit required proof that individual claims "necessarily will affect later claims," Judge Weinstein applied a "probable risk" standard. This standard required a showing only that there was a "substantial probability" that damages paid to early claimants would deplete the assets of the defendants. Judge Weinstein stated that a "substantial probability" can exist where there is less than a preponderance but more than a mere possibility. Upon a hearing before a master, defendants submitted financial information and the court concluded that a substantial risk of exhaustion of the defendants' assets existed with respect to the punitive damages claims. The court expressed the opinion that punitive damages should not be awarded against the defendants, but nevertheless stated that because a substantial probability existed that punitive damages might still be awarded, nothing prevented the court from certifying the 23(b)(1)(B) class for punitive damages.

Rule 23(b)(1)(B) class actions for punitive damages in mass toxic tort litigation solve some of the problems associated with punitive damages awards. The mandatory nature of the (b)(1)(B) class action would assure that only a single punitive damages award would be assessed against the defendants for the conduct of which the plaintiffs complained, thus avoiding any due process problems of multiple punitive damages awards. Of course, for this device to be effective it is necessary for a nationwide class to be certified so that additional claims are not left hanging.

d.   *Rule 23(b)(2) Class Actions*

The 23(b)(2) class action is designed to reach litigation in which final injunctive relief or declaratory relief is sought affecting the entire class. The Advisory Committee notes make clear, however, that this kind of class action "does not extend to cases in which the appropriate final relief relates exclusively or predominantly to money damages." Fed. R. Civ. P. 23, adv. comm. note. The classic (b)(2) case is a case alleging the violation of civil rights. Most toxic tort actions, even where they seek injunctive relief, will seek money damages as well, thus rendering the 23(b)(2) class action inappropriate.

Some toxic tort actions may seek primarily injunctive relief. A 23(b)(2) class will still probably be inappropriate, however. For example, a public nuisance action often seeks abatement of the nuisance. *See, e.g.*, Village of Wilsonville v. SCA Services, Inc. (Ill.1981) (disposal of hazardous waste). When brought by a municipality to vindicate a public right, a class action is rendered unnecessary. When brought instead by private individuals who have suffered a special injury, it is likely that money damages would be requested in addition to an injunction, rendering 23(b)(2) inappropriate. *See generally* Chapter Two, Sec. C(3)(b), *supra*. Thus, the 23(b)(2) class action is of very limited use in toxic tort litigation.

e. *Rule 23(b)(3) Class Actions*

By far the most common kind of federal class action in the toxic tort context is the 23(b)(3) class action. In many ways, the 23(b)(3) action is a catch-all provision with less stringent or arcane

requirements than the other 23(b) types. Moreover, it is more flexible in that it permits class
members to opt out of the class action to pursue
their own individual lawsuits.

In certifying a 23(b)(3) class action, the court
must determine that the common questions of law
or fact that had been found to exist in the 23(a)
prerequisite inquiry actually predominate in the
litigation over the questions affecting individual
class members. Further, the court must find the
class action device superior to other means of handling the complex litigation. Rule 23(b)(3) offers
the following factors to assist the court in its determination of whether this type of class action should
be certified:

> (A) the interest of members of the class in indi-
> vidually controlling the prosecution or defense of
> separate actions; (B) the extent and nature of
> any litigation concerning the controversy already
> commenced by or against members of the class;
> (C) the desirability or undesirability of concen-
> trating the litigation of the claims in the particu-
> lar forum; (D) the difficulties likely to be encoun-
> tered in the management of a class action.

The Advisory Committee notes emphasize that a
mass tort action "is ordinarily not appropriate for a
class action because of the likelihood that significant questions, not only of damages but of liability
and defenses to liability, would be present, affecting
the individuals in different ways." The Advisory
Committee was concerned that class certification in

litigation involving numerous individual questions would "degenerate in practice into multiple lawsuits separately tried."

Notwithstanding these concerns, courts have read the Advisory Committee notes as not prohibiting the use of the 23(b)(3) class action device in mass torts, but rather emphasizing the predominance and superiority requirements. In the Agent Orange litigation, Judge Pratt examined the claims in light of the 23(b)(3) factors and held that certification of a (b)(3) action was warranted. Judge Pratt's approach was oriented toward maximizing judicial economy. Accordingly, he developed a case management plan that addressed the most common issues first (such as the government contractor defense, negligence, product defectiveness, and general causation). If the plaintiffs' claims had survived challenges on those grounds, individual trials would have been held on the questions of individual causation and assessment of damages.

Judge Weinstein, agreeing with Judge Pratt's decision to certify a 23(b)(3) class action, stated that so long as common questions of law or fact constitute a "significant aspect" of the case and are appropriate for resolution on a class basis, the predominance requirement is met. In the Agent Orange litigation, significant common questions existed on certain defenses that were applicable to the class as a whole. This, the court held, sufficed to meet this test. As to the individual questions of causation, the court found that no barrier to the certification of a 23(b)(3) class action existed provided that the plaintiffs' counsel chose representatives for each type of injury alleged. Judge Weinstein further held that the superiority requirement was met. The defendants argued that the fact that the separate substantive product liability law of the individual states would be applied to the individual plaintiffs' claims even if the action were to proceed as a class action was a deterrent to certifying the class. Judge Weinstein rejected this argument, concluding that sufficient general uniformity existed among the states to render that objection inadequate. Because the Agent Orange litigation settled prior to trial, there was no opportunity to evaluate the success of class treatment in the factfinding process.

In contrast, an effort to certify a 23(b)(3) class action in the Dalkon Shield litigation ultimately failed. The Ninth Circuit reversed a conditional certification of a statewide class in California limited to the issue of Robins's liability for the manufacture and sale of the Dalkon Shield. The Ninth Circuit concluded that too many issues requiring individual determination were present in the case, including individual case histories of plaintiffs regarding their use of the Dalkon Shield and their alleged injuries. *See* In re Northern Dist. of California "Dalkon Shield" IUD Prods. Liab. Litig. (9th Cir.1982). The district court judge who had originally certified the class, Judge Spencer Williams, has criticized the Ninth Circuit's decision, insisting that his certification of an "issues-only" class precluded a challenge on the predominance grounds because individual questions were not part of the matters certified. *See* Hon. Spencer Williams, *Mass Tort Class Actions: Going, Going, Gone?*, 98 F.R.D. 323 (1983).

Problems of causation are at the basis of the reluctance of many courts to certify 23(b)(3) class actions in toxic tort litigation. Thus, the court in Mertens v. Abbott Laboratories (D.N.H.1983) held that proof of general causation of the adverse effects of in utero exposure to DES did not constitute a predominating common question, because individual proof would be required of each plaintiff on the matter of specific causation. Likewise, in Yandle v. PPG Industries, Inc. (E.D.Tex.1974), an asbestos case, the court denied class certification because "there is not a single act of negligence or proximate cause which would apply to each potential class member and each defendant in this case."

In contrast, in Payton v. Abbott Labs (D.Mass. 1979), another DES case, the court allowed a class action, defining the class as persons who were exposed to DES, but who had not developed injury. The purpose of this class was to make certain determinations regarding novel issues of law, such as whether a plaintiff could maintain an action without being able to identify the precise manufacturer of the DES to which the plaintiff was exposed and whether claims would be maintainable on a theory of increased risk of disease. The *Payton* court found sufficiently common questions as to periods of negligent conduct on the part of the defendants and the defendants' knowledge of the hazards of DES. When the court, by its own ruling or by questions certified to the Supreme Judicial Court of Massachusetts, had satisfactorily determined a number of the class issues, it decertified the class. Payton v. Abbott Labs (D.Mass.1983).

Courts give considerable attention to judicial management, and it is important to remember that the superiority requirement of 23(b)(3) must be satisfied as well as the predominance requirement. The interest in economical judicial management of mass litigation must not outweigh the due process rights of the parties in individualized decisionmaking. With trial courts attempting to structure new and effective ways to handle mass toxic torts, it was inevitable that appellate courts would be called upon to draw the due process line. The line may lie somewhere between two asbestos cases managed by Judge Robert Parker, then of the Eastern District of Texas. Judge Parker has been praised as one of the leaders in using innovative procedures to handle mass tort actions. In Jenkins v. Raymark Industries, Inc. (5th Cir.1986), the Fifth Circuit affirmed Judge Parker's certification of a 23(b)(3) class action primarily on the issue of state-of-the-art, going to both ultimate liability of the defendants and to punitive damages.

When Judge Parker attempted to use the class action device in a more complicated scheme involving causation and damages in over 3,000 consolidated asbestos cases, the Fifth Circuit reversed on the ground that individualized adjudication was warranted. In this case, In re Fibreboard Corporation

(5th Cir.1990), Judge Parker had consolidated 3,031 pending actions for a single trial on state-of-the-art and punitive damages and had certified a 23(b)(3) class for the issues of exposure and actual damages. The trial was to proceed along these lines in two phases. Phase I was a consolidated trial on product defects, state-of-the-art defense, and punitive damages issues. Phase II involved the trial of eleven representative cases, with further evidence from thirty additional plaintiffs on liability and damages. The Fifth Circuit rejected the Phase II procedure, stating that it improperly assumed that proof of general causation could suffice to prove specific causation. Moreover, the court pointed to different diseases, occupations, and periods of exposure among the plaintiffs, all leading to the conclusion that common questions did not predominate.

The foregoing cases demonstrate the difficulty courts have in both identifying an appropriate class and deciding whether common questions predominate in toxic tort actions. As a result, it is difficult to predict with certainty how a court will decide the certification question, as the determination is fact-specific to the particular litigation.

f. Notice in 23(b)(3) Class Actions

An integral part of the 23(b)(3) class action is the notice requirement, which is mandated by due process in order to give class members the opportunity to opt out and pursue individual actions. Rule 23(c)(2) provides that in a 23(b)(3) class action, "the best notice practicable under the circumstances" must be given to the class members, "including individual notice to all members who can be identified through reasonable effort." These requirements reflect the general procedural due process requirements set forth in Mullane v. Central Hanover Bank & Trust Co. (S.Ct.1950). Rule 23(c)(2) also provides that the notice shall state that the class member may affirmatively opt out of the action by a certain date and that if the class member does not opt out, any judgment in the action will become binding on the class member.

The notice ordered by Judge Weinstein in the Agent Orange litigation demonstrates the lengths to which courts may have to go to assure that due process is satisfied in notifying class members in a 23(b)(3) action. Judge Weinstein ordered notice in several different forms, in a hierarchy that related to the ability of the plaintiffs' attorneys to identify class members individually. Thus, where class members had already participated to any degree in litigation on Agent Orange or were represented by counsel, or were listed in the V.A.'s "Agent Orange Registry," the court ordered individual mailings. For the remainder of the class, notice was appropriate by radio and television announcements or in newspapers and magazines, each providing an 800 telephone number to direct class members as to how to obtain further information about the class action. Moreover, the court ordered notice to the Governors of the states to identify potential class members who may be known to state organizations established to assist Vietnam veterans. *See* In re "Agent Orange" Prod. Liab. Litig. (E.D.N.Y.1983).

5. Settlement of Class Actions

Rule 23(e) provides that a class action may not be dismissed or settled without court approval and that notice of the dismissal or settlement must be given to all class members. Approval of a class action involves, first, a preliminary hearing on fairness which can include information from expert witnesses designated by the parties or from court-appointed experts. If the settlement seems appropriate after the preliminary hearing, the court should order that notice of a formal fairness hearing be made to class members. The notice should invite class members who may have objections to the settlement to file written objections with the court. *See* Federal Judicial Center, Manual For Complex Litigation (Second) § 30.44 (1985). Objectors may not opt out of the class action at this stage, but they may notify the court of the reasons that they believe the settlement is unfair.

In the Agent Orange litigation, the court received numerous objections to the proposed settlement provisions. In the "Fairness Opinion" approving the settlement, Judge Weinstein explained that class consensus was virtually impossible to gauge and could not form the basis for a determination of the fairness of the proposed settlement. Thus, although the court received hundreds of responses to the proposed settlement, there was what the court called "an overwhelmingly large silent majority."

Even though individual approval of the settlement provisions and individual execution of the settlement documents were not possible under the circumstances, the class members nevertheless would be bound to its terms. *See* In re "Agent Orange" Prod. Liab. Litig. (E.D.N.Y.1984) (Fairness Opinion).

The court applied the following test in deciding whether the settlement was fair and reasonable:

"(1) The complexity, expense and likely duration of the litigation," . . . . "(2) the reaction of the class of [sic] the settlement," . . . . "(3) the stage of the proceedings and the amount of discovery completed," . . . . "(4) the risks of establishing liability," . . . . "(5) the risks of establishing damages," . . . . "(6) the risks of maintaining the class action through the trial," . . . . "(7) the ability of the defendants to withstand a higher judgment," . . . . "(8) the range of reasonableness of the settlement fund in light of the best possible recovery," . . . [and] "(9) the range of reasonableness of the settlement fund to a possible recovery in light of all the attendant risks of litigation," . . . .

Id. (quoting City of Detroit v. Grinnell Corp. (2d Cir.1974)). The court considered in detail the objections of the class members as well as the overall social effect of the Agent Orange litigation. Judge Weinstein stated that the most important issue in determining the fairness of the proposed settlement was the plaintiffs' likelihood of success on the merits in light of the amount offered in settlement. The court considered the weaknesses of the plaintiffs' case, particularly causation ("[T]he evidence presented to the court to date suggests that the case is without merit ...."), the strength of the defendants' defenses, and other risks of establishing liability and damages and concluded that the settlement was fair.

B. OTHER AGGREGATIVE PROCEDURES

1. Multidistrict Litigation Transfer

Congress has granted authority to the Judicial Panel on Multidistrict Litigation (MDL) to transfer actions "involving one or more common questions" pending in different federal districts to any single district for pretrial proceedings, provided that the transfer "will be for the convenience of parties and witnesses and will promote the just and efficient conduct of such actions." 28 U.S.C.A. § 1407(a) (1993). As the provision states, the panel is authorized to make such transfers for pretrial purposes only, including settlement.

The MDL transfer has been used to aggregate more than 26,000 asbestos cases in the Eastern District of Pennsylvania before Judge Charles Weiner. *See* In re Asbestos Prods. Liab. Litig. (Jud. Pan. Mult. Lit. 1991). Transfer was carried out even though a substantial group of plaintiffs objected. The rationales for the transfer to Judge Weiner's court were that the greatest number of the cases was already pending in that district and that Judge Weiner brought to the litigation a high level of experience in such matters. It is the responsibility of the transferee judge to establish procedures to expedite the litigation, and the judge may seek the assistance of other experienced judges in advancing the procedures.

Similarly, thousands of cases alleging personal injuries from silicone gel breast implants have been transferred to the court of Judge Sam Pointer in the Southern District of Alabama by the MDL Panel since 1992. These cases had been brought in or removed to other federal districts. In 1994, Judge Pointer provisionally certified a 23(b)(3) class action for the purpose of settlement. In late 1994, the settlement was approved. In re Silicone Gel Breast Implant Prods. Liab. Litig. (MDL 926) (S.D.Ala. 1994).

2. Consolidation

In the federal courts, consolidation of actions is governed by Federal Rule of Civil Procedure 42(a), which provides that the court may order that actions with at least one common question of law or fact be consolidated. Consolidation may be for pretrial and trial purposes, or merely for discovery. Although use of this device has been attempted where many individual cases are involved, it appears that the device is most appropriate under relatively narrow circumstances.

In general, broad discretion is vested in the trial court to determine whether consolidation is appro-

priate in a given case. The need for judicial economy must be balanced against due process considerations. Consolidation must not be imposed at the
substantial risk of prejudice or jury confusion. Attempts at the use of consolidation in asbestos litigation give some sense of the difficulties faced by
courts. The asbestos litigation was particularly
suited to innovative attempts at collective resolution. As one court observed: "Finding an appropriate forum to resolve all these [asbestos] claims with
minimal delay is the goal.... Pre-trial consolidation for the purposes of discovery, the appointment
of special masters to expedite settlement, and, especially, the liberal use of consolidated trials have
ameliorated what might otherwise be a sclerotic
backlog of cases." Malcolm v. National Gypsum
Co. (2d Cir.1993). But the case law indicates that
consolidation may not be appropriate in all circumstances in which multiple lawsuits threaten to seriously backlog the system.

In Johnson v. Celotex Corp. (2d Cir.1990), the
court upheld the district court's consolidation of
two asbestos cases. The court applied a balancing
test that weighed the risk of prejudice and confusion against the advantages of collective factfinding.
These advantages included judicial economy, avoiding conflicting results on issues of fact and law, and
reducing the hardship on the parties and witnesses.
The court also stated that trial courts should explore the possibility of minimizing prejudice and
confusion by providing specific instructions to jurors or employing other devices. The *Johnson*

court followed other courts in employing the following criteria when deciding whether consolidation is appropriate in asbestos litigation: " '(1) common worksite [of plaintiffs]; (2) similar occupation; (3) similar time of exposure; (4) type of disease; (5) whether plaintiffs were living or deceased; (6) status of discovery in each case; (7) whether all plaintiffs were represented by the same counsel; and (8) type of cancer alleged ....' " (quoting In re All Asbestos Cases Pending in the United States Dist. Court for the Dist. of Maryland (D.Md.1983)). The court determined that these criteria were met.

A much larger number of asbestos cases was consolidated by Judge Weinstein in In re Eastern & Southern Dists. Asbestos Litig. (Brooklyn Navy Yard) (E. & S.D.N.Y.1991). In that case, Judge Weinstein divided the consolidated action into three phases for trial, depending upon the percentage of each plaintiff's exposure to asbestos that occurred in the Navy Yard. Judge Weinstein rejected later objections to the consolidation, and the defendant did not appeal that issue. The cases that were consolidated in the Brooklyn Navy Yard litigation all arose out of exposure at that particular geographical site, which during all relevant times was owned by the United States Government. Further, the sellers of the asbestos used at the Yard were somewhat consistent, as they were contractors hired by the Government, presumably to comply with certain specifications. Also, due to the uniformity of the uses to which the asbestos products were put at the Yard, it was reasonable to assume that the circumstances under which the plaintiffs were exposed to asbestos were reasonably consistent.

Not all consolidated asbestos cases exhibited the level of consistency that was present in the Brooklyn Navy Yard litigation. In Malcolm v. National Gypsum Co. (2d Cir.1993), the court reversed the consolidation of 600 asbestos cases in which each plaintiff had been exposed to asbestos through work in one or more of more than 40 powerhouses. The court applied the criteria referenced in the *Johnson* case, but found that they were not met. The most significant problem for consolidation cited by the court was the lack of a "primary worksite" such as had existed in the Brooklyn Navy Yard case. The court determined that too many variables existed, which in turn led to an avalanche of evidence requiring a jury to make distinctions that were too difficult and confusing.

C. TRIAL MANAGEMENT

Regardless of the aggregative procedure employed to bring together numerous cases, issues remain as to management of the postaggregation course of the litigation. For a detailed exploration of postaggregative procedure in two case studies involving toxic torts, see Linda S. Mullenix, *Beyond Consolidation: Postaggregative Procedure in Asbestos Mass Tort Litigation*, 32 Wm. & Mary L. Rev. 475 (1991). One of the areas in which judges have been especially innovative is the management of trial.

One of the cases followed by Professor Mullenix, and an example of judicial efforts in trial management, was Cimino v. Raymark Industries, Inc. (E.D.Tex.1990), another mass asbestos litigation assigned to Judge Parker in the Eastern District of Texas. Over 3,000 asbestos cases were certified in a 23(b)(3) class action. Judge Parker established a procedure for trial in three phases, obviously mindful of the problems encountered with the trial plan in *Fibreboard*. Phase I addressed the fact questions in the issues of product defect, appropriateness of warnings, state-of-the-art, and punitive damages. Part of this process involved assigning a figure by which compensatory damages would be multiplied to obtain the amount of punitive damages.

Phase II was to require the jury to make findings regarding nineteen worksites; but instead, the parties entered into a stipulation on causation and exposure. The issues in this phase involved determining the time frame when asbestos products were used at each site, identifying the jobs in which the products were used and whether the amount of exposure in a job would be sufficient to produce injury, and apportioning liability among the defendants. The stipulation regarding Phase II was based upon a list compiled by the court of various work sites and specific jobs. Judge Parker stated: "It was contemplated that any plaintiff whose work history did not include a threshold amount of time in any of the worksites would have the exposure issue tried in an individual mini-trial." Essentially, the parties agreed to assess ten percent causation to each of the nonsettling defendants and thirteen percent to the settling defendant, Johns–Manville Corporation.

Finally, Phase III addressed damages by dividing the class into five categories of disease. The court randomly chose sample plaintiffs, ranging from fifteen to fifty persons for each category, to be tried to a jury. The amounts determined by the jury served as a basis for awards to be given to the remaining class members. As to method, Judge Parker said: "The Court finds no persuasive evidence why the average damage verdicts in each disease category should not be applied to the nonsample members." He further stated that the "averages are calculated after remittitur and take into consideration those cases where plaintiffs failed to prove the existence of an asbestos-related injury or disease resulting in a zero verdict." He said the result achieved a 99% confidence level, leaving a one percent likelihood that the aggregate result would have been substantially different in individual adjudications. The class members waived objections to the dollar outcomes of the awards, and the defendants waived the right to challenge the awards on the ground that individual verdicts would have been different.

Although Judge Parker expressed confidence in the scheme developed in *Cimino*, stating that it satisfied the Fifth Circuit's concerns in *Fibreboard*, he was left with some lingering due process concerns. He concluded, however, that he would "leave it to the academicians and legal scholars to debate whether our notion of due process has room for balancing [the] competing interests [of the defendants and the plaintiffs]."

The example of the asbestos litigation demonstrates that the use of aggregative procedures will be important in the future of toxic tort litigation. *See generally* Glen O. Robinson & Kenneth S. Abraham, *Collective Justice in Tort Law*, 78 Va. L. Rev. 1481 (1992) (proposing use of statistical claim profiles derived from earlier cases and settlements, or models, to provide baseline values for individual claims). Legitimate concerns exist regarding due process, however, and future attempts by innovative judges to address the problems associated with collective resolution of mass toxic torts will no doubt result in a compilation of effective alternatives from which courts may draw when faced with similar challenges. For a discussion challenging the widely accepted notions of party control in traditional tort litigation and demonstrating that using such preconceptions as a standard against which aggregative procedures are measured may be faulty, see Deborah R. Hensler, *Resolving Mass Toxic Torts: Myths and Realities*, 1989 U. Ill. L. Rev. 89 (1989).

D. SETTLEMENT

Another area in which innovative approaches have been attempted is settlement. Toxic tort plaintiffs often seek remedies beyond traditional compensatory damages, or even punitive damages. Consequently, parties and courts have attempted to fashion creative settlement provisions to accommo-

date these requests. Some of the more innovative
settlement provisions that have been proposed address plaintiffs' concerns about future illness, or
respond to counsel's concerns for future claimants.

1. Medical Monitoring

Plaintiffs concerned about future injuries associated with the defendants' conduct may seek to
include some form of medical study or care in the
settlement agreement. For example, In re Fernald
Litig. (S.D.Ohio 1989) (approving settlement) involved claims by residents alleging exposure to hazardous substances, including uranium, as a result of
the operation of the nearby Feed Material Production Center of the U.S. Department of Energy. The
plaintiffs sought medical monitoring in the lawsuit.
The settlement required the defendants to pay $73
million to the plaintiffs for future medical monitoring. The money was to be placed in a fund managed by trustees (special masters) who were also
designated to establish the monitoring program.
Appropriate uses of the funds included medical examinations, diagnostic tests, and epidemiological
studies. Subsequently, in a separate class action
brought by former employees of the Fernald plant
against NLO Inc., which operated the plant for the
Government, the parties reached a settlement during trial that included lifetime medical monitoring
for the employees. As part of the settlement, an
independent three-member panel would evaluate
physical injuries or illnesses and determine whether
they should be compensable under workers' com-

pensation. The Government has agreed not to challenge the workers' compensation claim decisions of the panel. *See* Day v. NLO (S.D.Ohio 1994) (transferring case for review of fairness of proposed settlement).

In the Three Mile Island litigation, which arose from a release of radiation at a nuclear facility in Harrisburg, Pennsylvania, a class of plaintiffs sought medical monitoring for all persons residing within a certain distance of the plant. Under the terms of the settlement, the defendants established and financed a Public Health Fund to conduct studies of the public health effects of the release at the facility and of the effects of low-level radiation generally, as well as public education programs. *See* In re Three Mile Island Litig. (M.D.Pa.1982).

2. Class of Future Victims

In perhaps the most innovative settlement effort, the Center for Claims Resolution, a consortium of twenty asbestos defendants, initiated negotiations to develop a broad settlement of numerous claims, present and future, arising from exposure to asbestos-containing products. The one-billion dollar settlement was negotiated before any actions had been filed, and the settlement was filed in the Eastern District of Pennsylvania together with the complaint and third-party complaint against 80 insurers of the defendant companies. The settlement was subsequently approved by the district court. *See* Carlough v. Amchem Products, Inc. (E.D.Pa.1993).

The terms of the settlement were quite revolutionary. Some of the class representatives alleged no present injury and sought to settle the future claims of other, unidentified persons who were not presently suffering any injury. This matter alone generated a stir among the plaintiffs' bar. *See* Frederick M. Baron, *Carlough v. Amchem: Prepackaged Future Claimants Class v. Article III*, 8 Toxics L. Rep. 24 (June 9, 1993). The settlement covered a period of ten years and established a mechanism for compensating approximately 10,000 cases per year of persons having or developing certain designated malignancies and non-malignant conditions associated with asbestos exposure. The schedule of compensation has been developed from average jury verdicts and settlements over a period of four years prior to the settlement. The agreement also addressed the situation of plaintiffs with lesser injuries who develop more serious injuries later on. It provided that plaintiffs who have noncompensable injuries, but who develop related compensable conditions at a later date, may resubmit their claims when the later injury occurs. Likewise, plaintiffs compensated for a non-malignant condition who later develop a malignancy may obtain further compensation when the malignant condition develops.

The settlement allocated a percentage of liability to each defendant, regardless of whether the specific claimant was exposed to a particular defendant's products. Accordingly, joint and several liability would not apply.

Finally, the settlement agreement contained a limited opt-out provision that allowed one percent of qualified claimants per year to pursue individual claims. These tort claims are limited, however, and plaintiffs would not be allowed to sue for punitive damages or for increased risk.

The *Carlough* case and related litigation continue to be the subject of legal activity. The ultimate result in this litigation will serve as an example for other actions in which courts and parties attempt to fashion innovative mechanisms for resolving mass toxic tort litigation.

3. Bankruptcy

In 1982, the Johns–Manville Corporation, the major manufacturer of asbestos products, filed for protection under Chapter 11 of the federal bankruptcy laws on the basis of projected liabilities in current and future asbestos-related claims. The company estimated its liabilities at two billion dollars. The estimate was based upon both current claims and future claims calculated on the basis of the number of persons who had been exposed to Johns–Manville asbestos-containing products, but who had not yet manifested disease symptoms. A reorganization plan was created in 1986 that involved establishing the Manville Personal Injury Settlement Trust to pay asbestos personal injury claims. All claims, present and future, were required to be presented to the Trust; no claimant could bring a tort action against Manville in court. No recovery for punitive damages was to be allowed by the Trust. *See* In re

Johns–Manville Corp. (Bkrtcy. S.D.N.Y.1986). After the plan was approved by the Second Circuit in
1988, Kane v. Johns–Manville Corp. (2d Cir.1988),
the Trust received an infusion of cash in the
amount of $909 million, as well as stocks and bonds.
The aggregate value of the Trust was in the vicinity
of $2.5 billion.

The Trust began processing claims, but by 1990
the cash reserves were almost empty. Until that
point, the Trust had provided compensation for
more than 20,000 claims at an average value of
$42,000. In 1990, the Plan came under the control
of Judge Weinstein for restructuring so that the
early claimants would not deplete the funds. A
class was certified, and a settlement was proposed
allocating the Trust payments with priority based
upon seriousness of illness. The Second Circuit
rejected the restructured plan in 1992, In re Joint
E. & S. Dists. Asbestos Litig. (2d Cir.1992), in part
because it identified certain subclasses—for example, those claimants who had held a higher priority
under the original Plan—whose interests were not
adequately represented by the class representatives.
Later, however, the Second Circuit modified its
ruling, holding that subclasses were not necessary
and allowing further negotiations to go forward.

The result was a settlement plan approved by the
court. In re Joint E. & S. Dists. Asbestos Litig. (E.
& S.D.N.Y.1995). The settlement contained a
scheduled value of claims based upon previous settlements under the Trust and recent settlements of
tort actions. The settlement plan created a matrix

of values for seven diseases on which the payments would be based. Nevertheless, claimants objecting to the scheduled amount could request individual claim review. The plan provided for initial payments to be made based upon ten percent of the scheduled value of claims, ranging from $1,200 to $20,000.

In addition to the scheduled values, another significant feature of the settlement was the inclusion of the claims of co-defendants who alleged that they were forced to pay to claimants the Trust's share of liability while the stay on Trust payments was in effect. The sum of $55.7 million was set aside to reimburse the co-defendants.

The settlement also provided for the continued immunity of the new Manville Corp. and the Trust from asbestos-related lawsuits. Its scope was far-reaching, including claims by current claimants, persons who may become ill in the future (represented by counsel), co-defendants, and Manville's distributors and judgment creditors. The settlement of the Manville Trust claims demonstrates the results that can be achieved through tenacious judicial management. The settlement's sweeping scope was intended to provide a mechanism to eventually put to rest the thousands of claims associated with the operation of Johns–Manville Corporation as an asbestos manufacturer and seller.

4. Contribution Claims

Successful settlement of a mass toxic tort action may be impeded by disagreement among defendants as to the contribution rights available to each. The situation becomes particularly complex when fewer than all of the defendants in a mass tort action reach a pretrial settlement with the plaintiff. The most hotly debated issue in this situation is the determination of the amount by which the subsequent judgment against the nonsettling defendants is to be reduced. This reduction, called a credit or set-off, is significant in that it defines the remaining liability that is the responsibility of the nonsettling tortfeasors.

Notwithstanding the existence of two model acts to guide the states in this area of the law—the Uniform Contribution Among Tortfeasors Act, 12 U.L.A. 57 (1975), and the Uniform Comparative Fault Act, 12 U.L.A. 43 (Supp. 1993)—a remarkable lack of uniformity exists. Indeed, these two model acts contain conflicting provisions on some of the basic issues involved in the resolution of contribution claims. Moreover, application of these acts in the individual states has become a complex matter of legislative and judicial interpretation, further fragmenting the legal doctrines. *See generally* Jean Macchiaroli Eggen, *Understanding State Contribution Laws and Their Effect on the Settlement of Mass Tort Actions*, 73 Texas L. Rev. 1701 (1995).

The vast majority of states provide for a right of contribution among tortfeasors insofar as a tortfeasor has paid a judgment in an amount in excess of the tortfeasor's pro rata share. *See* Unif. Contribution Among Tortfeasors Act, 12 U.L.A. § 1(b), at 63 (1975). Many states interpret the term "pro rata" to mean the tortfeasor's equitable share of liability as determined according to the rules of comparative negligence in effect in the relevant jurisdiction. *See, e.g.*, Pesaplastic, C.A. v. Cincinnati Milacron Co. (11th Cir.1985) (applying Florida law). But some states retain the original definition of pro rata as "per tortfeasor" equally. In the situation in which some, but not all, of the tortfeasors settle with the plaintiff, most states prohibit a settling tortfeasor from seeking contribution from a non-settling tortfeasor. *See, e.g.*, Ark. Code Ann. § 16–61–202(3) (Michie 1987); Md. Ann. Code art. 50, § 17(c) (1994). The states are split, however, on the question whether nonsettling tortfeasors may obtain contribution from a settling tortfeasor, with the majority denying such a right of contribution. *See, e.g.*, N.Y. Gen. Oblig. Law § 15–108(b) (McKinney 1989) (no right of contribution against settling tortfeasor). *But see, e.g.*, Del. Code Ann. tit. 10, § 6304(b) (1974) (allowing nonsettling tortfeasor to obtain contribution from settling tortfeasor).

The states are also split on the set-off effect to be given to the settling tortfeasor's payment. Each state seems to believe that its particular approach most successfully encourages settlement and promotes judicial economy. The majority employs the pro tanto rule, whereby the plaintiff's judgment is off-set by the dollar amount paid by the settling party, or any other amount so designated in the release. *See, e.g.*, Cal. Civ. Proc. Code § 877(a) (West Supp. 1994); Minn. Stat. Ann. § 604.01 (West Supp. 1994). Under this scheme, and assuming the applicability of joint and several liability, if the settling tortfeasor settles for less than its equitable share of the judgment, and the jurisdiction does not permit the nonsettling tortfeasors to seek contribution from the settling tortfeasor, the nonsettling tortfeasors could end up paying a share of the judgment in excess of their equitable shares without recourse. On the other hand, if a tortfeasor settles for an amount in excess of its equitable share, the nonsettling tortfeasors would enjoy a windfall by having less than the aggregate of their equitable shares left to pay, especially considering that most states prohibit a settling tortfeasor from seeking contribution. *See, e.g.*, Martinez v. Lopez (Md. 1984) (applying pro tanto set-off in medical malpractice case with result that nonsettling defendant paid nothing). Thus, there may be little incentive for the remaining defendants to settle following a settlement by one defendant under the pro tanto rule.

A second, minority, approach to this situation is to reduce the plaintiff's judgment by the released tortfeasor's equitable share—percentage of fault—regardless of the amount that the tortfeasor paid in settlement of the claim. *See, e.g.*, Ky. Rev. Stat. Ann. § 411.182(4) (Baldwin 1991). This apportioned share rule protects the nonsettling defendants by assuring that the judgment is credited with the equitable share of the settling tortfeasor. If the settling tortfeasor settled the claim for an amount that turned out to be in excess of its equitable share, however, the plaintiff could realize a windfall by receiving the settlement plus the judgment (which judgment would be the equivalent of the aggregate equitable shares of the nonsettling tortfeasors). Nevertheless, some courts are undisturbed by this possibility. *See* Charles v. Giant Eagle Markets (Pa.1987) (" 'Plaintiffs bear the risk of poor settlements; logic and equity dictate that the benefit of good settlements should also be theirs.' ") (quoting Duncan v. Cessna Aircraft Co. (Tex.1984)).

As a result of these and other problems in choosing between one of the above rules, some parties employ a release that allocates a specific set-off amount, sometimes designated as the settling tortfeasor's equitable share to be determined at trial. In addition, some states have developed a set-off rule that combines features of the pro tanto rule and the apportioned share rule. Thus, New York has enacted a rule that mandates that the plaintiff's judgment be reduced by the amount paid in settlement or by the settling tortfeasor's equitable share, whichever is larger. N.Y. Gen. Oblig. Law § 15–108(a) (McKinney 1989). This combined approach seeks to avoid windfalls to plaintiffs in the same manner as the pro tanto rule. *See* Williams v. Niske (N.Y.1993).

Recently, the United States Supreme Court has advocated the use of the apportioned share rule. In McDermott, Inc. v. AmClyde (S.Ct.1994), an accident case arising under the admiralty jurisdiction of the federal courts and therefore decided under federal law, the Court opined that the apportioned share set-off rule was preferable to the pro tanto rule both because it was consistent with the trend toward proportionate share liability and because of its settlement-inducing qualities. The court was not particularly concerned with the possibility of windfalls to plaintiffs if the apportioned share rule were to be applied. The Court stated that "[t]he law contains no rigid rule against overcompensation" and "making tortfeasors pay for the damage they cause can be more important than preventing overcompensation."

This array of contribution and set-off rules can create significant problems in mass toxic tort litigation. Some rules favor settling defendants, whereas others favor plaintiffs or nonsettling defendants. These problems may arise in "smaller" mass litigation (one plaintiff, several defendants), but they are exacerbated in the situation in which numerous cases—perhaps hundreds—have been aggregated. Sometimes these cases arrive with some defendants having settled with the plaintiff, while others remain in the action. In attempting to fashion a global settlement for such mass litigation, the court may encounter strong objections from defendants to the proposed means of handling contribution claims and to the chosen method of set-off. Consequently, the defendants may resist settlement if they believe that the proposed rules do not benefit their cause. Because contribution and set-off rules vary from state to state, a defendant may feel that its own state's rules are more favorable than any rule chosen by the court to bind all defendants. This, in turn, raises choice-of-law questions in the mass tort litigation context. *See* Section E(2), *infra*.

5. Alternative Dispute Resolution

Some types of alternative dispute resolution (ADR) have appeared in mass toxic tort litigation to help move the parties toward settlement. Because the substantive and procedural issues in mass toxic tort litigation are typically quite complex, parties may not have a clear sense of their likelihood of success on the merits. Thus, they may resist reasonable settlement proposals for lack of their own ability to properly assess their litigation risks. ADR has been used to provide some of the information that they lack. The ADR methods used in this context are broadly defined, as the results would not necessarily displace the judicial process, but would supplement it and assist in the management of the litigation. The more traditional forms of ADR—arbitration and mediation—typically will be less effective mechanisms in mass toxic tort litigation because of the problems generated by the complex nature of the litigation. Several more innovative methods have been used, however, that are designed to enhance fact availability and to induce settlement. Two such methods are summary jury trials and mini-trials.

a. Summary Jury Trials

The use of the summary jury trial was initiated in 1981 by the Honorable J. Thomas Lambros of the Eastern District of Ohio, but has since been adopted by judges around the country. Its initial use to encourage settlement appeared to be quite effective. The summary jury trial is intended to result in an advisory verdict for use by the court and the parties in developing an approach to settlement. An actual jury is used, but both voir dire and "trial" are conducted by a truncated procedure that may relax the rules of evidence. Typically, each side has a set amount of time to present its case, with the overall time frame ranging from a day to a few weeks, depending upon the complexity of the litigation. Jurors may be asked to provide detailed information by means of interrogatories, with the possibility of the judge and parties being allowed to question the jurors after the verdict. During the SJT, the jurors may or may not know that the verdict will be non-binding. The participants then use this information for the purpose of fashioning a settlement.

By its nature, the summary jury trial requires that discovery and other pretrial procedures be completed by the commencement of the SJT. The procedure can be somewhat costly, but the cost may be warranted in cases, such as complex toxic tort actions, that are sure to be lengthy if they go to trial. In some instances, the SJT may just point out the arbitrariness of a jury's verdict. In Stites v. Sundstrand Heat Transfer, Inc. (W.D.Mich.1987), a case arising out of the contamination of a drinking water supply with the chemical TCE, the court impanelled twelve jurors who deliberated in two separate groups of six. The SJT used one test plaintiff and consisted of closing arguments only, with use of discovery materials. The first jury found for the plaintiff in the amount of $2.8 million. The other jury found for the defendant; when asked, the second jury valued the case at $300,000. Despite such contradiction, this information in itself is valuable to the parties. When a case could easily go either way, settlement may be attractive. And, indeed, the *Stites* case settled after the SJT.

The SJT is a voluntary procedure. Courts may not require parties to submit to an SJT, at least in the absence of a court rule. *See* In re NLO, Inc. (6th Cir.1993); Strandell v. Johnson County (7th Cir.1987). An SJT could require parties to divulge litigation strategy and privileged work product. But where used with the consent of the parties in cases that otherwise would be hard to settle, the SJT can be quite effective in its goal to achieve settlement.

b. *Mini-Trials*

A mini-trial is essentially the private sector equivalent of an SJT. Unlike the SJT, however, the parties in a mini-trial make their presentations of the evidence to the principals. Ideally, these individuals would have authority to enter into a binding settlement. A judge or other neutral third party may preside over the mini-trial as a facilitator, but does not make legal rulings. *See generally* Green, *Growth of the Mini–Trial*, 9 Litig. 12 (Fall 1982). No advisory verdict results from the mini-trial. Rather, its chief advantages are in providing an early neutral evaluation of the case and in bringing the parties together to initiate settlement on equal ground.

E. OTHER PROCEDURAL ISSUES

1. Collateral Estoppel

a. *Basic Concepts*

The doctrine of collateral estoppel, or issue pre-clusion, operates to bar relitigation of certain issues in subsequent litigation. The basic rules of collateral estoppel require that "once an issue is actually and necessarily determined by a court of competent jurisdiction, that determination is conclusive in sub-sequent suits based on a different cause of action involving a party to the prior litigation." Montana v. United States (S.Ct.1979). Only parties and their privies may be bound by a prior judgment. *See* Restatement (Second) of Judgments § 29 (1980) (does not use the term "privity," but adopts con-cept). Privies are entities whose relationship to a party is so close that it does not violate due process to bind the entity to the prior judgment. Typically, privies fall into one of several categories. They may be representatives of a party to the prior action, such as the administrator of an estate. Privies could also be successors in interest to property belonging to a party, when the property was the subject of the prior action. Or, privies could be entities that effectively controlled the prior litiga-tion. Privity is not established by a mere "inter-est" in the outcome of litigation. Those entities that are not parties or privies are considered "strangers" to the prior litigation; and strangers may not be bound to the results in the prior litigation.

Traditionally, the doctrine of mutuality of estoppel limited the operation of collateral estoppel. Mutuality provided that because a stranger could not be bound to a prior judgment, the stranger would not be permitted to benefit from it. How might a stranger seek to benefit from the determination of a particular issue in the earlier litigation? If the issue had been decided in a manner favorable to the stranger's position in the subsequent litigation, the stranger may seek to prevent his or her opponent from relitigating the issue. The stranger may want to use the issue defensively—i.e., when the stranger is in the defensive posture defending against a claim brought by the party to the earlier litigation—or offensively—i.e., when the stranger affirmatively asserts a claim against the party. In any event, under mutuality, the stranger was not allowed to benefit from this situation, either defensively or offensively.

By now, mutuality has been all but abandoned in the states and the federal court system. *See, e.g.*, Blonder–Tongue Laboratories, Inc. v. University of Illinois Foundation (S.Ct.1971); Bernhard v. Bank of America National Trust & Savings Assn. (Cal. 1942). In general, jurisdictions have demonstrated more reluctance in abandoning mutuality when a stranger seeks to use collateral estoppel offensively, rather than defensively. Offensive, nonmutual collateral estoppel has been accepted when certain safeguards apply to prevent its abuse by parties or its inequitable application. In Parklane Hosiery Co. v. Shore (S.Ct.1979), the Supreme Court set forth some significant limitations on the use of offensive, nonmutual collateral estoppel in the federal courts. In *Parklane*, the Court stated that the trial court has broad discretion in deciding whether collateral estoppel should be applied, but with some guidelines: "[T]he general rule should be that in cases where a plaintiff could easily have joined in the earlier action or where the application of offensive collateral estoppel would be unfair to a defendant, a trial judge ... should not allow the use of offensive collateral estoppel." *Accord* Restatement (Second) of Judgments § 29 (1982) (providing that offensive collateral estoppel should be allowed "unless the fact that he lacked full and fair opportunity to litigate the issue in the first action or other circumstances justify affording him an opportunity to relitigate the issue"). At least some states have incorporated the *Parklane* rule into their collateral estoppel doctrines. *See, e.g.*, Bichler v. Eli Lilly & Co. (N.Y.1982).

Courts have been especially concerned about the situation involving multiple plaintiffs with claims against the same defendant arising out of the same or related conduct. *See generally* Brainerd Currie, *Mutuality of Collateral Estoppel: Limits of the Bernhard Doctrine*, 9 Stan. L. Rev. 281 (1957). This is precisely the configuration of mass toxic tort litigation. A simple hypothetical will illustrate the problem. Assume a bus accident occurs and that all

50 passengers were injured. Passenger #1 brings an action against the bus company and driver, but cannot prove negligence. Passenger #2 (and any other passenger) has a right to bring an independent action against the same defendants, claiming negligence. This is because Passenger #2 is a stranger and cannot be bound to the result in Passenger #1's action. (Passenger #2 is not in privity with Passenger #1; their similar interests in holding the bus company negligent are not sufficient to constitute privity.) Suppose Passengers #2 through #15 all sue separately and all are unable to prove that the bus company was negligent. Then Passenger #16 sues and *wins*. Should Passengers #17 through #50 be allowed to use offensive collateral estoppel, based upon Passenger #16's favorable finding that the bus company was negligent, so as to prevent the bus company from relitigating the issue of negligence? Put otherwise, may Passengers #17 through #50 win on summary judgment on the issue of liability, on the basis of Passenger #16's favorable finding? The problems here are clear, not the least of which is the fact that a substantial number of cases had been tried earlier with a different result.

b. Application to Toxic Torts

Toxics torts compound the above problems. Because statutes of limitations have been relaxed to accommodate latent disease claims, actions accrue later and later. This does not create the "wait-and-see" situation of the bus accident, in which all plaintiffs were injured at the same time and some chose to sit out and wait for a favorable verdict, then come in and attempt to use collateral estoppel. Rather, in latent disease cases, many plaintiffs have no choice but to wait, as their illnesses will be manifested at different future dates.   Further, in toxic torts, claims may arise from the same general conduct of the defendant, but the circumstances of the plaintiffs' exposures may vary considerably.   In Hardy v. Johns–Manville Sales Corp. (5th Cir.1982), the court applied the rule of *Parklane* and found enough problems with allowing the use of offensive collateral estoppel that its utility in toxics tort litigation is seriously in question.

Hardy involved consolidated actions brought by various asbestos workers against various manufacturers, distributors, and sellers of asbestos products.   The plaintiffs alleged claims of strict liability, negligence, and breach of warranty.   The trial court accepted a standard of industry-wide liability and issued an omnibus order approving the use of collateral estoppel on issues of marketing an unreasonably dangerous product, state-of-the-art, and general causation.   The plaintiffs sought to use issues determined in Borel v. Fibreboard Paper Products Corp. (5th Cir.1973) which were favorable to asbestos workers seeking to recover damages from asbestos companies on product liability theories.   On interlocutory appeal from the omnibus order, the Fifth Circuit in *Hardy* reversed the district court and held that the use of collateral estoppel was not appropriate.

The Fifth Circuit conducted separate discussions of those defendants in *Hardy* who had also been defendants in *Borel* (the "*Borel* defendants") and those defendants who had not been defendants in the *Borel* lawsuit ("non-*Borel* defendants"). The distinction was warranted because the *Borel* defendants, as parties to the earlier action, could be bound. The non-*Borel* defendants, on the other hand, appeared to be strangers, although the plaintiffs argued that they should be considered privies. The Fifth Circuit noted that the district court had not distinguished between these two classes of defendants.

The Fifth Circuit first addressed the collateral estoppel issues involving the non-*Borel* defendants. Initially, the court determined that no privity existed between the non-*Borel* defendants and the *Borel* defendants. A mere "identity of interests" between these two groups of defendants was insufficient to constitute privity. For privity to exist, the non-*Borel* defendants would have had to have controlled the litigation in *Borel*. Quoting the Restatement (Second) of Judgments § 39, comment c (1982), the court stated: " 'To have control of litigation requires that a person have effective choice as to the legal theories and proofs to be advanced in behalf of the party to the action. He must also have control over the opportunity to obtain review.' " The mere fact that the non-*Borel* defendants, like the *Borel* defendants, were manufacturers of asbestos-containing products did not transform them into privies.

The court's analysis of the *Borel* defendants was different, as they clearly could be bound to the results in *Borel* under appropriate circumstances. Those circumstances were not present in this case, however. The court found that the basic requirements of collateral estoppel—that the issue be identical, that the issue was actually litigated in the prior action, and that the issue was necessary and essential to the judgment in the prior action—were not met because of the ambiguity of the findings on which the *Borel* judgment was based. *See also* Restatement (Second) of Judgments § 29, comment g (1982) (providing that collateral estoppel is not appropriate where the prior judgment is ambivalent). The Fifth Circuit closely examined the special interrogatories given to the jury in *Borel* and held that their lack of specificity made it impossible to determine the jury's precise findings on issues that were critical to the *Hardy* litigation (e.g., when the duty to warn attached, the exact composition of the various products). Because *Hardy* involved persons exposed to various products over differing periods of time, absolute clarity of the issues resolved in *Borel* was essential before collateral estoppel could be allowed. The Fifth Circuit stated that *Borel* did not decide that all manufacturers of asbestos-containing products knew or should have known their products were dangerous at all times relevant to the plaintiffs in *Hardy*.

In the alternative, the Fifth Circuit found that the use of collateral estoppel in *Hardy* was inappropriate under the rule of *Parklane*. The court held that application of collateral estoppel would be unfair to the defendants for two main reasons. First, numerous other asbestos cases had been tried, at least half of which had resulted in verdicts inconsistent with *Borel*. As in the bus accident hypothetical above, the court was concerned that selecting *Borel* to provide the basis for offensive collateral estoppel was arbitrary and unfair. Second, the court concluded that the defendants could not have foreseen that their liability to the plaintiff Borel, amounting to $68,000 (even though Borel sought damages far in excess of that amount), would have grown to a multimillion dollar liability in *Hardy*. This lack of foreseeability may have meant that the defendants did not have sufficient incentive to vigorously litigate the issues in the earlier litigation.

One might argue that had the court in *Borel* used a special verdict or a general verdict with detailed interrogatories, the *Hardy* court may have reached a different result, at least in part. But the incentive of the plaintiffs in an earlier action to accommodate any future plaintiffs may be low. In addition, it would be a difficult task indeed for a judge to fashion interrogatories in one asbestos case that would cover all conceivable situations in the thousands of other cases. *Hardy* reflects a circumspect judicial attitude toward use of offensive collateral estoppel in toxic tort litigation. The fact that some of the court's rationales for denying the use of collateral estoppel seem strained is an indication of just how strict courts are when faced with a stranger-plaintiff's proposal to prevent relitigation of key, disputed issues.

2. Choice of Law

The substantive law to be applied in mass toxic tort litigation is almost exclusively state tort doctrines. When brought in federal court, these actions are typically brought under the diversity jurisdiction of the federal courts. Pursuant to the *Erie* doctrine, state law, including state common law as well as statutory enactments, applies to diversity actions. *See* Erie Railroad Co v. Tompkins (S.Ct. 1938). The federal court sitting in diversity is under an obligation to apply the choice-of-law rules of the forum state. Klaxon Co. v. Stentor Elec. Mfg. Co. (S.Ct.1941). As a result, a different choice-of-law rule may apply in federal courts in different states. Moreover, when an action has been transferred to a federal district different from the one in which it was commenced, the transferee court is mandated to apply the law that the transferor court would have applied. *See* Ferens v. John Deere Co. (S.Ct.1990); Van Dusen v. Barrack (S.Ct. 1964). These basic rules make for some complicated choice-of-law questions in mass tort litigation.

Because tort law is a matter of high state interest, it has been subject to idiosyncratic interpretations and applications that vary from state to state. These state-to-state variations create an additional layer of complications when toxic tort actions have been aggregated. The claims of the individual plaintiffs may be subject to different state laws and,

therefore, different tort rules. This may lead to
conflicting results among similar claims that have
been consolidated in one forum.

Further, practical problems arise from the stale-
mate that choice-of-law issues often create. The
time for resolution of a mass tort action may become protracted when the choice of law is unclear.
This is particularly true when there is an attempt
to settle numerous actions. Judicial management
issues become even more critical if the parties do
not achieve settlement, for the court must determine an appropriate manner to handle the litigation when different state laws apply.

A few efforts have been made to supplant state
tort doctrine with federal common law in mass tort
litigation. In the Agent Orange litigation, Judge
Pratt initially held that federal common law should
apply to the product liability claims of the class
members against the manufacturers of the defoliant. The court applied a three-part test to determine the propriety of developing federal common
law. First, the court identified substantial federal
interests in the lawsuit in the relationship between
the military service personnel and the Government
and in the Government's interest in protecting its
relations with suppliers of war material. Second,
the court found that the federal interests would be
adversely affected by the application of state law
because state law would lead to inconsistent results
and, ultimately, to uncertainty for all parties. Con-
versely, the court found no adverse effect on state
interests if state law were to be supplanted by

federal common law. This was partly because the narrow question of a military contractor's liability to servicemen was not a matter of settled law in the states.

The Second Circuit reversed, finding that no substantial federal policy was at stake in the litigation. *See* In re "Agent Orange" Prod. Liab. Litig. (2d Cir.1980). The court examined the existing legal precedent and concluded that because the claims in the Agent Orange litigation were not brought by or against the United States Government, no rights or duties of the Government were directly raised by the litigation. The court stated:

> Since this litigation is between private parties and no substantial rights or duties of the government hinge on its outcome, there is no federal interest in uniformity for its own sake.... The fact that application of state law may produce a variety of results is of no moment.... That alone is not grounds in private litigation for judicially creating an overriding federal law.

Additionally, the court noted that the two federal interests identified by Judge Pratt competed with one another to some degree, thus fracturing the uniformity sought from a federal common law. This reasoning seemed to foreclose any use of federal common law in mass tort litigation within its reach. *But see* Boyle v. United Technologies Corp. (S.Ct.1988) (developing federal common law of government contractor defense).

The Fifth Circuit reached a similar conclusion with respect to asbestos litigation. In Jackson v. Johns–Manville Sales Corp. (5th Cir.1985), the Fifth Circuit reaffirmed the state interest in tort litigation, even when the litigation occurs on a massive scale. Further, the court expressed concern for the unfettered spread of federal common law beyond asbestos litigation if allowed under the circumstances of the case. Accordingly, the court concluded that in the absence of legislative action, use of federal common law was inappropriate. Of some significance, however, was the existence of a substantial dissent in *Jackson*, thus demonstrating judicial interest in a federal law alternative.

In the Manville Trust litigation, Judge Weinstein ultimately reached the same conclusion. *See* In re Joint E. & S. Dists. Asbestos Litig. (E. & S.D.N.Y. 1991). Judge Weinstein identified substantial federal interests—upholding the reorganization plan under the Bankruptcy Code and effecting a settlement of a tort action of massive scope, encompassing more than 150,000 claimants. Nevertheless, he rejected the application of federal common law mostly for reasons of federalism. Even though the states had individual tort laws that could cause choice-of-law problems, a legislative enactment by Congress, not a rule imposed by judicial edict, was the appropriate solution. Thus, the judiciary should not intervene to create a federal common law in the absence of action by Congress. He stated: "We are loath to cut the Gordian Knot presented by state tort law diversity using the sword of federal common law without Congressional warrant."

Earlier, however, in the Agent Orange litigation, Judge Weinstein did take steps to create and apply what essentially amounted to a federal common law, but was characterized as "national consensus" law. Similarly, commentators have offered strong arguments in favor of considering federal common law as a solution to the choice-of-law problem in mass torts. *See, e.g.*, Georgene M. Vairo, *Multi-Tort Cases: Cause For More Darkness on the Subject, or a New Role For Federal Common Law?*, 54 Fordham L. Rev. 167 (1985). *See also* Linda S. Mullenix, *Federalizing Choice of Law for Mass–Tort Litigation*, 70 Tex. L. Rev. 1623 (1992) (stating that "the legal profession has a longstanding, collective psychological block with regard to even the mention of federal common law"). While all are in agreement that something must be done to remedy the problems associated with choice of law, it appears for the moment that no clear solution has emerged.

CHAPTER TEN

A PARADIGM: THE CASE OF ENVIRONMENTAL TOBACCO SMOKE

Attention to the effects of tobacco smoke on nonsmokers has grown during the 1990s. Considerable activity has occurred simultaneously on all fronts—scientific, legislative, regulatory, and judicial. As a result, environmental tobacco smoke ("ETS")—also called "passive smoke" or "secondhand smoke"—is emerging as a model of the evolution of a "toxic tort." Thus, it is instructive to examine the law of ETS as a paradigm of the modern toxic tort. This law is incomplete, evolving, and fraught with gaps and conflicts. In short, it is the very picture of the *process*—both public and private—from which a toxic tort emerges.

Although many suits by *smokers* against the cigarette manufacturers have entered the legal system over the past decade, claims by nonsmokers have heretofore only trickled into the system. The expectation is that such claims will multiply rapidly as the scientific evidence accumulates. Smokers have yet to recover a verdict against the cigarette manufacturers, however. Nevertheless, important distinctions between the claims of nonsmokers and those of the smokers may warrant different treatment. The Supreme Court decision in Cipollone v. Liggett Group, Inc. (S.Ct.1992) restricted the kinds of claims for which the manufacturers could be held liable on federal pre-emption grounds; but the same case articulated areas in which viable claims may still be fashioned. Moreover, good reason exists to argue that *Cipollone* does not restrict nonsmokers' claims in the same manner that it restricts the claims of smokers. *See* Chapter 6, Sec. E(2), *supra*. Thus, *Cipollone* is a watershed case, not only for smokers seeking to recover from the tobacco companies, but also for nonsmokers claiming injury as a result of ETS.

The steady flow of scientific studies tending to demonstrate a relationship between a variety of illnesses and ETS has fostered a remarkable interest in both judicial and regulatory quarters. Far from being deterred by the lack of success on the part of smokers' lawsuits, proponents of legal reforms related to ETS have been fueled in the 1990s by the increasing number of scientific studies. *See, e.g.*, Dwight T. Janerich et al., *Lung Cancer and Exposure to Tobacco Smoke in the Household*, 323 New Eng. J. Med. 632 (1990) (reporting increased risk of lung cancer in nonsmokers associated with their exposure to passive smoke in the home). In addition, individuals claiming to have suffered injuries as a result of exposure to ETS differ significantly from smokers, in that the former often have been involuntary consumers of tobacco smoke.

The legal context of ETS has become a paradigm of toxic torts: emerging scientific evidence, latent illness in the absence of a signature disease, significant workplace issues, private lawsuits against cigarette manufacturers, and regulatory movement on the federal, state, and local levels. It is an emerging paradigm, however. It is most significant in that the various fronts on which legal action is being taken have converged at approximately the same moment in time. Thus, ETS gives a unique glimpse into the development of a paradigm in the new area of the law known as toxic torts.

A. RISK OF DISEASE FROM EXPOSURE TO ETS

1. Scientific Studies

Emerging scientific evidence points to the conclusion that ETS poses many of the same health risks to exposed persons as direct smoking does to smokers. ETS has been defined as follows:

[E]nvironmental tobacco smoke is composed of mainstream smoke exhaled by the smoker and sidestream smoke emitted from the burning tobacco between puffs. Sidestream smoke is the main component of environmental tobacco smoke. The great majority of smoke emitted from a lit cigarette is sidestream smoke rather than smoke that is actively inhaled. Sidestream and mainstream smoke contain many of the same air contaminants. Sidestream smoke has more particles with smaller diameters, and these particles are therefore more likely to be deposited in the most distant regions of the lungs.

Carl E. Barticchi et al., *The Human Costs of Tobacco Smoke*, 330 New Eng. J. Med. 907, 907 (1994). The Surgeon General issued two reports, in 1979 and 1986, that ultimately concluded that passive smoking was capable of causing lung cancer in exposed nonsmokers. The Surgeon General further declared that "simple separation of smokers and nonsmokers within the same air space may reduce, but does not eliminate, the exposure of nonsmokers to environmental tobacco smoke." U.S. Dep't of Health and Human Services, The Health Consequences of Involuntary Smoking, A Report of the Surgeon General 7 (1986). A string of reports has followed, substantiating these conclusions and detailing the effects of exposure to ETS on a variety of persons in various contexts, culminating in an EPA report in 1992 that classified ETS as a Group A carcinogen. Environmental Protection Agency, Respiratory Health Effects of Passive Smoking: Lung Cancer and Other Disorders (1992).

A recent report has extended concern for the hazards of ETS beyond lung disease. The study has identified ETS as being associated with as many as 47,000 deaths from heart disease annually and up to 150,000 non-fatal heart attacks annually. 24 J. Am. Coll. Cardiol. 546 (1994). The statistics in this study demonstrated a stronger connection than those obtained in previous studies.

Notwithstanding the mounting studies tending to demonstrate an association between ETS and various health conditions and illnesses, the tobacco industry has denied a causal connection between smoking and most ill health effects. Accordingly, the industry has steadfastly refused to settle private lawsuits and has undertaken affirmative challenges to legislative restrictions on smoking. Moreover, the industry has taken the offensive in several instances, as where it brought an action challenging the EPA report that classified tobacco smoke as a human carcinogen. Flue–Cured Tobacco Cooperative Stabilization Corp. v. EPA (M.D.N.C.1994) (denying EPA's motion to dismiss and holding that report constituted final agency action subject to review under Administrative Procedure Act). As a result of its perseverance, the industry has been successful in keeping liability at bay, but it remains to be seen how long it will continue to stave off the onslaught of litigation and regulation.

2. Supreme Court Recognition of Hazards

The risks inherent in exposure to ETS that have been identified in the medical literature have found a powerful ear in the United States Supreme Court. In Helling v. McKinney (S.Ct.1993), the Court ruled on the question whether a prisoner's forced confinement in a prison cell with a cellmate who smoked five packs of cigarettes a day constituted cruel and unusual punishment within the meaning of the Eighth Amendment to the United States Constitution. In response to the prisoner's civil rights claim

pursuant to 42 U.S.C.A. § 1983 (1994), the prison
officials argued that the Eighth Amendment did not
apply in situations in which a prisoner was subjected merely to a *threat* of future physical health
effects. The Court held that the conditions of the
prisoner's confinement provided a valid basis for his
claim of cruel and unusual punishment. In so
doing, the Court recognized that the *risk* of future
health effects associated with ETS constituted a
legally cognizable basis for the prisoner's particular
claim. The Court stated: "We have great difficulty
agreeing [with the prison officials] that prison au-
thorities ... may ignore a condition of confinement
that is sure or very likely to cause serious illness
and needless suffering the next week or month or
year."

Beyond its immediate criminal-law issue, *Helling*
is significant to the law of toxic torts because of its
recognition of the risk of future illness as the basis
for a legal claim. With respect to the specific threat
of ETS exposure, *Helling* lends legal credibility to
claims by plaintiffs that are based upon the health
risks associated with ETS.

B. WORKPLACE ISSUES AND ETS

1. Workers' Compensation

As discussed in Chapter 4, an employee's exclusive remedy for work-related injuries is to file a
claim pursuant to the workers' compensation system. Employers have resisted, and courts have
demonstrated a suspicion of, workers' compensation

claims for illnesses based upon exposure to ETS. Because ETS compensation claims are claims for occupational illness, rather than a workplace accident, they experience the same legal restrictions as other occupational illness claims. Thus, typically, an ETS claimant must demonstrate that the illness is peculiar to the claimant's employment and not an ordinary disease of life. This may be difficult to prove. *See* Chapter 4, Sec. A(2), *supra*.

Courts are split on the treatment of ETS-related illnesses and conditions under the workers' compensation systems of the various states. In Johannesen v. New York City Dep't of Housing Preservation & Development (N.Y.App.Div.1989), the claimant complained of asthma that developed after a period of employment in an office filled with ETS. The workers' compensation board interpreted the claimant's injury as an "accidental injury" within the compensation statute and held that the claim was covered. Similarly, in Schober v. Mountain Bell Telephone (N.M.Ct.App.1978), the court held that the claimant's allergic reaction to ETS was compensable because "accidental injury" was broad enough to include a gradual occurrence that resulted in an accidental injury.

In contrast, the court in Palmer v. Del Webb's High Sierra (Nev.1992), refused to interpret the state occupational disease statute to cover the claimant's claim for ETS-related lung disease. The claimant had worked as a pit boss in a casino for more than twenty years. He alleged that many casino patrons smoked and that the casino encouraged them to smoke by providing free cigarettes. In 1988, the claimant developed respiratory symptoms of chronic obstructive pulmonary disease and was later specifically diagnosed as suffering from reactive airways disease, severe bronchitis, and asthma. As the claimant had been a relatively athletic person who engaged in many outdoor activities when not working, nothing in the record indicated that he had any significant exposures to ETS other than in his workplace. The key issue in the case was whether ETS-related lung disease was sufficiently related to the character of the employer's business so as to satisfy the work-relatedness requirement of workers' compensation. The court held that it was not. The court reasoned that nothing in the nature of the employer's business gave rise to the claimant's injury. The court contrasted black lung disease, which is directly related to the nature of the business of mining coal. Rather, the court likened the claimant's ETS-related injuries to ulcers, colds, and migraine headaches, all of which could occur as a result of workplace conditions, but which were not covered by the state workers' compensation provisions.

If one were looking hard for a distinction between the reasons for the results in the above cases, one might point to the allergic reactions in the former set of cases as being in the nature of acute attacks. In contrast, the claimant's illness in *Palmer* developed slowly over a period of time and was a chronic condition. This distinction might be one factor contributing to the different results. More likely, however, the difference was more arbitrary in nature. The results likely were driven by the difference in judicial interpretation of the respective state occupational disease schemes, with some states focusing more restrictively on the nature of the employer's enterprise and whether the illness or condition sought to be covered was incidental to the character of the enterprise.

In one case where the workers' compensation board held that the claimant's lung condition was not within the coverage of the state occupational disease statute, the claimant was allowed to bring a tort action against the employer. In McCarthy v. Department of Social & Health Servs. (Wash.1988), the board had held that the claimant's illness did not satisfy the statutory requirements. When she brought the tort action, the court held that the plaintiff had stated a cause of action because the illness fell outside of workers' compensation. Furthermore, the court recognized a common law duty of employers to provide a safe workplace.

As did the *McCarthy* plaintiff, and in light of judicial resistance to workers' compensation claims based upon exposure to ETS, claimants have looked to other private legal avenues for redress for ETS-related injuries in the workplace. These have taken the form of actions for injunctive relief and, in some cases, actions based upon discrimination claims.

2. Injunctive Relief

A court may reasonably exercise its equitable powers to grant injunctive relief to a person injured in the workplace as a result of exposure to ETS. In Shimp v. New Jersey Bell Telephone Co. (N.J.Super.Ch.1976), the court ordered injunctive relief in favor of an employee who suffered from an allergy to cigarette smoke. Taking judicial notice of "the toxic nature of cigarette smoke and its well known association with emphysema, lung cancer and heart disease," the court explained that its authority in equity extended to granting relief to the injured employee "by ordering the employer to eliminate any preventable hazardous condition which the court finds to exist." Accordingly, the court ordered the employer to limit smoking to restricted areas, such as the company lunchroom and lounge. *See also* Smith v. Western Electric Co. (Mo.Ct.App. 1982).

The equitable relief granted in *Shimp* was in addition to whatever remedies may have been available under the state workers' compensation law. Such relief is complementary to, rather than in conflict with, the workers' compensation system. Notwithstanding the broad equitable powers of the court to grant relief so as to assure a reasonably safe workplace for employees, cases fashioning such a remedy are few. This may reflect a concern for balancing the equities when only one of many employees has complained of ETS in the workplace. *See* Gordon v. Raven Systems & Research Inc. (D.C.Ct.App.1983) (holding that employer is not required to make changes to workplace merely to accommodate the sensitivities of a single employee).

3. Discrimination Claims

Some employees who claim to have suffered injuries as a result of exposure to ETS have sought a remedy through the federal anti-discrimination laws. Two important federal laws may provide relief. The older of the two—the Federal Rehabilitation Act, 29 U.S.C.A. §§ 701–797b (West Supp. 1994)—is restricted to programs receiving federal money. The recent Americans with Disabilities Act (ADA), 42 U.S.C.A. §§ 12101–12213 (West 1990 & Supp. 1994), reaches private employment situations. Essentially, both acts require employers to provide reasonable accommodations for employees with disabilities. *See generally* Chapter Four, Sec. E, *supra*.

The first issue raised in the passive smoking context is whether sensitivity to ETS constitutes a disability giving rise to the protection of the federal statutes. In Gupton v. Commonwealth of Virginia (4th Cir.1994), the court held that an allergy to smoke by itself does not necessarily constitute a disability under the meaning of the Rehabilitation Act. The court stated that the plaintiff must show that the allergic condition prevented her from obtaining "the type of employment involved." This focus on the type of employment would prevent many ETS claimants from using the discrimination laws because, presumably, they would be suited to obtain the same type of employment in a smoke-free workplace. Only the most severe ETS reactions may qualify, and only where the individual was greatly restricted in the general activities of life as a result of the condition.

The second issue raised in discrimination claims arises after the individual is found to have a disability within the meaning of the relevant act. If so, what constitutes an appropriate "reasonable accommodation" for the person's disability? Is the employer required to alter the entire workplace to accommodate the individual? Prior to bringing suit, the *Gupton* plaintiff had complained to the employer regarding her allergy to smoke. She was relocated to a nonsmoking area approximately 60 feet from a smoking area, but continued to suffer symptoms, taking an unpaid leave of absence from work. When the employer eventually offered the plaintiff a position at a different—smoke-free—location, the plaintiff apparently declined to accept.

Although the *Gupton* decision did not turn on the type of accommodation offered, that case raises some important issues for both employers and smoke-sensitive employees. The Rehabilitation Act contemplates that the reasonable accommodation should offer the same opportunities for salary and advancement as the former position. But more subtle issues may arise with respect to the perception by the employer and co-employees of the complaining employee. Moreover, the plaintiff in *Gupton* may have felt that the relocation to a different building burdened her in some way that was unreasonable.

Is an accommodation that continues to allow smoking in certain areas near the plaintiff reasonable? In one of the rare cases under the ADA on the subject of ETS, the court in Harmer v. Virginia Electric and Power Co. (E.D.Va.1993) held that a partially smoking-restricted workplace constituted a reasonable accommodation. The plaintiff, who suffered from bronchial asthma, sought a complete ban on smoking in the workplace. The employer had undertaken measures to limit smoking to smokers' own cubicles and to diminish the spread of smoke to areas where nonsmokers were located. The measures included air purifiers, fans, and smokeless ashtrays. In finding the accommodation reasonable, the court noted that the plaintiff had been capable of performing his job with the accommodation and had, in fact, received favorable performance evaluations.

A further issue may arise when the employer can identify no reasonable means of accommodation for the affected employee. In Pletten v. Department of the Army (M.S.P.B.1981), a nonsmoker who suffered from chronic asthma was required, as part of his regular duties, to travel among different offices and buildings where he was exposed regularly to ETS. Although the Merit Systems Protection Board had found that his condition constituted a disability under the Rehabilitation Act, the review board refused to require the employer to institute a pervasive smoking ban in the workplace. The review board found that the only effective accommodation for the employee's condition would be an outright ban throughout the workplace, but also found that such a ban would be unreasonable within the meaning of the act.

C. PRODUCT LIABILITY CLAIMS

The judicial system is beginning to process claims brought against the cigarette manufacturers by nonsmokers who have been exposed regularly to ETS. The early claims tend to be brought by employees who claim injury as a result of workplace exposures. But conceivably, these product liability claims could extend to individuals who allege exposure under other conditions. Beyond the workplace, however, there are some powerful deterrents to such claims. First, if a plaintiff alleges exposure in the home, he or she will encounter issues relating to the contributing conduct of the smoker or smokers producing the ETS. These would often be family members, potentially creating great discomfort in the plaintiff at the prospect of taking an adversarial posture with respect to the smoker. Second, the workplace is a more controlled situation in which exposures to ETS are identifiable and, to some extent, quantifiable. In addition, workplace exposures may be documented by the employer and other employees. Other settings may not have such objective measures of exposure.

The litigation with the greatest potential for a far-reaching impact is Broin v. Philip Morris Cos. (Fla.Dist.Ct.App.1994). This class action was commenced on behalf of 60,000 nonsmoking flight attendants, claiming a variety of illnesses and physical conditions as a result of exposure to ETS on airline flights during the course of their employment. The illnesses claimed go beyond respiratory distress to cancers of the lung and numerous other organs, heart disease, and infertility. The action alleged product liability theories, including strict liability, breach of implied warranty, negligence, and fraud. After experiencing a defeat on the issue of class certification at the trial court level, the plaintiffs were successful in having their class action reinstated by the appellate court. The results of such litigation as the flight attendant class action and similar lawsuits will have significant ramifications in future litigation involving exposure to ETS. *See also* Butler v. R.J. Reynolds Tobacco Co. (S.D.Miss.1993) (ruling on procedural motion); *Family of Deceased Barber Files Tort Suit Seeking $650 Million Against Makers*, 9 Tox. L. Rep. 1415 (May 18, 1994) (describing product liability action filed against six cigarette manufacturers by representative of deceased barber shop owner, claiming that lung cancer from which decedent died was caused by 30 years of inhaling ETS in workplace and alleging that had he known of danger, he would have enforced a nonsmoking policy).

In many ways, product liability claims against cigarette manufacturers for injuries due to exposure to ETS have the same problems as claims brought by smokers. They are dependent upon whether the plaintiffs can demonstrate that cigarettes are a defective product as well as the extent to which the

manufacturers' conduct may have been inappropriate in researching and testing their products. A
significant issue in this context is the extent to
which the United States Supreme Court's important pre-emption opinion in Cipollone v. Liggett
Group, Inc. (S.Ct.1992) applies to claims brought by
nonsmokers. A strong argument is that the warnings mandated for cigarette packages are directed to
smokers only. The content of the warnings refers
to the hazards of "smoking." Moreover, those
most likely to see the warnings are those using the
product or those reading the product's advertisements. Indeed, many nonsmokers are exposed to
ETS involuntarily, and those who do so in a manner
that could be viewed as "voluntary" may be doing
so as a matter of domestic necessity or to keep a
desired job. These issues will likely be addressed
before nonsmokers' claims against the cigarette
manufacturers are resolved.

D. LITIGATION BY PUBLIC ENTITIES

It is evidence of the substantial public interest in
the hazards of ETS that the subject has generated
not only actions by private citizens, but also litigation by public entities seeking to protect the health
of their citizens. In this respect, ETS blurs the
boundaries between private law and public law.
Because toxic torts present significant issues regarding the public health, and because there is
often a potential to affect large numbers of persons,
it is logical for the state or other public entities to

take action when the public interest has been burdened.

Thus, the Texas Attorney General has filed an action on behalf of the State against the major fast food chains, alleging that they improperly exposed young people to ETS. *See* Texas v. McDonald's Corp. (complaint filed 2/16/94). The action alleged violation of the Deceptive Trade Practices Act, Tex. Bus. & Com. Code §§ 17.41 to -.63 (West 1987 & Supp. 1995), by advertising the availability of both smoking and nonsmoking sections, but using a single ventilation system. The complaint further alleged that the fast food chains were exposing mostly children to the hazards of ETS because most of their employees were children.

In a different approach, some states recently have authorized their attorneys general to commence actions against the cigarette manufacturers to recover the health care costs of smoking-related illness in Medicaid recipients. Such actions take notice of the enormous profits realized by the tobacco industry in relation to the fact that numerous persons with smoking-related disease are required to seek public assistance for their medical bills. *See* Mass. Ann. Laws ch. 118E, at 22 (1994). *See also* Minnesota v. Philip Morris, Inc., Minn. Dist. Ct. No. 94–8565 (filed 1994) (action brought by State and large health insurer for reimbursement of sums spent in treating smoking-related illnesses); Mississippi v. American Tobacco Co. (filed 1994) (action brought by state Attorney General, and opposed by Governor, seeking reimbursement for smoking-related health care costs). These actions have generated an aggressive legal response by the tobacco industry. *See* Associated Industries of Florida v. Florida Agency for Health Care Administration (filed 1994) (action brought by tobacco and business groups challenging Florida law allowing suit on grounds that it unconstitutionally eliminated certain defenses and allowed the use of mere statistical evidence as proof of causation; bill repealing law later passed by legislature).

E. ANTI–SMOKING LEGISLATION

An assortment of federal laws and regulations ban smoking in a variety of locations. These include most federal buildings, 41 C.F.R. § 101–20.105–3 (1993), parts of federal prisons, 28 C.F.R. § 551.160 (1993), domestic airline flights, 49 U.S.C.A. § 137(d)(1) (1993), and interstate bus trips, 49 C.F.R. § 1061.1 (1992).

In addition to federal measures, a variety of state legislation and, in some cases, municipal regulation limiting smoking on the basis of the hazards of ETS has occurred in recent years. Legislative concern has focused on certain public places and on private establishments in which smokers are likely to linger and smoke, thus creating an environment filled with ETS.

For example, in Utah, the state legislature enacted a ban on smoking in public places, state buildings, schools, and child care facilities. In enacting the law, the legislature found that ETS was a "public health nuisance and a cause of material annoyance, discomfort, and physical irritation to nonsmokers," making it necessary to regulate so as "to protect the health, safety, welfare, comfort, and environment of nonsmokers." Utah Code Ann. § 76–10–106 (1986). *See also, e.g.*, Minn. Stat. Ann. § 144.414 (1986); Neb. Rev. Stat. § 71–5704 (1981).

With respect to workplace legislation, Washington has prohibited smoking in all enclosed offices, whether the employer is public or private. *See* Wash. Rev. Code § 70.160.060 (1994). The only exception is offices equipped with separate ventilation systems. Washington also has provided for diminution of the amount of outdoor smoke (from employees who smoke outside the workplace on breaks or otherwise) that enters the interior workplace by requiring employers to take measures to prevent the smoke from entering through doorways, windows, and air intakes. The regulations call for notification of employers for initial violations and fines up to $200 for each subsequent violation. The Washington smoking ban has been challenged by tobacco companies and other businesses on the ground that it was not based on substantial evidence of the hazards of ETS in offices. An appeal for an emergency stay of the rule was rejected in late 1994. *See* Aviation West Corp. v. Washington, Wash. Sup. Ct. No. 62408–9 (filed 1994).

An extensive workplace ban promulgated in Maryland includes restaurants and bars, locales that typically attract a clientele who will be smoking.

The Maryland legislation has traveled a rocky course toward implementation. The tobacco industry and businesses brought suit challenging the ban as overly extensive and likely to cause economic injury to business. The regulation was to go into effect on August 1, 1994, but a court ordered an injunction temporarily imposing a stay on implementation of the ban. Eventually, the Maryland Court of Appeals lifted the injunction, and the ban has gone into effect, with further action on the tobacco industry's case yet to take place. *See* Fogle v. H & G Restaurant (Md.1995).

More broad-based federal legislation and/or regulation may be on the way. In recent sessions of Congress, legislation has been introduced that would prohibit smoking in certain locations. For example, the Smoke–Free Environment Act has been offered by Representative Henry Waxman of California. The bill included provisions to ban smoking in most buildings and contained fines for violation as steep as $5,000 per day. Such legislation was opposed by the Bush administration, but has been supported by the Clinton administration. Similar concerns have been voiced in the perennially proposed Indoor Air Act, sponsored by Representative Joseph Kennedy. This proposed legislation would address indoor air pollution generally, but would include specific restrictions on ETS. Despite such proposals, Congressional action does not appear poised to occur.

Administrative action appears to be moving at a similarly slow pace. Since 1991, OSHA has been

taking steps toward regulating indoor air quality,
including ETS.   In 1994, OSHA proposed standards
for indoor air quality that contained restrictions on
smoking in the workplace.   *See* 59 Fed. Reg. 15968.
The proposed rule would require employers in non-
industrial settings such as office buildings and
health care locales to establish and implement indoor air plans for managing indoor air pollutants in
their workplaces.   The rule includes what amounts
to an outright ban on smoking.   The proposed
indoor air rule—in particular, the portion addressing smoking—has drawn substantial comment and
criticism from industry, labor unions, and citizens.
The tobacco industry has objected to the use of non-
workplace scientific data on the hazards of ETS for
the purpose of standard-setting in the occupational
context.   The OSHA rulemaking process is a protracted one, however, and a final rule on these
issues could take several years.

INDEX

References are to Pages

†